AF560305

Essays on Contemporary Indian Economy

Essays on Contemporary Indian Economy

Neeraj Jain

ESSAYS ON CONTEMPORARY INDIAN ECONOMY
Neeraj Jain

First Published, 2016

ISBN 978-93-5002-410-2 (Hb)

Published by
AAKAR BOOKS
28 E Pocket IV, Mayur Vihar Phase I, Delhi 110 091
Phone : 011 2279 5505 Telefax : 011 2279 5641
aakarbooks@gmail.com; www.aakarbooks.com

in association with
LOKAYAT
129 B/2, Erandwane,
Pune 411 004
lokayat.india@gmail.com
www.lokayat.org.in

Printed at
Sapra Brothers, Delhi 110 092

CONTENTS

LIST OF TABLES, CHARTS AND BOXES

Tables

Charts

Boxes

INTRODUCTION

NEW ECONOMIC POLICIES AND THE PARADIGM SHIFT: MARGINALISING THE MAJORITY*

Arun Kumar
Retired Professor of Economics, JNU

The book at hand focuses on the recent period in Indian economic policy making and connects it to the New Economic Policies (NEP) launched in June 1991 by the Narasimha Rao Government soon after it took office. These were launched with the promise that they would help overcome the crisis plaguing the economy at that juncture in a decade. It was argued that after some pain, the common man would soon benefit.[1] It was also said that there is no alternative (TINA), a term first used by Margaret Thatcher in 1978 when she came to power in the UK and initiated rabid pro-business policies. The book brings out that the pain continues for the people of India 25 years after the launch of the NEP while the benefits have largely been cornered by businesses, especially the multinational corporations (MNCs).

The book consists of five essays covering different aspects of the NEP. The first essay analyses the fiscal deficit in the budget and the implications of curtailing it, especially for the poor. The second essay deals with the Union Budget 2015–16. The third essay discusses the implications of opening up of the insurance sector in India and the fourth essay goes into the implications of allowing foreign direct

* *Based substantially on the author's book, "Indian Economy Since Independence: Persisting Colonial Disruption".*

investment in the multi-brand retail sector. The final chapter analyses the likely impact of spread of the habit of consuming fizz drinks made by the MNCs Coca-Cola and PepsiCo on health and environment, and why MNCs are able to make such toxic drinks and successfully market them in such a big way globally.

Overall, the book spells out the adverse impact of indiscriminate opening up of the Indian economy on the common people of India. It becomes clear that the Indian ruling elite is conniving in this with international finance capital which now has the Indian economy firmly in its grip. Policy space for independent or pro-poor policies has diminished/vanished. The book points to the distress of the common people in various ways over the last 25 years. It is not that before 1991, the poor were not suffering. There was a gradual change in the lot of the poor prior to 1991, but since then it has deteriorated faster. This decline is sought to be masked by the policy makers through the greater availability of a large number of consumer goods. The middle classes and the lower classes who are aspiring for a better life are taken in by the glitz and glamour of malls, mobile phones, cars and electronic goods which gives the impression of rapid material progress since 1991.

The book suggests mobilisation by the people to resist the NEP based on neoliberal policies. There is a sense of urgency that action is needed sooner than later before matters worsen further. There has to be mobilisation of the different segments of the population. People have been fighting against displacement, exploitation, destruction of natural resources, and so on. There is a need for these different movements to come together. One needs to understand the impediments in the way of mobilisation of the people. These are philosophical in nature since there is a basic change in the thinking of the ruling elite and the middle classes that aspire to join the elite. The poorer sections have also been affected by these philosophical changes.

The Present Day Contradictions

Indian society is full of contradictions. It is one of the world's fastest growing economies but with rapidly increasing inequality. India has the most number of poor and illiterate people in the world. Its rivers and the air in its cities are amongst the most polluted in the world. This is a result of the pursuit of the strategy of 'growth at any cost' based on what has been referred to as the Washington Consensus.[2] It is pushed by international agencies like the World Bank. Who bears the cost? Of course, the environment, the workers and the farmers. Within these groups the burden has fallen disproportionately on the unorganised sector which employs 93 percent of the work force.[3]

A basic feature of the neoliberal policies imposed on the developing world since the 1980s became clear rather quickly. Namely, that these policies hit the marginalised sections in society hard so that they need a 'safety net'.[4] After all, these policies were designed to be pro-business and therefore are not inclusive. The Indian rulers accepted this only in the early part of the last decade as social strife and political instability increased all through the 1990s. To mitigate the ill effects of the policies being pursued, the UPA Government initiated the Rights approach to poverty by implementing the Right to employment in the form of MGNREGS and the Right to food and education. These Rights were granted only so that the social situation does not deteriorate further. They do not resolve the basic problem which is leading to the worsening social situation. They only patch up a declining situation and do not lead to the basic changes that are needed.

Be that as it may, the political will to implement these Rights has been weak with vested interests substantially subverting them via corruption and on the plea of shortage of resources. Thus, on the one hand, resources are not adequately budgeted and on the other hand what is allotted does not reach the beneficiaries due to leakages. Is there a shortage of resources? This is a political question, namely, where to raise the resources from and how to spend them.[5] Every nation has the resources for its own development provided it pursues its own policies based on its own requirements. However, this has not been possible in today's world because policies are imposed on nations under conditionalities imposed by the IMF and the World Bank and the requirements of WTO. They are forced explicitly or implicitly to pursue another's path.

Following Another's Path

China has been copying the capitalist path of development in the post-Mao period since the late 1970s even though it is called a path with a difference. Deng Xiaoping, who took over the reins after Mao, said, 'How does the colour of the cat matter as long as it catches mice,' thereby implying that it is growth alone that matters and not how one gets it. China has had tremendous growth but history will judge its costs in due course of time. It has experienced massive pollution, exploitation of workers and rise in corruption. The book at hand spells out some of the costs the Indian people are paying. This is true everywhere in the developing world since that is the nature of globalisation today.

The Greek situation is before us. In early 2015, the new Syriza Government took over the reins of office on the promise of opposing the austerity programme being imposed on the Greek people by international finance capital and which was causing the Greek people tremendous hardship. After resisting for seven months, it capitulated and promised to implement an even harsher austerity programme than earlier. It had not worked out an alternative and had hoped that the troika of Germany, European Central Bank and the European Commission would give in to its demands. However, the troika is made of sterner stuff and knew that Greece was not prepared to stand alone because it had not worked out an alternative. It had not even prepared to issue its own currency in a short time. Without an alternative, the economy was beginning to collapse and Tsipras, the Greek PM, had to capitulate. The Greek Parliament also backed him and passed the austerity programme. An example has been set for any developing country that resists international finance capital.

One-Way Globalisation

To understand the nature of globalisation confronting the developing world today, one needs to understand its philosophical roots.[6] Globalisation stands for exchange of ideas, technology, capital, goods and services and people across nations. Globalisation is not new since it has been going on for long. India has been trading with the South East Asians, Arabs and East Africans for thousands of years. Buddhism went from India up to Japan. This globalisation was two-way, since ideas, trade, etc. went in both directions.

It is after 1750 that the process has become one-way with ideas coming from outside at a more and more rapid pace with India contributing little to generation of new ideas. The language we use, the clothes we wear, the food we eat, the sports we play, the goods we buy have been strongly influenced by the West. The technology that has transformed our lives over the last 250 years has mostly come from there. Thus, life in India has changed to a Western pattern. Our notions of beauty, music, art and culture are strongly influenced by Western trends. Our films and advertising often copy Western themes. Even success means going West or is measured in Western terms.

This one-way globalisation did not begin in 1991 or in 1982 or in 1975. These only represent the changing phases of one-way globalisation. Independence in 1947 also saw a new phase of one-way globalisation wherein we attained political independence but chose a path of Western development. A crucial phase was the beginning of a new education policy following the *Minutes of Education* of 1835 authored by Lord Macaulay, which brought in English as the medium of instruction in higher education and turned Indian intellectuals into 'derived' intellectuals.

Colonisation and Disruption of Indian Society

Numerous studies have shown that India was a dominant manufacturing power in the world in 1750 but had lost its position by 1900.[7] This was a result of colonisation, a form of globalisation, which led to de-industrialisation in the mid-nineteenth century. The socio-economic conditions deteriorated all through the colonial period. However, the biggest setback was the disruption in society and loss of dynamism. These have continued in the post-independence period. Under colonial rule, the ruling elite in the country was answerable to British power and not to the people. The leadership of the national movement emerged from this elite which was enamoured of Western modernity but was feudal in outlook.

This leadership which took over the reins of power in 1947 was self-centered and decided to copy the path of Western modernity rather than working towards an Indian modernity. It chose a top-down path of development rather than a bottom-up approach. It copied the two paths then available in the West—central planning from the Soviet Union and market from the Western bloc. Both were paths of top-down development.

The paradigm of development in 1947 was based on the idea that the individual is not responsible for her/his problems since they have a social basis. The experience of the national movement was that poverty, unemployment, illiteracy and ill-health were due to the socio-economic conditions under colonisation. Thus, the collective had to solve these social problems. As such, the state was given a large role in the economic sphere.

Infrastructure for education, health, transport and communication was set up rapidly. The rate of growth of the economy went up sharply after 1947. However, given the focus on copying Western modernity and the top-down approach, the problems of the people persisted and led to crisis after crisis after the 1960s.

The ruling elite faced the dilemma that while for strategic reasons the Soviets were India's allies, emotionally they wanted to copy the elites of the West and were enamoured of their consumerism. This led to confusion in policy, growing pressure to end the austerity policies and spread of corruption. There was a rapid rise of the black economy and illegality in the economy which subverted economic policies.[8] Not only was growth held back by this, it led to failure of state intervention in the economy and to louder calls for change of policies from the state to the market.

The ground for this switch was prepared at the start of the Emergency in 1975. It marks the beginning of the rightward drift in Indian society. Indians from the World Bank and the IMF were brought in growing numbers to policy making positions in government. Indian intellectuals were invited to serve as consultants in these institutions with the lure of high salaries. Official reports on different aspects of the economy were written by many of them, uniformly suggesting a retreat of the state and an advance of the market in the economy. A revolving door policy followed wherein policy makers rotated between government jobs and these international institutions.[9]

Globalisation as Marketisation

Two oil crises (1979 and 1989) led to deterioration in India's balance of payment position and by 1990 the Indian economy was on the verge of collapse. The rapid decline of the Soviet Union from the mid-1970s and the U-turn taken by China added to the ideological pressure in India to jettison the mixed economy model and go for a market economy. The collapse of the Eastern Bloc in 1989 and the demise of the Soviet Union in 1990 added to the pressure for a paradigm shift in Indian economic policies. They were turned on their head.

Under pressure from the IMF and the World Bank, the new paradigm became that individuals are to blame for their problems and the collective was no more responsible for them. Thus, the individual must go to the market to solve her/his problems of health, education, employment and poverty. With this started a new phase of one-way globalisation of Indian society which may be referred to as 'marketisation'. This paradigm shift affected all policies. One needs to understand its philosophical underpinnings to realise its deep impact on the thinking of the people.

We have argued elsewhere that marketisation is based on the notions of 'dollar vote', 'more is better', rational profit-maximising individuals, and so on.[10] These principles lead to consumerism, the 'marginalisation of the marginal', environmental degradation, atomisation and treatment of man as a cog in a machine. Markets are only an institution for exchange of goods and services. By themselves they have no values, so they tend to be amoral and immoral. Values come from society, but it is in retreat. Society says that narcotic drugs or cigarettes are harmful to people, but the markets make no such value judgment and supply these goods to whosoever demands them. The same is the case with fizz drinks which the markets supply. There is a new international division of labour with clean technology production in the advanced countries and dirty production in the developing world. Thus, the developing world is destroying its environment while the advanced countries have greatly improved theirs while consuming more and more. There is domination of finance over the rest, greed has been raised to a new high pedestal and today the 1% rule over the 99%, thereby subverting democracy.

Capital has become mobile but labour remains restricted within the boundaries of the nation state. This has enabled capital to extract concessions from nation states by making them compete with each other, and one of the ways in which it has forced them to compete is to restrict trade unions and lower labour costs. Thus, collective action has become difficult and trade unions have weakened. This has led to growing inequality within nation states and a rising income gap between the 1% and the 99% globally.

Today, globalisation is globalisation of the elite of the world. The Indian elite want to join the global elite. The state is giving concessions to corporations in the form of lower taxes and easy and cheap access to land, air, water and other infrastructure. Thus, where markets did not exist they have been created, and people are being dispossessed on a large scale.

Global strategic interests of the US and other Western powers have led them to interfere in other nations to control their raw material resources. It has led them to intervene for petroleum products in the Middle East. They have also intervened on a large scale in Africa, Eastern Europe and Central Asia. The consequence has been a wide arc of instability in the world from Central Asia to the Middle East to Africa. Many nation states have been completely destroyed as a result of Western interference in their internal politics. This is true of Iraq, Afghanistan, Syria, Yemen and Libya. Many others have become destabilised and are becoming 'failed states', like Pakistan, Sudan, Nigeria and Ukraine. The sudden rise of IS and the rising tide of refugees is also a consequence of one-way globalisation in the world.

Consequences of Marketisation

Marketisation has brought about a fundamental change in thinking in society and has helped justify a more unjust and more unequal society. Pursuit of material well-being over all else has become central since Man is treated as homo-economicus. Politically, consumerism has enabled leaderships all over the world to divert attention of the people from the more important national tasks. The image of a good life based on greater material prosperity in the future has held many in its thrall and reduced resistance to neoliberal policies. It has also impacted media and the judiciary in a big way. Media is increasingly controlled by the corporate sector and therefore marginalises the real issues, like poverty and inequality, by sanitising them and swamping people with the image of a good life. Further, the advertising and entertainment dished out by the media is substantially based on sex and violence. The media managers are not bothered about its long term impact on the people and especially on children, as the aim is to sell.

Courts have also changed their stance towards labour and capital, favouring the latter over the former. The gains that labour made in the period after independence and up to the 1980s have been reversed in many cases. Collective action, a tool of labour to counter the money power of capital, has been greatly diluted. Corporates have with impunity used more and more contract labour rather than permanent employment to whittle down the organised sector and weaken it. Ninety three percent of the work force is in the unorganised sector, working at low wages and without any social security, and it constitutes a large reserve army of labour.

The organised sector workers fear losing their well paid jobs and their privileges and therefore tend to stay away from collective action. Post-1991, protection of the courts to labour from arbitrary actions of managers has declined. In brief, the pull of consumerism and the fear of being sacked are the twin forces that have weakened the labour movement in the country, and this has emboldened businesses.

In the name of labour flexibility, businessmen have been demanding policies of 'hire and fire' to further weaken labour. They argue that this would lead to employment generation, but have no answer to the question as to why the unorganised sector is not generating enough jobs when it has complete flexibility. Most unorganised sector jobs are residual and not generated by the system. Further, there is tremendous underemployment in this sector and that results in poverty. There is no social security in this sector so that it is afflicted by health and old age related issues. These further add to the costs of living of workers, and make them even more insecure.

As argued earlier, marketisation is based on the retreat of the state from economic activity. However, it is a strategic retreat in favour of capital and away from labour. We have pointed out elsewhere that the philosophical underpinning is that there should be no interference in the pricing mechanism; the new philosophy is 'let prices prevail'.[11] Thus, there should be no minimum wage, no subsidy, no fixed prices for essential goods, no differential taxes on luxury and essential goods, and so on.

This principle of non-interference in the market by the state means that there should be no differential treatment of MNCs compared to local capital. Under WTO, national treatment has to be given to foreign capital. Foreign Direct Investment (FDI) and Foreign Institutional Investment (FII) are welcome. Prior to 1985, the developing countries used to get aid since they were recognised to be economically weak. More importantly, there was the fear that if they were pushed too hard then they may tilt towards communism and ally with the Soviet bloc. Vietnam was a lesson that the poor could revolt and turn communist. When the threat of the Soviet bloc disappeared, the gloves came off and now the developing nations have to attract capital by granting concessions (instead of getting concessions).

The Solution is the Problem

These features of one-way globalisation and marketisation help one understand the concerns expressed in the different chapters of this book.

The budgetary calculus and the attempts to restrict the fiscal deficit are a ploy to restrict the role of the government in the economy and give it a pro-business twist. It enables businesses to maintain an upper hand in the economy. The economy's health remains in their hands so that they can extract concessions from society in the name of boosting the economy. This is what has happened in the current juncture when the economy has slowed down.[12] When tax revenues are not buoyant, then a reduction in the fiscal deficit leads to curtailment in government's expenditures. So, essential expenditures on social sectors and on the Plan have been reined in as a percentage of the GDP.

In the period since 2011, private sector investment has been declining due to lack of demand in the economy. Public sector investments have been held back due to cuts in Plan expenditure, thereby leading to a further decline in the investment rate in the economy which has dropped from 38 percent of the GDP in 2007–08 to the current level of 28 percent. The decline in the rate of investment in the economy has led to a fall in the rate of growth of the economy.

Using the excuse of a decline in the investment rate, the government has been arguing for the need to attract foreign investment. Hence the move to give concessions to MNCs and open up sectors like multi-brand retail trade, airlines, insurance and defence production. However, foreign investment has typically been around 10 percent of the total investment in the economy. It usually takes time for investment to materialise and therefore no immediate effect is likely. At best it may raise the investment rate by one or two percent of the GDP, and therefore cannot make up for the 10 percent decline in the investment rate, and hence it cannot be the solution. Rather the solution has become the problem.

Why is the government keen on reducing the fiscal deficit? This is because the IMF and the international credit rating agencies watch this parameter like a hawk. If it rises, they downgrade the economy and that raises the cost of raising funds abroad. Why do these agencies watch this parameter of the economy? Because that is the best way of restricting the role of the government in the economy and strengthen the private sector and more specifically the MNCs.

Linking the Theoretical Framework to the Chapters

So, why is the government doing what has become the problem? It has conceded policy space to international finance capital and cannot follow independent policies that can take care of the interests of its people.[13] No wonder it is said globally today that Wall Street (world of finance) dominates over Main Street (rest of the economy). The financial sector corporations brought about the global financial crisis and also benefited the most by extracting concessions from governments. They did not get punished on the plea that they are 'too big to fail'.

Globally, governments have lost the capacity to pursue policies in the interests of their people, and the same has happened in India since the 1980s and more so after 1991. Hence today, even if the costs of FDI in multi-brand retail or insurance are far more than the benefits, it does not matter. The objective is not to benefit the people but a small group of elite in the country and the MNCs. This is consistent with the desire of the ruling elite to join the elite of the world and that is what globalisation means for them. Their emotional attachment with the nation is over. They can become NRIs and espouse the interest of the MNCs as the interest of the nation, even if this hurts the common people. They do not even take a stand against corporations like Coca-Cola whose fizz drinks are known to be harmful to children.

The fiscal deficit can be reduced if the government is willing to tackle the black economy which is now 56 percent of GDP and could yield an additional tax-GDP ratio of 22 percent. This would lead to the fiscal deficit turning into a surplus of 18 percent of GDP. This could provide adequate investment in education, health, employment generation, energy, transport, and so on. But a government consisting of the elite and beholden to them cannot be expected to tackle its own constituency's illegality. So the nation does not lack the resources, but the government is not willing to lay its hands on them. If the black economy were to be tackled effectively, the waste in society would decline and the rate of growth would go up. We have shown elsewhere that the country has lost on an average 5 percent rate of growth due to the existence of a substantial black economy since the mid-1970s.[14] If this problem had been dealt with, the economy would have been 7 times larger today, at $14 trillion. In effect, the missed development annually is $12 trillion.

Call for Action

Given the adverse consequences of the NEP for the Indian people, this book repeatedly calls for urgent mobilisation and action to check and reverse these policies which have been implemented by successive governments since 1991. Their ideology has not come in the way of implementing these policies. Many of them have come to power opposing these policies but after coming to power they have implemented them with vigour. For instance, the NDA Government came to power in 1998 on the 'swadeshi' plank, but on attaining power it pushed the 'videshi' interest even more strongly than the earlier regime that it had opposed. The UF Government with the Left as one of its components made P. Chidambaram its finance minister who completely marginalised the poor and welcomed foreign capital.

The unanimity among political parties on implementation of the anti-people neoliberal policies is a result of the fact that ideology has taken a back seat to getting to power to benefit vested interests and one's own personal interest. The entire elite ruling class is complicit in this.

This state of affairs has come about because there is a lack of an alternative backed by social groups. There is a lot of action and agitation in the nation against the NEP but it is splintered. Movements against displacement, for right to work, food, education, information and so on are going on, but they are based on a single agenda and with a limited perspective. They lack a wider vision which can unite them all onto a common political platform. They are unable to counter the underlying philosophical underpinnings of the marketisation process. The vested interests are all too happy to see these groups divided and unable to mount a wider challenge. Governments have even conceded some of the rights being demanded to deflate the movements, but implementation is lacking since the commitment is missing.

Everyone is active in life but based on his/her consciousness at that moment of time. Currently that is informed by marketisation which 'marginalises the marginal'. If action has to be in the right direction and energies are not to be frittered away, a basic change in consciousness is needed. For this, not only should everyone have good education, but its content is equally crucial and it should be democratic in content.

Gandhi said that education in India is alienating, and that remains true to this day since it does not link up with life and does not give a wider understanding of society. It does not give hope to the young for the future and given the weak employment generation, they have turned despondent. They are open to irrationalities of various kinds, such as the idea of a glorious past. This leads them to accept divisive agendas and become pawns in the hands of vested and sectional interests.

In brief, a basic rethink of the top-down development strategy adopted by the ruling elite in India since independence is required. One-way globalisation needs to be challenged in totality. A basic reform of our decrepit education system is needed so that socially relevant knowledge may be generated. None of this is feasible without social action which needs to be accelerated; action and thought need to iteratively inform each other for success.

References

1. A. Kumar, *Proposals for a Citizens Union Budget for the Nation for 1994–95: An Alternative to the Fund–Bank Dictated Union Budget for 1994–95*, Presented to the Citizens' Committee on February 12, 1994 at Gandhi Peace Foundation, New Delhi. Prepared for the Preparatory Committee for Alternative Economic Policies.
2. J. Williamson, *What Washington Means by Policy Reform*, in J. Williamson (ed.), "Latin American Readjustment: How Much Has Happened?" Institute for International Economics, Washington, 1989.
3. M. Kelly and Deepika D'Souza (eds.), *The World Bank in India: Undermining Sovereignty, Distorting Development*, Orient Blackswan, New Delhi, 2010, pp. 27–36.
4. G. Cornia, R. Jolly and F. Stewart, *Adjustment with a Human Face*, Clarendon Press, Oxford, 1987.
5. A. Kumar, *Proposals for a Citizens Union Budget for the Nation for 1994–95: An Alternative to the Fund–Bank Dictated Union Budget for 1994–95*, op. cit.

6. A. Kumar, *Indian Economy Since Independence: Persisting Colonial Disruption*, Vision Books, New Delhi, 2013.
7. See for instance: P. Kennedy, *The Rise and Fall of Great Powers: Economic Change and Military Conflict from 1500 to 2000*, Random House, New York, 1988.
8. A. Kumar, *The Black Economy in India*, Penguin (India), New Delhi, 1999.
9. M. Kelly and Deepika D'Souza (eds.), *The World Bank in India: Undermining Sovereignty, Distorting Development*, op. cit.
10. A. Kumar, *Indian Economy Since Independence: Persisting Colonial Disruption*, op. cit.
11. A. Kumar, "Structural Adjustment Policies: Loss of Sovereignty and Alternatives", *Lokayan Bulletin,* November–December 1991, pp. 5–23.
12. A. Kumar, "Indian Economy and the Crisis of a Borrowed Development Strategy", *Mainstream*, Independence Day Special, Vol. LI, No. 35, August 17, 2013.
13. For an exposition of the clout of the corporates, see: D.C. Korten, *When Corporations Rule the World*, Kumarian Press, Connecticut, 1995.
14. A. Kumar, "India's Black Economy: The Macroeconomic Implications", *Journal of South Asian Studies*, South Asia, Vol. 28, No. 2, August 2005. pp. 249–263.

I

IS THE GOVERNMENT REALLY POOR?*

1. India: Economic Superpower?

India has been globalising its economy for more than two decades now.

Corporate honchos, management gurus, influential economists, top academicians, intellectuals writing for prominent newspapers and appearing on television talk shows, leading journalists, celebrities, government bureaucrats and leading politicians of both the ruling and opposition coalitions (who keep interchanging their chairs)—are all ecstatic about globalisation. They are all in agreement that because of the economic reforms, the country is on its way to becoming an economic superpower.

Table 1.1: Average Decadal Growth Rate, India, 1970–2010[1]

Decade	*Average Growth Rate (% per annum)*
1970–71 to 1979–80	3.0
1980–81 to 1989–90	5.6
1990–91 to 1999–2000	5.8
2000–01 to 2009–10	7.2

Globalisation has indeed led to an increase in the country's GDP growth rate (see Table 1.1), making the country one of the world's fastest growing economies during the decade 2001–10. Till before the economy started slowing down since 2011, analysts had in fact been predicting that the country was all set to overtake China as the

* *This essay was written in August 2014, a few months after the new BJP Government assumed power.*

world's fastest growing major economy by 2015.[2] The country's real GDP growth rate accelerated to nearly 8 percent in 2003–04, and remained at above 9 percent during the three years 2005–06 to 2007–08.[3]

One consequence of these high growth rates is that India has now become the world's third largest economy[4] in terms of purchasing power parity*.

The Rich Becoming Richer

These high growth rates have led to a huge increase in the wealth of the country's super-rich. To quote one newsreport, "India's billionaires have never had it so good."[5] India now boasts of 56 billionaires with a collective net worth of $191.5 billion, as per the 2014 list of the world's billionaires released by *Forbes* magazine. That amounts to …er, Rs 11.7 lakh crore, or one-tenth of India's GDP for 2013–14.[6] India now has the sixth largest number of billionaires in the world.[7]

In 2013, the number of 'Ultra High Net Worth' individuals in India, defined as those having net assets (meaning company shares, real estate, cars, planes, yachts, etc.) of above $30 million (Rs 200 crore or so), increased by 120 to reach 7850, and their total wealth grew to $935 billion or Rs 56 lakh crore. To give an idea of what this means, this amount was just a tad above 50 percent of India's GDP for 2013–14.[8]

And the Poor Poorer

On the other hand, globalisation has also pushed crores of ordinary people down to fourth world immiseration. They have never had it so bad! This is evident from a host of government data.

In the 1970s, based on the recommendations of an expert committee, the Planning Commission defined the poverty line as that particular level of total spending per capita on all goods and services whose food spending part satisfied the nutrition level of 2,200 calories

---

* *Purchasing power parity is used to compare economies by adjusting for differences in prices in different countries.*

of energy intake per day in rural India, and 2,100 calories per day in urban areas. As per these norms and basing herself on data from official surveys (called National Sample Surveys or NSS), the noted economist Utsa Patnaik has estimated that:

- In 2004–05, 69.5 percent people in rural India were unable to access 2,200 calories; this percentage increased to 75.5 percent in 2009–10!
- 64.5 percent of the urban population was unable to reach 2,100 calories energy intake in 2004–05; this percentage too had risen to 73 percent in 2009–10.[9]

These shocking data are also confirmed by other nutritional and health surveys. Thus:

- According to the latest available National Family Health Survey–3 (NFHS–3, conducted in 2005–06), more than 48 percent of children under the age of five are stunted (low height for age, indicating chronic malnutrition).[10]
- In 2011, a large-scale survey by civil society organisations across 100 districts found that rates of stunting among children below the age of five had gone up to 59 percent, 11 percentage points higher as compared to NFHS–3.[11]
- According to the UNICEF, one in every three malnourished children in the world lives in India; malnutrition is more common in India than in sub-Saharan Africa.[12]

Other 'Human Development' indicators are equally abysmal. Thus, India claims that it is becoming a knowledge superpower. Ever since the government opened up the higher education sector for the private sector to invest and make profits, the number of colleges and universities in the country has zoomed:

- The number of universities in India rose from 256 in 2000–01 to 700 in 2012–13, a two-and-a-half fold increase in just 12 years; and the number of colleges zoomed to 35,539 in 2011–12 from 12,806 in 2000–01, a three-fold increase in just over a decade![13]

However, this growth is mainly at the higher education level, and most of these new educational institutions are in the private sector. Being private-sector led, this boom is obviously oriented towards catering to children from the middle and upper classes. So far as the poor are concerned, 42 percent children drop out of school without completing basic schooling (elementary education). The drop-out rates at the elementary level for scheduled caste and scheduled tribe students are even higher, at 51.25 percent and 57.58 percent respectively![14]

Two Questions . . .

Malnourishment impairs the mental and physical development of children. How can a country which is home to one-third of the world's malnourished children claim that it is on its way to becoming an economic superpower?

Education is fundamental to development; it not only benefits those taking education, it benefits society as a whole, which is why an important characteristic of all developed societies is universal, high-quality education. In the words of Amartya Sen, "Nothing really is as important in the world as getting children to school, especially female children."[15] How can a country which is not concerned with imparting even elementary education to the vast majority of its children call itself a knowledge superpower?

India's Biggest Scam

Despite these appalling poverty and hunger levels and development indicators, India's ruling classes are reducing the government's welfare expenditures—designed to make available essential services like food, education and health to the poor at affordable rates—and transferring the savings to the super-rich!

Sounds unbelievable, but is absolutely true. It is actually India's biggest scam—to the tune of lakhs of crores of rupees!

And how has the government been able to get away with this, without it creating an uproar across the country? To justify this, the establishment economists have cooked up an economic theory—that may be called the 'Fiscal Deficit Reduction Theory'—and have been able to 'market' it so well that it has become an economic gospel today.

This essay seeks to expose this gigantic scam being perpetrated on the Indian people.

But before we go ahead, let us first discuss an issue that we have raised at the beginning of this essay: if the poverty levels in the country are so huge and growing, then how come the country has seen such high growth rates during the past more than a decade? Why has the country's much hyped GDP growth rate of 8–9 percent per annum (before the present slowdown since 2011) not trickled down to the ordinary people?

2. The GDP Obsession

Gross domestic product, or GDP, measures the total market value of all the goods and services produced (and sold) in an economy. The problem lies in this supposed gauge itself, that economists have traditionally relied on to assess societal well-being. A few examples will illustrate why this gauge is faulty:

- If a certain quantity of goods are produced but not sold, and instead consumed by the producer, then they do not add to the GDP. Therefore, most of India's small farmers, who produce for self-consumption, do not contribute to the country's GDP. But when they are driven out of their lands, and their lands are taken over by giant corporations to set up villas/golf courses/expressways/airports/industrial projects, this contributes to the GDP and is called development. But what about the destruction of farmers' livelihoods? That is of no consequence; in any case, they were not contributing to the GDP. This is precisely the 'development model' that the Modi Government is seeking to implement at an accelerated pace by modifying the Land Acquisition Act, so as to make acquisition of land of small farmers easier.
- If a corporation increases production and at the same time reduces the number of workers employed by it, since the

profits of the corporation increase, this is supposed to be good for the economy, never mind the destruction of workers' livelihoods.

- When a public transport system is deliberately dismantled to promote the growth of private cars, this is supposed to be good for economic growth, even though the resulting traffic congestion contributes to increased pollution, more accidents, and much time of people wasted in traffic jams.
- A living forest does not contribute to GDP growth, but when its trees are cut down for timber, that contributes to growth; and then when a factory is set up in place of the forest, that contributes to still more GDP growth.
- Water available in underground aquifers for the common usage of all does not contribute to GDP growth. But when Coca-Cola sets up a bottling plant, extracts millions of litres of this water, bottles and sells it, this contributes to GDP growth. In the village of Plachimada in Kerala, where Coca-Cola had set up one such bottling plant, this over-exploitation of groundwater created severe drinking water shortages for the local people and adversely affected agriculture. Women were forced to walk as much as 10 km to fetch drinking water. Additionally, toxic waste from the plant polluted the local lands and water bodies. The local people eventually said, 'Enough is enough', and launched an agitation that forced the plant to shut down. Their livelihoods and health were thus saved, but it adversely affected the country's GDP!
- When farmers save seeds and use them for next year's crop, or engage in organic farming, since they are no longer buying seeds, chemical fertilisers and pesticides from the market, this negatively affects the country's GDP growth. But when they buy Monsanto's genetically modified seeds, and do chemical intensive farming, this adds to the country's GDP, even though these agricultural practices have pushed crores of Indian farmers into indebtedness and have led to more than three lakh farmers' suicides in the past two decades.

That this obsession with GDP growth rate does not take into account the destruction of livelihoods and environment caused by economic growth, and so is a false measure of the wealth of nations, is now admitted even by some of the world's leading economists like Joseph Stiglitz and Amartya Sen. In a study done for French President Nicolas Sarkozy in 2009, these economists called for the adoption of new tools to measure how well the economy is doing, that incorporate a broader concern for human welfare and environmental sustainability than just economic growth. Their report, titled *The Measurement of Economic Performance and Social Progress Revisited*, said:

> Developing countries may be encouraged to allow a foreign mining company to develop a mine, even though the country receives low royalties, even though the environment may be degraded, and even though miners may be exposed to health hazards, because by doing so GDP will be increased.

The authors of the report noted that over the course of recent decades, GDP was rising in most of the world, even as the median disposable income* was falling in many countries, meaning that economic growth was benefiting the wealthy at the expense of the rest. The Stiglitz–Sen Commission report calls on policy makers to focus on the material well-being of typical people by measuring income and consumption, along with availability of health care and education, instead of being obsessed with increasing the production of goods and services in the economy.[16]

Despite these limitations with the concept of GDP, the Indian Government, ever since it began the globalisation of the economy in 1991, has single-mindedly focussed on adopting policies to increase the GDP growth rate of the economy. Why? Because it gives the government an excuse to implement policies that maximise profits of giant corporations, even though they have caused enormous destruction of livelihoods, massive impoverishment of people, and

---

* *Median income for a country is that income such that half the people earn above that amount, and half below it (it is different from mean income, which is total aggregate income divided by number of people); disposable income is income after payment of taxes.*

mind-boggling environmental destruction.

And why is our government bent upon adopting such anti-people policies? Why have our country's rulers divorced themselves from the ordinary people, and have so totally aligned themselves with the elites? To understand this, we need to go back two decades, to 1991 . . .

3. Why Globalisation?

Debt Entrapment

After India won independence in 1947, the economic model implemented in the country by the Nehru Government was essentially a model of autonomous capitalist development. Its most essential features—the mixed economy model, the Industrial Policy Resolutions of 1948 and 1956, and restrictions on foreign capital inflows—closely followed the economic plan proposed by the 'Post-War Economic Development Committee' set up by the Indian capitalists in 1942. The committee comprised of eight leading Indian industrialists, including Purshottamdas Thakurdas, J.R.D. Tata, G.D. Birla and Sri Ram. Its proposal, titled *A Plan of Economic Development of India*, popularly came to be known as the *Bombay Plan* or the *Tata–Birla Plan*.[17]

Due to many reasons, by the late 1980s, this model was in crisis. One of the consequences of this crisis was that the Indian economy was trapped in an external debt crisis and was on the verge of external account bankruptcy (see Box 1.1).

The developed capitalist countries, who not very long ago were the imperial masters of the entire Third World*, were looking for just such an opportunity. They had been forced to retreat and grant independence to India and other Third World countries after a tidal wave of powerful independence struggles had swept across these countries in the years after the end of the Second World War. By the

* *Third World: This term is used to define the 'developing' (actually underdeveloped) countries of Asia, Africa and Latin America, most of whom were colonies or neo-colonies of the developed countries in the 19th and early 20th centuries.*

early 1970s, the post-War boom in the economies of the developed countries had come to an end, and 'stagnation' returned to afflict their economies once again, that is, their economies began to slow down once again.*

Box 1.1: Some Economics

An external debt is different from an internal debt. For a Third World country like India, the government can repay its internal debt by, say, increasing taxes on the people. However, an external debt is in international currency, like dollars, and it cannot be repaid in rupees. When for a country like India, its foreign exchange outflows (due to imports, profit repatriation by foreign companies in India, etc.) are more than its foreign exchange earnings (from exports, tourism earnings, remittances by workers abroad, etc.), one way of paying the difference, called the current account deficit, is by taking a dollar loan from abroad. But an interest has to be paid on this foreign debt, which also needs to be paid in dollars. Thus, debt servicing of the external debt leads to still more debt.

Since it was no longer possible for them to outright colonise the Third World countries as before, they now began looking for alternative ways to bring the former colonial world back under their hegemony and ensnare it once again in the imperialist network, so that they could once again control its raw material

---

* *The giant monopoly corporations dominating the economies of the advanced capitalist countries have an enormous capacity to expand production, as well as earn super-profits. And so the capitalist system in these countries has come to be gripped by a problem of finding profitable investment opportunities to invest the growing pool of accumulated capital. The result has been a slowdown in the rate of growth, along with rising unemployment and falling rate of utilisation of productive capacity. This crisis, which is different from the temporary crisis of recession faced by these economies in the 19th century, is defined as stagnation. While during the small-scale capitalism of the 19th century, rapid growth was the norm and economic crisis the exception, now, in the monopoly capitalism of the 20th–21st century, 'stagnation is the norm, good times the exception'. (For more on stagnation, see: Paul M. Sweezy, "Why Stagnation?"* Monthly Review, *June 2012, http://monthlyreview.org.)*

resources and exploit its markets.[18]

With the Indian economy caught in an external debt trap, the Western imperialist powers sensed that the time was opportune to force the Government of India to submit to a restructuring of the Indian economy and open it up to foreign capital flows and imports. The World Bank (WB), an international financial institution that is decisively controlled by the US and West European countries, submitted a memorandum to the Indian Government in November 1990 'suggesting' economic reforms like opening up the economy to foreign investment, liberalising trade, privatisation of the public sector, reforming the financial sector, and so on. Simultaneously, the Western creditors put on hold fresh loans to the Indian Government, demanding that it first implement these policy changes.[19]

Globalisation Begins

The Nehru Model of capitalist development sharply polarised Indian society. Society split into two camps. In one camp are the capitalists, big farmers, big traders, politicians, bureaucrats, blackmarketeers, smugglers, mafia, dealers, distributors, etc.—the parasites. They comprise less than 5 percent of the population. In the other camp are the working people, the students and youth, and the pro-people intellectuals—the ordinary folk. These are 95 percent of the population. It is the first camp which controls political power in the country. All major political parties serve only its interests.

By the late 1980s, the path of relatively autonomous capitalist development chosen by the Indian ruling classes was beset with severe structural crisis. The capitalist classes now came to the conclusion that in order to expand their profit accumulation, they must abandon their dream of independent capitalist development and become active collaborators of the imperialists.

And so, in mid-1991, the Indian Government, in return for a huge foreign loan to tide over the foreign exchange crisis, signed an agreement with the World Bank and the International Monetary Fund (IMF) pledging a thoroughgoing restructuring of the Indian economy. The main elements of this Structural Adjustment Programme (SAP) accepted by the Government of India are:[20]

1. **Free Trade:** Removal of all curbs on imports and exports.

2. Free Investment: Removal of all restrictions on foreign investment in all sectors of the economy.

3. Free Market: No government interference in the operation of the market. This means:

i) Ending of all subsidies to the poor, including food, health and education subsidies;
ii) Privatisation of the public sector, including essential services like drinking water, health and education;
iii) Removal of all government controls on profiteering, even in essential services.

It is this 'restructuring' of the Indian economy at the behest of the country's foreign creditors that has been given the high sounding name, *Globalisation.*

Globalisation is the consensus policy of the entire Indian ruling class. And so, ever since 1991, while governments have kept changing at the Centre, globalisation of the Indian economy has continued unabated. The first budget of the new BJP-led government makes it obvious that despite its rhetoric of *Swadeshi* or indigenous development, it is going to implement globalisation at an even faster speed than the previous UPA Government.

In consequence of the second conditionality—'free investment'—imposed by the World Bank, for the last two decades, the Indian Government has gradually allowed foreign corporations to enter each and every sector of the Indian economy. It is allowing them to take over our mineral resources, agricultural lands, public sector corporations and even our public sector financial institutions. Most recently, the new NDA–BJP Government that has come to power at the Centre has even permitted foreign direct investment (FDI) in defence. More than two centuries ago, the British had to use force to colonise this country. Now, our rulers are themselves allowing foreign corporations to enter and take control of the country's economy.

The upshot of the third conditionality—'free market'—is that successive governments at the Centre (and the states too) have been running the economy solely for the profit maximisation of giant foreign corporations and their collaborators, the big Indian business houses.

Simultaneously, they have also been reducing government expenditures on welfare services and gradually privatising them, so that they can be taken over by private corporations and transformed into instruments for naked profiteering.

Goebbelsian Propaganda

The Indian elites are euphoric about globalisation. Their wealth has increased at a brisk pace—the number of Indian households with a minimum net worth of more than Rs 25 crore doubled over the four-year period 2011–14.[21] Foreign corporations are entering each and every sector of the Indian economy; some of India's big capitalists have become their junior collaborators; others are benefiting through dealerships, sub-contracts, etc. Hoarders and blackmarketeers are having a field day—laws controlling their activities are being relaxed in the name of freeing the market. Due to financial liberalisation, the speculators have never had it so good. India's swanky middle classes are in raptures over globalisation—the world's most trendy consumer brands are now available in the country. And so leading Indian intellectuals and media houses—faithful servants of the capitalist classes—have launched a massive propaganda campaign to convince the Indian people about the benefits of globalisation.

The country is on *SALE*. And yet, how do you convince people that this is beneficial for the country? So, the propaganda machinery has launched a huge indoctrination campaign about the benefits of 'FDI'—that it will lead to creation of jobs, fall in prices, make available high quality goods and technology, enable Indian industry to become more competitive, blah blah blah.

But how do you convince people that cutbacks in government spending on education, health, ration system and other welfare services are good for the economy? For that, they have come up with an economic theory—that 'reduction in fiscal deficit' is good for development. The government is claiming that its expenditures on welfare services are very high, are 'unsustainable', and need to be reduced for economic growth, employment generation, bringing down inflation, blah blah blah.

4. Fiscal Deficit Reduction Gospel

Fiscal Deficit

Fiscal deficit is the excess of government expenditures over its revenue from all sources.

- Fiscal Deficit = Government Expenditures – Revenues

Government revenues include both income from taxation (from both direct and indirect taxes), as well as non-tax revenues such as profits of public sector enterprises and revenues from sale of state-assets.*

Reduction of Fiscal Deficit: An Economic Canon

That high levels of fiscal deficit relative to GDP adversely affect growth is an economic gospel today. All the leading establishment economists, each and every economist associated with international financial institutions and every renowned management guru—are in agreement that India needs to rein in its fiscal deficit if it is to maintain its growth rate and become an economic superpower in the near future. To quote a few of the present and former leading economic advisors to the Government of India:

- **Kaushik Basu**, World Bank Chief Economist and former Chief Economic Advisor in the Finance Ministry, Government of India (2012): "Government's top across politicians together are mature enough that they realise that the path of fiscal consolidation is extremely important."[22]
- C. **Rangarajan**, Chairman, Prime Minister's Economic Advisory Council (2013): "I think there has been an effort to reduce subsidies (given by the government). We need to do more."[23]
- **Raghuram Rajan**, former Director, Research Department, IMF, and presently Governor, RBI: "The government has to be commended for its efforts to revive growth, narrow the current account deficit, and meet fiscal targets.... Going

* *All these economic terms are explained in detail in Essay II.*

> forward, however, we need to continue on the path of fiscal consolidation—constantly improving the sustainability and quality of fiscal adjustment."[24]

Ever since India began globalisation, controlling the fiscal deficit has been a key aspect of budget making of the Government of India. All the finance ministers of all the governments that have come to power at the Centre since 1991 have focussed on reducing government expenditures and bringing down the fiscal deficit to 'sustainable levels'. The Indian Parliament even passed a law in 2003 requiring the reduction of the fiscal deficit to 3 percent of GDP by 2008. This deadline was subsequently suspended because of the 2007 international financial crisis. Nevertheless, P. Chidambaram, the finance minister in the UPA Government that recently demitted office (2014), promised to bring down the fiscal deficit to this level by 2016–17.[25] He brought down the fiscal deficit from 4.8 percent in 2012–13 to 4.5 percent in 2013–14; and then set a target for further reducing it to 4.1 percent for the year 2014–15 in his interim budget presented just before the 2014 Lok Sabha elections.[26]

Now, a new BJP-led NDA Government is in power at the Centre. The new Finance Minister Arun Jaitley, soon after being sworn in, declared that the immediate focus of the government would be on curbing the fiscal deficit.[27] In his first budget speech, he vowed to adhere to the "daunting" fiscal deficit target of 4.1 percent of GDP for the year 2014–15 set by his predecessor, and further affirmed that the fiscal deficit would be brought down to 3.6 percent in 2015–16 and 3 percent by 2016–17 (Chart 1.1).[28]

Every news channel and newspaper every other day carries a newsreport highlighting the disaster that awaits us if we don't control our fiscal deficit. And so, most people have come to accept this as a gospel truth.

Chart 1.1: Fiscal Deficit of the Central Government[29]
(% of GDP)

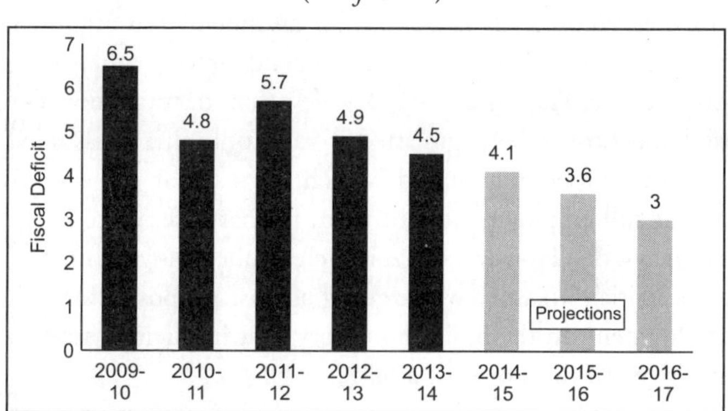

Humbug of Finance

The fact is, and this may sound unbelievable to most of our readers, the economic theory that the government must balance its expenditure with its income, that is, must bring down its fiscal deficit to near zero, is plain humbug. John Maynard Keynes, considered by many to be the greatest economist of the twentieth century, had convincingly demolished it long ago in his opus *The General Theory of Employment, Interest and Money* published in 1936.

Before that, that is, till the 1920s, economic theory held that governments must seek to balance their expenditure and income, and that the most desirable policy for an economy is zero fiscal deficit. For instance, a White Paper of the British Treasury, written in 1929 in response to Lloyd George's (British Liberal politician and former prime minister) suggestion that Britain should undertake public works for reducing unemployment which at that time stood at 10 percent (the Great Depression was just beginning, unemployment was to reach 20 percent later), based itself on this economic logic. The White Paper argued that in any economy there was at any time only a certain pool of savings, and that if more of it was used for public works financed by government borrowing, then less was left over for private investment. It follows then that public works can never increase total employment in an economy since the increase in employment brought about by public works would be exactly counterbalanced by the reduction in employment arising from reduced private investment.

Keynes exposed the fallacy of this argument. His argument was simple: total savings in an economy depend, among other things, on its total income. The British Treasury view that the total pool of savings is fixed and cannot be augmented is valid only if it is assumed that income cannot be augmented, which means that the economy is already at full employment. But then, in that case, there is no need for public works. However, what if there is unemployment? It follows that the British Treasury was arguing against proposals for reducing unemployment on the basis of a theory that implicitly assumed that unemployment did not exist at all!

Keynes explained in the beginning of his magnum opus that the orthodox economics of his day assumed that unemployment was an aberration, and that the natural state of the economy was full employment. However, the reality was, this hardly ever existed under capitalism. Keynes showed that there is a natural tendency for an advanced capitalist economy to run into chronic stagnation, with permanent unemployment. (Keynes did not develop an actual theory of stagnation; that was done by other economists, like Michael Kalecki, Josef Steindl, Paul Baran and Paul Sweezy.)

In an economy where there is unemployment, it means economic resources (labour, machinery, etc.) are lying idle due to lack of demand. Keynes argued that in such an economy, the government can, and in fact should, expand public works and generate employment by borrowing, that is, enlarging the fiscal deficit. Far from there being any adverse effect of this on private sector expenditure, such government action in fact would stimulate private sector expenditure through the "multiplier" effect (the employment created due to government investment would stimulate demand, and hence would lead to larger output and employment in the private sector too). It would not generate any significant inflationary pressures too. Keynes went on to show that the fiscal deficit (that is, the additional investment by the government) would eventually result in accrual of an equal amount of savings in private hands (which can be invested). A fiscal deficit in other words finances itself.

Keynes in fact stated that to argue against the mitigation to human suffering that an increased fiscal deficit can provide is sheer "humbug of finance".[30]

Return of the Humbug

All developed countries (especially in Western Europe) and many newly independent countries initially adopted Keynesian economic principles after the Second World War, thus giving rise to what has come to be known as the welfare state.

During the 1950s–60s, the changed economic conditions after the Second World War and historical conditions led to rapid economic growth in the advanced capitalist countries. However, by the 1970s, the special factors that had caused this growth were mostly on the wane.[31] These economies started to slow down, and entered a long period of stagnation, that has continued till today.

Among the various strategies adopted by the ruling classes of the developed countries to keep the profit accumulation process going, one important strategy was to *withdraw the welfare benefits given to the poor and transfer them to the rich*. To legitimise this assault on the welfare state, the 'voodoo economics' of the 1920s, dubbed by Keynes as *humbug of finance*, was revived—that government budgets must be balanced (and hence welfare expenditures must be cut). Josef Steindl, the great Austrian economist, called it a "counter-revolution, the return of the Bourbons" in economics. Meanwhile, transfers to the rich were justified in the name of promoting entrepreneurism. An economic theory was also invented to back it up—'supply-side economics'—which claimed that tax breaks to the wealthy would help boost investment. The theory was of course silent on who would buy the goods thus produced in an economy already in the grip of saturation.*

* *To explain this point further: In an economy gripped by stagnation / recession, the problem is not that the capitalists do not have money to produce goods, the problem is there is a surplus of goods in the market which are not being sold. (For more on this, see Paul M. Sweezy, Harry Magdoff, "Supply-Side Economics", Monthly Review, March 1981, http://archive.monthlyreview.org; "Notes from the Editors",* Monthly Review, *October 2010, https://monthlyreview.org.)*

This capitalist offensive on the working classes was first launched in the United States and Britain in the early 1980s, during the days when the conservative governments of Ronald Reagan and Margaret Thatcher were in power. Since then, these policies have continued, irrespective of the shade of government in power, and have spread to rest of Europe as well.[32]

Meanwhile, by the same time, the economies of most Third World countries or 'developing countries' too became crisis-ridden. Many of these countries had achieved independence from colonial rule after the Second World War, and the native ruling classes that had come to power had adopted a model of autonomous capitalist development (similar to the economic model implemented in India)—one of whose key elements was limiting the penetration of imperialist capital into their economies. However, there are inherent limitations to independent capitalist development in the Third World countries,[33] and by the 1970s, their economic models had started failing. These countries then started taking loans from the imperialist countries. Gradually, the external debt accumulated, and eventually became unpayable. In the early 1980s, several Third World countries approached international financial agencies (World Bank, International Monetary Fund) for quick loans to avoid external account bankruptcy. The IMF–WB readily agreed, but in return, forced these countries to undertake a thorough restructuring of their economies (the so-called *Structural Adjustment Programme*). They were forced to dismantle the restrictions imposed on inflows of foreign goods and capital into their economies. Another important conditionality imposed on these debt-laden underdeveloped countries was that they implement the Reagan–Thatcher economic model and reduce their fiscal deficit, that is, reduce their subsidies to the poor and privatise welfare services. Simultaneously, they were encouraged to transfer ownership of public resources and public sector institutions to private sector corporations and give the latter 'incentives' to 'accelerate GDP growth'.[34]

The consequences of this economic model have been catastrophic for the people of these countries. It has led to massive destruction of livelihoods and huge rise in hunger, poverty, disease and destitution all across the Third World.[35] Nevertheless, the ruling classes of these countries have been willing accomplices of the corporations and governments of the developed countries. They have faithfully implemented the WB–IMF dictated economic model on their people, an important reason being that the rich of these Third World countries have actually benefited by these economic reforms—similar to what is happening in India today.

The Humbug Imposed on India

Till about 1990, hardly anyone in India mentioned the 'fiscal deficit'. The term is not even to be found in the *Economic Survey 1989–90.* Till then, what used to be discussed was the budget deficit—the printing of money by the central bank to meet government spending needs. [Budget Deficit = Government Expenditures – (Government Tax and Non-tax revenues + Government Borrowings)]

One of the conditionalities of the World Bank–dictated SAP imposed on India following the foreign exchange crisis of 1990–91 was that the government must stop the printing of money to finance its deficit, that is, it must phase out its budget deficit. Instead, the World Bank asked the government to resort to borrowing from the market to meet its deficit—this borrowing is what is called the fiscal deficit.[36] Further, it asked the government to strive to reduce its fiscal deficit; according to the World Bank, reduction in India's fiscal deficit "would materially increase growth and reduce inflation."[37] And so, the term 'fiscal deficit' made its first appearance in the *Economic Survey 1990–91* presented to the Parliament by Finance Minister Manmohan Singh on July 20, 1991.[38]

Since then, each and every budget of the Government of India (even though the coalition at the Centre has been changing) has made reduction in fiscal deficit a central task of the budget. The pimps who masquerade as intellectuals have been writing lengthy articles in the media warning of impending doom unless the fiscal deficit is curtailed.

Of course, neither the World Bank, nor any of our finance ministers—from Manmohan Singh and Yashwant Sinha to P. Chidambaram and now Arun Jaitley—have really been concerned about reducing the fiscal deficit. This is obvious from the way they have been handling the various components of the government's expenditures and revenues. The fiscal deficit is the excess of the government's expenditures over receipts. Even a cursory look at the policies being pursued by the Government of India reveals that it is giving away lakhs of crores of rupees as subsidies to the rich. Had it really been concerned about the fiscal deficit, it could have easily reduced these mind-boggling give-aways! But in the new economic lexicon preached by the High Priests in Washington, these concessions are called 'incentives' and are considered essential for 'growth'. On the other hand, the concessions given to the poor, which are aimed at making available essential welfare services like education, health, food, transport and electricity to them at affordable rates, are given the derisive name 'subsidies' and are being drastically reduced in the name of containing the fiscal deficit. Not only that, these essential services are also being privatised—resulting in fabulous profits for the private sector.

5. The Fiscal Deficit Fraud

A. Incentives to the Rich

Those who take the meat from the table
Teach contentment.
Those for whom the taxes are destined
Demand sacrifice.
Those who eat their fill speak to the hungry
Of wonderful times to come.
Those who lead the country into the abyss
Call ruling too difficult
For ordinary folk.

– Bertolt Brecht

Let us take a look at some of these so-called incentives being given to the rich, especially the giant foreign and Indian business houses that today dominate the Indian economy and exercise enormous control over government policies.

i) Tax Concessions to the Rich

While presenting the 2013–14 budget, Finance Minister P. Chidambaram admitted that the ratio of taxes to GDP in India was "one of the lowest for any large developing country", and that it would "not garner adequate resources for inclusive and sustainable development." However, in the same breath, he also stated that there was very little potential for raising taxes to improve the tax–GDP ratio: "In a constrained economy, there is little room to raise tax rates or large amounts of additional tax revenues."[39]

Chidambaram is a bare-faced liar! Every year, for the past several years, the budget documents have included a statement on the estimated revenue forgone by the government due to exemptions in major taxes levied by the Centre. The budget documents reveal that for the year 2013–14, the government gave away Rs 5.32 lakh crore in tax exemptions/deductions/incentives to the very rich.* These major write-offs are in direct corporate income tax, customs and excise duties: corporate tax concessions amounted to Rs 76,116 crore, more than twice that sum (Rs 1,95,679 crore) was forgone in excise duty, and well over three times the sum was sacrificed in customs duty (Rs 2,60,714 crore).[40]

Had Chidambaram really been concerned about reducing the fiscal deficit, he could have reduced these tax concessions given to India's richie rich. *The total tax concessions given by him to the wealthy in 2013–14 of Rs 5,32,509 crore is more than our fiscal deficit for that year (Rs 5,24,539 crore)!*[41]

Successive governments at the Centre have been doling out these concessions to the 'corporate needy and the undernourished rich' for the last several years, ever since the economic reforms began. But we have data on revenue forgone only from 2005–06 (as it is only from 2006–07 that the budget documents started carrying these figures). They reveal that over the nine-year period 2005–06 to 2013–14, the tax write-offs given by the government to the super-rich total a mind-

---

* *The write-offs as mentioned in the budget are actually Rs 5.72 lakh crore. From that, we have deducted the Rs 40,000 crore forgone on personal income tax, since this write-off benefits a wider group of people.*

boggling Rs 36.6 lakh crore (Table 1.2)! To give an idea of the immensity of this figure, it is equivalent to roughly one-third of our 2013–14 GDP.[42]

These tax concessions are being given to some of the richest people in the world. *Forbes*, the oracle of business journalism, puts out a list of the world's billionaires every year. Its 2013 list included the names of 55 Indians, with an average net worth of around Rs 19,080 crore. Their total net worth was Rs 10.5 lakh crore, double our fiscal deficit for 2013–14.[43]

Table 1.2: Revenue Forgone Due to Tax Exemptions Given by the Central Government to the Rich, 2006–14[43]

	2005-06	*2006-07*	*2007-08*	*2008-09*	*2009-10*	*2010-11*	*2011-12*	*2012-13*	*2013-14*	*Total Revenue Forgone*
Revenue forgone, Rs lakh cr	2.29	2.73	3.03	4.21	4.37	4.23	5.07	5.33	5.32	36.59
Revenue forgone as % of GDP	6.20	6.36	6.07	7.48	6.74	5.43	5.65	5.25	4.68	

The obscenity of these tax concessions becomes evident from just a single statistic: in 2013–14, the single biggest chunk of customs duties forgone was on diamonds and gold, accounting for Rs 48,000 crore. The waiver on gold and diamonds in just three years (2012–14) was Rs 1.6 lakh crore—equivalent to 30 percent of our fiscal deficit for 2013–14. No wonder that three new Indian entrants to *Forbes* 2013 billionaires list were from the field of jewellery.[45]

India's Tax–GDP Ratio: Lowest in the World

It is because of these huge tax concessions that India's tax–GDP ratio (see Box 1.2 for definition), at 18.5 percent of GDP, is far below not only the 'advanced economies' (36.7 percent), but also the 'emerging market and developing economies' (27.9 percent). Even the countries of sub-Saharan Africa, considered to be one of the poorest regions in the world, have a tax–GDP ratio of 27 percent (Chart 1.2). It is thus obvious that there is a huge scope for increasing tax revenues in India.

> **Box 1.2: Tax-to-GDP Ratio**
>
> This ratio helps to understand how much tax revenue is being collected by the government as compared to the overall size of the economy.

The international credit rating agencies, the IMF and World Bank, the economic czars occupying prestigious chairs in the universities in New York and London, all of whom lecture us every day on the importance of reducing our fiscal deficit—none of them ever talk of our low tax–GDP ratio and the need to increase it to at least the level of the sub-Saharan African countries by reducing the subsidies given to our super-rich.

Chart 1.2: General Government Revenues of Developed Countries and India, 2007–11[46]

(% of GDP)

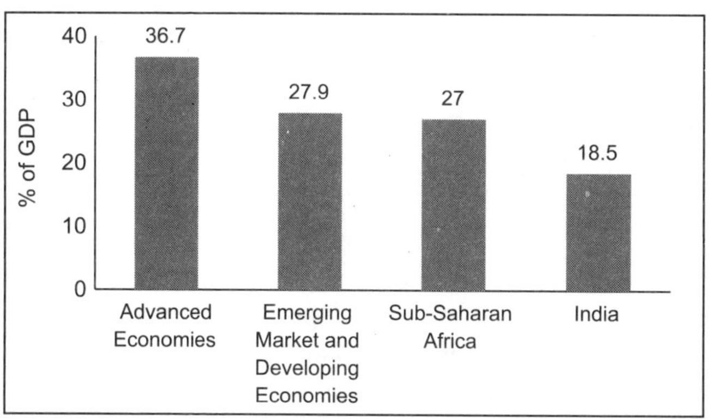

Why is the government giving such mind-boggling tax concessions to the already wealthy? This is revealed in the presentations made by Chidambaram to foreign investors during his trips to Singapore, Hong Kong, London and Frankfurt in January 2013. Wooing these brigands to invest their monies in India, he stated:[47]

> Among emerging markets India has one of the most favourable tax regimes, a very crucial factor for business growth.

BJP Government: Yet More Tax Concessions to the Rich

These mind-boggling transfers to the corporate trough are going to continue at an accelerated pace under the new government at the Centre. Arun Jaitley, the finance minister of the BJP/NDA Government, wants to outdo his predecessor in giving tax concessions to the super-rich. He has gone on record to say that the country had a "high tax regime", and that as the economy improves, he would announce more income tax concessions.[48]

(ii) Plundering Resources

a) Mother of All Scams: KG Basin Gas Scam

Though hydrocarbon reserves of the country belong to the people, bowing to World Bank conditionalities, the Government of India in 2000 handed over exploration of gas reserves in D-6 block of the Krishna Godavari basin to Reliance Industries Limited (RIL). The production sharing contract with RIL stipulated that RIL is to pay the government only 10 percent of the total revenue until it recovers 1.5 times its investment; thereafter, the government's share would increase.[49] RIL, in naked collusion with the government, through a series of manipulations, has indulged in absolutely mind-boggling plunder of the country's natural gas wealth. We briefly give three of these frauds below:

- In 2004, the government allowed RIL to over-invoice its capital expenditure in developing the D-6 block from the original estimate of $2.4 billion to $8.8 billion. This 'gold-plating' by RIL is estimated to have caused a loss to the government of at least Rs 37,000 crore.[50]
- In 2003, the public sector National Thermal Power Corporation (NTPC) agreed to buy gas from RIL for its thermal plants at the rate of $2.34 per unit of gas* for the next 17 years—even though Oil and Natural Gas Corporation (ONGC, a public sector oil and gas corporation) was supplying gas (to industries such as power and fertiliser) at

* *One unit of gas = One million British thermal units (mBtu)*

the rate of $1.83 per unit of gas. (According to one estimate, RIL's cost per unit of gas is $1.43; another estimate puts it at less than $1.)[51]

- And then, in 2007, the government allowed RIL to double the price of gas being supplied by it (to NTPC and other industries) to $4.20 per unit! The total additional profit to RIL due to this price increase—a cool Rs 1,20,000 crore (this is over and above the profit it was making when it was supplying gas at $2.34 per unit)![52] Three-fourth of the natural gas in the country is consumed by the power and fertiliser industries,[53] implying that this largesse to RIL is one of the reasons for the steep hike in the prices of electricity and urea fertiliser in recent years.

Adding up these figures, the total profit to RIL and loss to the exchequer from this illegal transfer of our natural gas reserves to RIL is going to be Rs 2 lakh crore at the minimum. This, for gas fields identified by the ONGC, which also has the necessary technology and expertise needed to explore and develop these gas fields—in other words, there was no need to transfer them to RIL!

b) Iron Ore Mining Scam

In 2005, the US–Korean multinational POSCO signed an agreement with the Odisha Government to build a steel plant in the state, along with a captive port and allocation of iron ore mines. The agreement allows POSCO to extract a total of 600 million tons of high grade iron ore for use in its proposed steel plant in the area, and also mine another 400 million tons of iron ore for export to its steel plants in South Korea. While the project is billed as India's largest FDI proposal, it is also going to result in stupendous profits for POSCO. We make a rough estimate of its profits below (for only its mining operations):[54]

- Let us take the cost of extraction, processing and transport of iron ore for POSCO to be a generous Rs 800 per ton. (These costs are Rs 400 per ton in Karnataka.)
- The government has fixed the royalty on the iron ore (to be

paid by POSCO to the government) at an absurdly low 10 percent of the sale price. Taking the market price of iron ore lumps to be Rs 5,000 per ton (an underestimate), this means POSCO will be paying a royalty of Rs 500 for each ton of iron ore mined.

- POSCO therefore stands to make a profit of at least Rs 3,700 [5000 – 800 – 500] for each ton of iron ore mined. POSCO will be mining 600 million tons of iron ore for its steel plant over the next 30 years—giving it a total profit of over Rs 2.22 lakh crore.
- Additionally, POSCO has been allowed to export 400 million tons of iron ore to South Korea—thus giving it an additional profit of Rs 1.48 lakh crore.

All this, just from mining iron ore, that belongs to the people of the country, when we have public sector companies with all the necessary technology and expertise needed to mine it.

That is just the *legal* iron ore mining scam. Apart from this, millions of tons of iron ore is being illegally mined and exported from the country. There are reportedly nearly twice as many illegal mines in the country as legal ones. Illegal iron ore mining scandals have come to light in at least five states—Karnataka, Andhra Pradesh, Chhattisgarh, Odisha and Jharkhand—with the chief ministers of at least three states directly involved in these scams.[55]

c) Coal Scam

Post-globalisation, the government began allocating coal blocks to private companies for private use. As of March 31, 2011, the government had allocated 194 (net) coal blocks to government and private parties. Wonder of wonders, these allocations were not done on the basis of any competitive bidding! When the Comptroller and Auditor General of India (CAG) investigated the coal block allocations to private parties, its report tabled in Parliament on August 17, 2012 contained damning findings. It estimated the financial gains accruing to the private block allottees in respect of the 57 open cast/mixed mines allocated to them to be a gigantic Rs 1.86 lakh crore![56]

(iii) The Great Land Grab

Tens of thousands of acres of land are being handed over to private corporations virtually for free to set up their projects. A few examples:

a) Land @ Re 1 per sq metre

The Gujarat Government allotted a staggering 14,305 acres—equivalent to 5.78 crore square metres—of land in Kutch to billionaire Gautam Adani controlled Adani Group at prices ranging from Re 1 to Rs 32 per sq metre (average price less than Rs 10 per sq metre). Adani paid less than Rs 60 crore for this huge chunk of land, whose market price was anywhere between Rs 1,000 to Rs 1,500 per sq metre. He then sublet a part of it to other companies, including state-owned Indian Oil, for as much as Rs 780 per sq metre.

Such scams abound in Gujarat. To give a few more examples: [57]

- The state government allotted 8 lakh square metres (80 hectares) of prime land to Larsen and Toubro in the industrial zone of Hazira in Surat also at Re 1 per sq metre;
- 24,021 hectares was gifted to Archean Chemicals Ltd and 26,746 hectares to Solaris ChemTech in the Rann of Kutch for manufacturing salt and salt-based chemicals, at just Rs 150 per hectare;
- The Essar Group, another Modi favourite, was allotted 2.08 lakh sq metres of Coastal Regulation Zone land and forest land—that can't be allotted as per Supreme Court guidelines—for a steel plant; as if to atone for this crime, Essar paid Rs 20 lakh as fine and peacefully continues to occupy the land.

b) Delhi–Mumbai Industrial Corridor (DMIC)

This proposal to construct a 1,483 km long 'industrial corridor' between Delhi and Mumbai that will pass through six states is probably the biggest land grab in India's history. The $90 billion project includes plans to develop 24 'industrial cities' over an area of 5,000–5,500 sq km, 3 ports, 6 airports, a high-speed freight line, and a six-lane 'intersection-free' expressway. In the first phase, by 2018, 7 cities will be developed, over an area of 2,000 sq km—to put this in perspective,

Delhi is around 700 sq km. The main beneficiaries of this project are expected to be Japanese firms, including Mitsubishi, Hitachi, Toshiba and JVC. The government subsidy for phase I: Rs 2,500 crore per city, or Rs 17,500 crore in all.[58]

iv) Direct Cash Transfers to Corporations

a) Costly People's Car

State governments are competing with each other to give thousands of crores of rupees as subsidies to private corporations for setting up projects in their states. After Tata Motors was forced to move out of Singur by a determined people's movement, Modi rolled out the red carpet to welcome Ratan Tata to Gujarat. It was a carpet with gold linings. Here is a brief list of the concessions given to the Tatas to set up the Nano car project in Gujarat:

- Tata Motors was allotted 1,100 acres of land for the project in Sanand, Gujarat at a discounted price of Rs 900 per sq metre, when its market rate was around Rs 10,000 per sq metre—a total concession of Rs 44,100 crore.
- On top of it, Tata Motors was given the facility of making the payment of Rs 400 crore for the land in 8 equal instalments at 8 percent compound interest with a moratorium of two years.
- The total project cost is estimated at Rs 2,200 crore. No financial institution grants a loan of more than 70–80 percent of the project cost; however, Tatas were given a soft loan of Rs 9,570 crore at an interest rate of 0.10 percent per annum, with repayment deferred for 20 years.
- The state government also volunteered to meet the cost of shifting the project from Singur, estimated to be Rs 700 crore.
- Tatas were exempted from payment of stamp duty, registration charges and transfer charges.
- The Gujarat Government promised to build a four-lane highway for the facility; it also agreed to acquire land for a railway line leading to the plant, for ancillary industries and for setting up a township for Tata Motors.

- Additionally, it agreed to provide 220 kv and 66 kv substations at the plant's doorstep for free, make provisions for supply of 14,000 cubic litres of water per day to the project site, and provide amenities such as a facility for disposal of hazardous waste, facility for a transport hub, and a pipeline for supply of natural gas to the project site.

The total cost to the Gujarat exchequer? Rs 33,000 crore over the next 20 years! The installed project capacity is 2.5 lakh small cars per annum, so the plant would be producing 50 lakh cars over these 20 years—implying that for each car produced, tax-payers would be shelling out Rs 66,000![59]

b) Multi-Billion Dollar Transfers to Car Industry

The Centre too is giving generous dole-outs to the car industry. On January 29, 2007, Prime Minister Manmohan Singh officially released the Automotive Mission Plan (AMP) 2006–16. The Plan, drawn up by the auto industry itself [with each sub-group chaired by the head of a top auto firm (Tata, Mahindra, Maruti)], envisions huge tax concessions and grants for the automobile industry, so as to help the industry increase its turnover from $35 billion to $145 billion and exports from $4.1 billion to $35 billion over the decade 2006–2016. The Plan includes a host of tax concessions and subsidies such as:

- tax holiday for automobile sector investments;
- 100 percent tax deduction on export profits;
- deduction of 30 percent of net income for ten years for new industrial undertakings;
- increase in deduction for R & D expenditure from 150 percent to 200 percent;
- exemption from electricity duty;
- government to give 100 percent grants for fundamental research, 75 percent for pre-competitive technology/application, and 50 percent for product development.

Media reports of course called these several thousand crore rupees of subsidies "incentives for the auto industry so as to make India a hub for automobile industry."[60]

c) PPPs in Infrastructure Sector

The economists sitting in Washington/Paris/London keep coming up with innovative ideas about how to transfer government funds to the private sector. One such concept that has been embraced by the Government of India in a big way is 'Public–Private–Partnership' (or PPP). Under this, the private partner is not only guaranteed a minimum rate of return on its investment (the government making up for any shortfall in profits), is not only given land and other resources at concessional rates, even the investment money is also often provided by the government in the form of long term loans at concessional rates. What a partnership!

One of the most common forms of PPP subsidy being given to private sector corporations investing in infrastructural sectors in India is what the government calls 'Viability Gap Funding' (VGF). Thus, the *Economic Survey 2008–09* argued that "Infrastructure projects ... are generally characterised by substantial investments, long gestation periods, fixed returns, etc.", and often have "an unacceptable commercial rate of return", and therefore, the private sector will only enter the field if it is given suitable financial incentives. And so, in the name of making their investments 'viable', the Government of India provides a direct subsidy to investors in the infrastructural sector of up to 40 percent of the project cost![61] And if the investor is somehow able to pad up his project cost, he/she can then extract an even higher subsidy!

The scale of the projects given subsidies under this scheme is enormous: the cost of projects completed, under implementation or in the pipeline as on March 31, 2012, was nearly Rs 13 lakh crore.[62] These projects are in highways, ports, airports, railways, power, urban infrastructure, and other sectors. Assuming that most of these projects are receiving VGF grants at the rate of 40 percent of the investment, the total public 'subsidy' for these projects works out to more than Rs 5 lakh crore.

Apart from VGF funding, the government also gives several other types of incentives to investors in the infrastructural sectors under the PPP model. Thus, private corporations building expressways and metro projects are additionally being given vast amounts of real estate for commercial use. To give an example, in the case of the infamous Yamuna Expressway built by the Jaypee Group under the PPP model, the Group was allowed to acquire five parcels of land along the expressway, each of 500 hectares, for township projects. The expressway cost the Jaypee Group roughly Rs 13,000 crore. The Group must have got 40 percent of this, that is, Rs 5,200 crore, as investment subsidy. But the real bonanza for the company was the 2,500 hectares of land allotted to it—it acquired this land from farmers for around Rs 1,500 crore (at the rate of around Rs 5 lakh to 60 lakh per hectare), and its present market value has zoomed to a whopping Rs 1.5 lakh crore (according to a *Forbes* newsreport)![63] That is some deal.

v) Firesale of PSUs to the Private Sector

One of the most important elements of the WB–imposed SAP is privatisation of public sector undertakings (PSUs). Governments of all shades that have come to power at the Centre since 1991 have dutifully implemented this diktat and have gradually been selling government equity in public sector companies to private investors; in many firms, the government has even sold majority stake and handed over management control to the private sector. Each and every such disinvestment in these PSUs, built out of the hard earned savings of the people of the country, has been done at scandalously low prices, resulting in huge losses to the government. This has been so from the very first round of disinvestment carried out in 1991–92—the CAG estimated the loss at Rs 3,442 crore, on receipts of just Rs 3,038 crore.[64] Ever since then, each and every privatisation deal has surpassed the record of previous sell-off in terms of the damage inflicted on the national exchequer and the fortuitous gain for the private buyers. Some more examples:

- In 2001, the then NDA Government sold 51 percent of Bharat Aluminium Company (Balco), the giant public sector aluminium producer, to Sterlite, a company notorious for its environmental abuses and bad safety record. The controlling stake in the company, valued at more than Rs 5,000 crore and with fixed deposits of Rs 350 crore, was handed over to Sterlite for just Rs 550 crore—an amount less than half the value of Balco's captive power plant![65]

- In 2002, the government handed over 25 percent shares and absolute control of Videsh Sanchar Nigam Ltd (VSNL), the telecommunications giant, to the Tatas for just Rs 1,439 crore. VSNL was a cash-rich company with cash reserves and surplus to the tune of Rs 6,000 crore and had made a profit of Rs 800 crore on a paid-up capital of Rs 285 crore in the year ending 2000. At the time of its sale, VSNL had a market capitalisation of about Rs 10,000 crore. In addition, it had prime properties in all major cities with a present market value of several thousands of crores of rupees. Tatas, who were more interested in leveraging the huge resources with VSNL to benefit their priority area of mobile telephony rather than further strengthen VSNL in its core competencies of long distance calls and internet services, very soon pumped out Rs 1,200 crore from VSNL to Tata Teleservices Ltd.[66]

India's rulers have become so shameless that they have actually been gloating over this sale of 'family jewels' at throwaway prices. During his roadshows across Asia and Europe in early 2013, the theme of the presentation made by Finance Minister P. Chidambaram before foreign investors was: "Why Global Investors Should Invest in India." One of the arguments he gave was that the government was going to sell-off shares in India's leading public sector corporations, and it presented investors with an "Opportunity to Reap High Yields".[67]

vi) Robbing Banks: Grandmother of All Scams

As if giving them tax concessions, cash transfers, control over the nation's natural resources and profitable public sector enterprises was not enough, the government is allowing private sector corporations to siphon off public sector bank funds too! It is the grandmother of all scams.

Small time bank robbers are put in jail (if caught); ordinary people defaulting on bank loans have their house/scooter/other assets seized; farmers are driven to suicide for not being able to pay the instalments on their bank loans. But when the super-rich default on their (public sector) bank loans, nothing happens to them, they go scot free, even their names are not disclosed; they continue to enjoy their heated swimming pools, rooftop helipads, foreign homes and fast cars. The banks simply write off their loans. In a presentation made to bankers, Reserve Bank of India Deputy Governor K.C. Chakrabarty revealed that over the past 13 years (2001–13), Indian public sector banks had written off a whopping Rs 2 lakh crore of loans, of which more than Rs 1 lakh crore was owed by corporate houses. He went to the extent of saying that while such a hue and cry was made when the finance minister had waived off loans to farmers of Rs 60,000 crore in 2008, the loan waiver given to corporate houses was much more than this.[68]

Loan write-offs, however, make bad news, both for corporate houses and banks/government. So public sector banks are adopting a new stratagem to provide succour to these 'helpless' rich—they 'restructure' their loans. That's the buzz word today, 'Corporate Debt Restructuring' (CDR). Under its name, the payback period may be extended, interest may be waived, a part of the loan may be converted into equity; the corporation is even given another loan to tide over its 'crisis'. Private corporations whose loans have been approved for restructuring include some of India's most well-known names:

- the Andhra Pradesh based infrastructural corporations IVRCL and Coastal Projects (CDR of Rs 11,000 cr);
- ABG Shipyard, the largest private sector ship builder in India (CDR of Rs 11,000 cr, including Rs 1,800 cr as fresh loan);
- Gammon India, India's largest civil engineering construction company (CDR of Rs 14,800 cr);
- Electrosteel Steels (CDR of Rs 6,000 cr);
- Suzlon Energy (Rs 11,000 cr CDR package);
- Orchid Pharma, a leading pharmaceutical company (Rs 3,000 cr CDR package);
- Lanco Infratech, one of India's largest conglomerates (Rs 7,000 cr CDR package); and so on.[69]

Data provided by the Reserve Bank of India shows that banks, led by state-run lenders, had cumulatively recast loans worth more than Rs 2.5 lakh crore under the CDR mechanism till June 2013. Another report by the industry body FICCI says that the total volume of restructured loans is much more than this, and stood at over Rs 4 lakh crore, as banks restructure loans outside the CDR cell too.[70]

This 'loan restructuring' subsidy being given to India's biggest corporate houses is all set for a massive hike in the coming years. A 2013 Credit Suisse report titled *House of Debt–Revisited* evaluated debt levels at ten of India's biggest corporate houses, including some owned by India's richest billionaires, and came up with stunning numbers: Anil Ambani's Reliance Group had a debt of Rs 1,13,543 crore on its books while London-based mining tycoon Anil Agarwal's Vedanta Group owed Rs 99,610 crore; the Essar Group had run up a debt of Rs 98,412 crore, while Gujarat billionaire Adani's group had a debt burden of Rs 81,122 crore. All other corporate houses investigated—the Jaypee Group, JSW Group, GMR Group, Lanco Group, Videocon Group and GVK Group—also had very high debt levels. The report predicted that banks will likely need to refinance/restructure most of these loans.[71] Its predictions did not take much time to come true. In December 2013, the newspapers reported that the government was considering restructuring the loans of the power companies of some of India's biggest corporate houses, including the Tata, Reliance, Adani and Essar Groups, worth more than Rs 2 lakh crore.[72]

With the government allowing corporate houses to plunder bank funds to the tune of lakhs of crores of rupees, obviously it will have to compensate the banks for this largesse—this roundabout subsidy to corporates has a fancy name called 'recapitalisation'. Over the last seven years, the government has poured in more than Rs 71,000 crore into public sector banks in the name of bank recapitalisation.[73]

vii) To Recap

Each of these above mentioned 'scams' involves the transfer of anything from 10–50 thousand crore rupees to a few lakh crore rupees of public money to the coffers of big business houses:

- ☞ Tax concessions to the wealthy (2006–14) ⇒ Rs 36.6 lakh crore;

- ☞ KG Basin gas scam ⇒ Rs 2 lakh crore;
- ☞ POSCO iron ore mining scam ⇒ Rs 3.7 lakh crore;
- ☞ Coal scam ⇒ Rs 1.86 lakh crore;
- ☞ Gujarat land scam ⇒ Rs 6,000 crore and counting;
- ☞ DMIC land subsidy (Phase 1) ⇒ Rs 17,500 crore;
- ☞ PPP subsidy to corporations for infrastructure projects ⇒ Rs 5 lakh crore and counting;
- ☞ Subsidies to automobile companies ⇒ Tens of thousands of crores of rupees;
- ☞ Sale of profit-making PSUs ⇒ Thousands of crores of rupees;
- ☞ Bank loan write-offs ⇒ Rs 1 lakh crore;
- ☞ Bank loan restructuring (most of it is eventually written off) ⇒ Rs 2–4 lakh crore.

And the above is just a cursory list. There would be dozens more of such scams.

The 'Bofors scam' that shook the nation in the 1980s was of only Rs 200 crore. Each of the above mentioned scams is at least a 100 to 1000 times bigger than the Bofors scam. However, only a few of these scams have hit the headlines, like the 2G spectrum scam and the coal scam, primarily because the Supreme Court has intervened in these cases. In most of the other cases of loot of public money by big corporations, the mainstream political parties (except the left parties to an extent), the country's leading intellectuals, and the media houses have chosen to maintain a conspiracy of silence—such is their collusion with big business today. That is why most people have not even heard of these scams. In fact, the country's rulers have become so audacious in their toadying to corporate houses that Prime Minister Manmohan Singh, defending the sale of '2G' telecom licences to corporate barons at a massive loss to the exchequer, compared this giveaway to top corporate firms with subsidies on the subsistence consumption of the poor, implying that it was a subsidy to corporations and therefore cannot be called a loss.[74] And Narendra Modi, when he was the chief minister of Gujarat, had the temerity to order an inquiry into who leaked the details of the concessions given to Tata's Nano project![75]

If the Government was Serious About the Fiscal Deficit . . .

This brazen loot of the nation's wealth has led to a sharp rise in the wealth of India's uber rich. Between 1996 and 2008, wealth holdings of Indian billionaires are estimated to have risen from 0.8 percent to 23 percent of India's GDP. Of the 55 Indian billionaires in the 2010 *Forbes* list, nearly half of them are involved in sectors which have directly benefited from privatisation and transfer of land and natural wealth (iron and steel, oil and natural gas, commodities, mining and metals, telecom, power, infrastructure and real estate) to corporate houses.[76]

This vampire-like plunder of the country's wealth and resources by the corporate sector has reached such rapacious proportions that even the RBI Governor Raghuram Rajan, himself an ardent votary of neoliberalism and globalisation, has lambasted the collusion between "venal politicians" and "crony capitalists". After observing that India has the second highest number of billionaires in the world per trillion dollars of GDP (after Russia), he pointed out that "three factors—land, natural resources, and government contracts or licenses—are the predominant sources of the wealth of our billionaires. And all of these factors come from the government."[77]

If the government was indeed serious about containing the fiscal deficit, the simplest way of doing so was to curb some of the above mentioned freebies to India's billionaires—withdraw some of the tax concessions given to them, ask them to pay more for their wives' jewellery, get them to pay market prices for the land they purchase, make them repay their bank loans, restrain them from plundering our natural resources . . .

But that is precisely the point we are trying to make: the government is not really interested in reducing the fiscal deficit.

B. Withdrawal of 'Subsidies' to the Poor

If that is so, then why have the IMF–WB and all the governments at the Centre since 1991 been harping upon the necessity of reducing the fiscal deficit? Because it provides them with a theoretical justification for drastically cutting down social sector expenditures of the government, and privatising these sectors. In a deft use of language, while the breathtaking 'subsidies' given to the rich are justified as being necessary 'incentives' for 'growth', the social sector expenditures—whose purpose is to provide the bare means of sustenance to the poor at affordable rates—are condemned as 'subsidies', as being wasteful, inefficient, benefiting the middle classes rather than the poor, promoting parasitism, and so on.

The neoliberal doctrine that each and every sector of the economy must be profitable is nothing but economic rubbish. A society provides free or low cost food, water, education, health, housing, sport, transport and other essentials to its citizens so that they can live like human beings and develop their abilities to the fullest extent. This 'subsidy' is actually an 'investment' for the future. Human beings are nature's highest creation, their potential is infinite. However, people must be given the appropriate social circumstances and opportunities to realise their inherent potential. When such human beings pool in their energies and engage in collective labour, they can create heaven on earth. The wealth they will create will be many times the 'subsidies' invested on them. This is simple economic commonsense. To give a quote from an absolutely mainstream document in support of this argument, even the *Human Development Report 1996* of the UNDP had stressed upon the vital importance of government policies in "spreading skills and meeting basic social needs" as a "springboard for sustained economic growth."[78]

India: Already at the Bottom

Most developed countries have a very elaborate social security network for their citizens, including unemployment allowance, universal health coverage, free school education and free or cheap university education, old age pension, maternity benefits, disability benefits, family allowance such as child care allowance, allowances for those too poor to make a living, and much more. Governments spend substantial sums for providing these social services to their people. People in the developed countries consider government investments on social security to be their right. In recent years, millions have come out on the streets in these countries to protest government attempts to reduce social sector spending.

The average public social sector expenditures of the 34 countries of the OECD* have been around 20 percent of GDP for the last many years, and for the EU–27 have been even higher at around 30 percent of GDP, touching 33 percent for France in 2013.

The average public social sector expenditures for the 21 countries of Latin America and the Caribbean have risen significantly over the past decade, from an average of 4.8 percent of GDP in 2001–02 to 18.6 percent in 2009–10. These expenditures are as high as 27.8 percent of GDP for Argentina, 27.1 percent for Brazil, and a fantastic 40.7 percent for Cuba (all figures for 2009).[79]

Chart 1.3: Public Social Sector Expenditures of Developed Countries and India, 2010[80] (*% of GDP*)

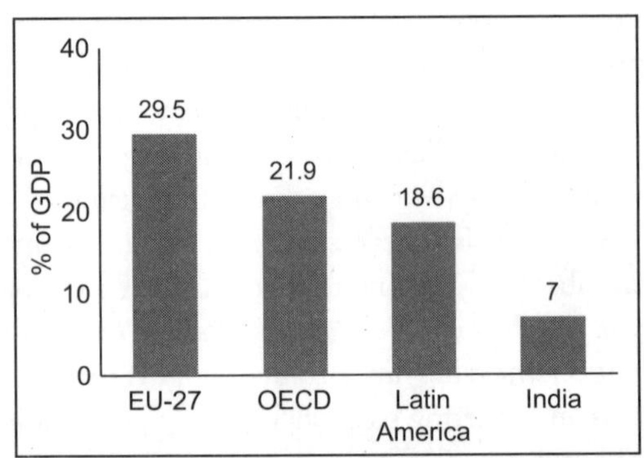

In contrast, the public social sector expenditures of the Government of India are very low! Jaitley and his predecessors in the Finance Ministry and the 'Chicago boys' who are their economic advisors are all blithely lying when they claim that our subsidies to the poor are very high! The total social sector expenditure of the Government of India (Centre and states combined) is barely 7 percent of GDP (Chart 1.3).[81]

It is because of this very low social sector spending that the *Human Development Report* released by the UNDP ranks India near the bottom with regard to overall human development. India's Human

* *OECD: Organisation for Economic Co-operation and Development, a grouping of 34 developed countries.*

Development Index ranking fell from 119 in 2010 to 135 in 2014 (in a list of 187 countries). According to the *Human Development Report 2011*, 53.7 percent of the Indian population is "multidimensionally poor"—a measure that captures how many people experience overlapping deprivations in living standards, health and education, and how many deprivations they face on the average.[82]

And yet the WB–IMF and the foreign corporate houses and their concubine governments are pressurising the Government of India to further reduce its social sector expenditures, and Delhi's badshahs are slavishly implementing their dictates. The Indian Government is cutting its already low expenditures on all social services, from education, health, electricity and public transport, to the public distribution system designed to provide food to the poor at affordable rates, to even drinking water supply. Worse, in the name of improving the quality of these social services, they are also being privatised—either through the infamous PPP route, or even outright. Private corporations are jumping with glee—being essential services, the scope for profits is huge.

We briefly discuss the abysmally low social sector expenditures of the Government of India in the areas of health and food security, and its consequences for the people.

Collapse of the Public Health System

The state of social services in the country was dismal even before the economic reforms began in 1991. The Indian ruling classes have always been very self-centred, to the extent of being short-sighted. All the high-flown talk of socialism was meant to hoodwink the people; the callous elites were never really concerned with the welfare of the ordinary citizens. Hence, public social sector expenditures were very low even before the reforms began in 1991.

With the onset of the reforms, the Indian rulers have willingly accepted World Bank instructions and are further reducing these already low expenditures. This is happening even in the vitally important health care sector too.

The World Health Organisation (WHO) recommends that countries should allocate at least 5 percent of the GDP for public health services. The advanced countries spend more than this; public health care spending as a percentage of GDP in 27 advanced economies rose from 5 percent to more than 7 percent over the period 1990–2008, with spending in 2008 ranging from 5.5 percent for Australia to 8.7 percent for France. Public health care spending in several 'emerging economies' is between 3 to 5 percent of GDP—especially in East European countries and several Latin American countries like Argentina, Brazil and Chile. It is because of these high expenditures on public health services that nearly all OECD countries have universal or near-universal access to health care; the same is the situation in most of Eastern Europe, and several developing countries in Asia, Africa and Latin America, including Costa Rica, Cuba, Argentina, Brazil, South Africa, Kenya, Iraq, Iran, Thailand and Sri Lanka.[83]

In contrast, in India, public health expenditure actually fell from 1.3 percent of GDP reached in 1985 to a shocking 0.85 percent in 2004–05.[84] In the Eleventh Plan (2007–12), the government promised to raise it to 3 percent of GDP, but it did not make the necessary financial allocations and hence budgetary allocation for health (both Centre and states combined) rose to only 1.29 percent of GDP in 2011–12.[85] According to the WHO, India's public health expenditure is amongst the lowest in the world, even lower than sub-Saharan Africa.[86]

This has forced citizens to bear the brunt of health spending. India has amongst the most privatised health systems in the world—households undertake nearly three-fourths of all health spending in the country (72 percent), public spending accounting for just 28 percent.[87]

Obviously, in such a situation, the poor are going to be the worst sufferers. An appalling 21 percent of Indians no longer seek medical treatment of any kind for their ailments—up from 11 percent a decade ago—because they cannot afford it.[88] Despite this terrible situation, the government is not willing to transfer even a wee bit of the subsidies given to the rich towards providing essential healthcare to the poor. An example is government funding for its much vaunted National Rural Health Mission, which was launched in 2005 and was aimed at strengthening the healthcare infrastructure in rural areas. A key component of it was upgrading every district headquarters hospital to provide quality health facilities to all by 2012. However, this has remained only on paper, with the government allocating only a minuscule 19.6 percent of the recommended outlay (Rs 544 crore out of Rs 2,780 crore) during the entire Eleventh Plan period (2007–12).[89]

The results of this neglect are predictable. India's health system is in "crisis", warn the editors of *The Lancet*, one of the world's most respected medical journals.[90] Some alarming statistics:

- India has not succeeded in controlling many infectious diseases, including tuberculosis, malaria, kala azar, filariasis, dysentry, typhoid, hepatitis and Japanese encephalitis. Malaria alone kills nearly two lakh people in India every year.[91]
- India is in the grip of a tuberculosis (TB) epidemic. WHO statistics for 2011 give an estimated incidence figure of 2.2 million cases of TB for India out of a global incidence of 8.7 million cases. WHO estimates that around 3 lakh people die of TB every year in the country, nearly 1000 a day.[92]
- According to the WHO (2008), of the total number of deaths due to disease in a sample of 192 countries across the world, India accounted for nearly one-fourth of the deaths due to diarrhoea, more than one-third of the deaths due to leprosy and more than half of the deaths due to Japanese encephalitis.[93]
- Children and women bear a particularly shocking and intolerable burden of death. Of the seven million children who died before the age of five in 2011 in the world, one-fourth deaths (1.8 million) took place in India. The bulk of these deaths are preventable, with an appalling one-third of the deaths being due to pneumonia and diarrhoea alone. India also accounted for one-fifth (56,000) of the 287,000 maternal deaths in the world in 2010, according to a UN report.[94]
- UNDP's *Human Development Report 2010* ranks India 143rd in infant mortality rate, 124th in maternal mortality rate, 132nd in life expectancy at birth, and 145th in under-five mortality rate.[95]

- Even as India has failed to tackle these long standing health challenges, it is also faced with another epidemic, of chronic diseases (like cardiovascular diseases, mental health disorders, diabetes and cancer). More than 50 percent of the deaths in India occur due to chronic diseases, with cardiovascular diseases being a major contributor. As a *Lancet* study points out, it is possible to address this challenge too, many inexpensive strategies are available, but again their implementation would require strengthening the public health system.[96]

According to *The Lancet*, the underlying reason for this health crisis gripping India is that its health system is solely "focused on technologically advancing medical care for the urban elite population", and "lacks an adequately functional public health infrastructure that is essential for prevention of disease in all communities."[97]

India's public health care system is seriously sick, it is in ICU (intensive care unit). But the thick-skinned ruling classes are unconcerned; they have become anti-people. While the government is unwilling to raise its meagre expenditures on public health in the name of 'keeping the fiscal deficit under control', it is giving huge subsidies to corporate houses for setting up five-star hospitals! For instance, several of Mumbai's leading private hospitals—from Jaslok to Breach Candy, Leelavati, Hinduja, Nanavati and Ambani Hospitals—have been given prime land at a fraction of the market value; several of them have in fact been given land on a token lease rent of one rupee per annum. Other concessions include additional FSI, concessional rates for water and electricity, low-interest loans from public sector banks, customs duty exemption on imported machinery, income tax exemption on more than 85 percent of their income, etc.[98] The majority of the Indian population is too poor to afford treatment in these elite hospitals. And so they are busy providing healthcare services to the rich from across the world. (Another example of how globalisation is bringing the world closer!)

The government is in fact promoting this—it earns the country much needed foreign exchange. It has even been given a name—

'medical tourism', and the Ministry of Tourism is organising road shows for this in the world's leading cities![99] India has become one of the world's most favoured 'medical tourism' destinations, and the country's medical tourism industry is growing at the rate of 30 percent per annum. Four lakh foreigners flew down to India in 2012 for medical treatment—treatment costs for them in India are 60–90 percent lower than in their countries![100]

India is on its way to becoming a Medical Superpower too! Hip-hip-hurray!

Rollback of Food Subsidies

Measuring Poverty Levels in India

Some time ago, the Planning Commission, the Government of India's think-tank, announced that poverty in the country had fallen over the past decade, from 41.8 percent to 33.8 percent in rural India and from 25.7 percent to 20.9 percent in urban areas over 2004–05 to 2009–10. It claimed that the overall percentage of population living below the poverty line had dipped by a huge 7.3 percentage points, from 37.2 percent in 2004–05 to 29.8 percent in 2009–10.[101]

Strangely, this fall in poverty comes at a time when the same National Sample Survey data from which the Planning Commission drew the above conclusions shows that the average intake of calories per head had actually fallen over the same period. And not just the average calorie intake, even the average protein intake per head had fallen (Charts 1.4 and 1.5).[102]

The discrepancy gets resolved when we examine the basis on which the Planning Commission has come to the conclusion that poverty in the country has fallen since 2004–05. According to the Commission, its figures are based on a monthly per-head poverty line of Rs 672.8 in rural and Rs 859.6 in urban areas, which works out to Rs 22.4 a day in rural areas and Rs 28.7 in urban areas.[103]

Clearly, the poverty line is absurdly low! The Planning Commission's figures become even more atrocious when it is kept in mind that they do not refer to food costs alone. These paltry sums are supposed to cover not only food but all non-food essentials, including clothing and footwear, fuel for cooking and lighting, transport, education, medical costs and rent![104] Even a school child knows that basic necessities, even just adequate food, cannot be obtained, nor working health be maintained, by spending so little. Amazingly, however, 30 crore Indians subsist below these levels. Clearly, India's poverty line does not measure poverty anymore; it measures destitution.

Chart 1.4: Per Head Calorie Intake[104]

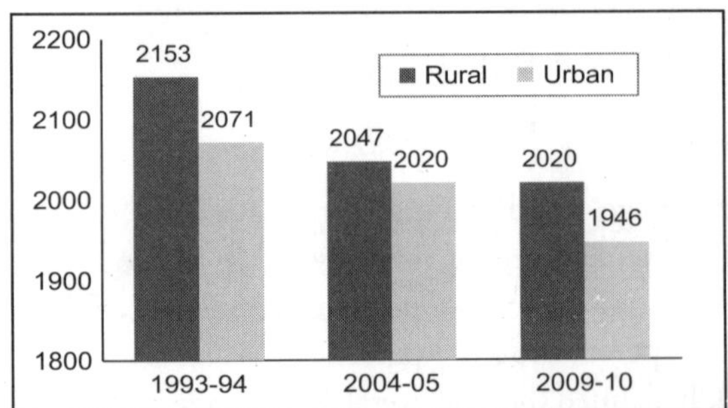

Chart 1.5: Per Head Protein Intake[105] *(in grams)*

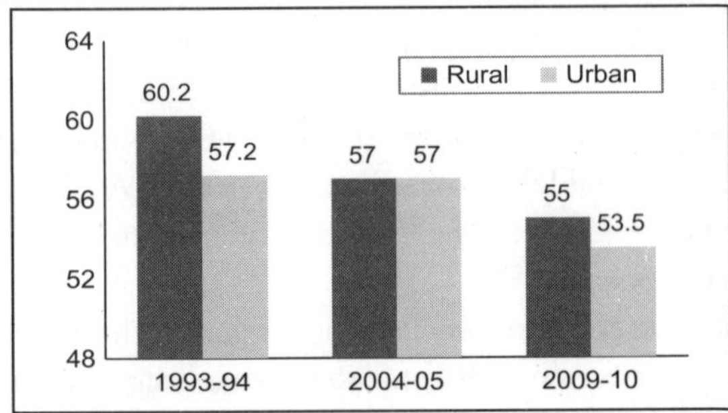

The reason why India's poverty line is so abysmally low has an interesting history. In the 1970s, based on the recommendations of an expert committee, the Planning Commission defined the poverty line as that particular level of total spending per capita on all goods and services whose food spending part satisfied the nutrition level of 2,400 calories of energy intake per day in rural India, and 2,100 calories per day in urban areas. The rural norm was soon after scaled down to

2,200 calories. The Planning Commission applied this definition only once, to NSS data of 1973–74, and then changed the definition in practice, *delinking it from the nutrition norm*. Ever since then, the new poverty line has had nothing to do with whether a person is able to access the minimum recommended calories. Thus, in 2009–10, while nutrition data from the NSS 66th Round showed that a person needed to spend Rs 1,100 in rural and Rs 2,120 in urban India a month to access 2,200 and 2,100 calories respectively, the official monthly poverty lines for that year were only Rs 673 and Rs 860, at which only 1,870 calories could be accessed in rural areas and 1,720 calories in urban areas.

The noted economist Utsa Patnaik has estimated the number of people in India living below the poverty line based on the original poverty line of the 1970s that was based on nutrition norms wherein all people unable to access 2,200/2,100 calories per day in rural/urban areas are considered poor. The data from the National Sample Surveys of 2004–05 and 2009–10 then show that:[107]

- In contrast to the claims of the Planning Commission, the number of people living below the poverty line had considerably gone up over this period.
- In 2004–05, the percentage of people in rural India unable to access 2,200 calories was 69.5 percent; this percentage had gone up to an appalling 75.5 percent in 2009–10!
- 64.5 percent of the urban population was unable to reach 2,100 calories energy intake in 2004–05; this too had gone up to 73 percent in 2009–10!

These figures are now in congruence with the data given in Charts 1.4 and 1.5 that indicate that calorie and protein intakes of Indian people had fallen over the period 2004–05 to 2009–10.

Under-Nutrition: A National Emergency

To most people fed on a daily diet of media propaganda that India is rapidly growing and is an emerging superpower, these figures that show three-fourths of the Indian people living in dire poverty would appear to be an exaggeration. But these distressing figures are borne out by other surveys too. According to the National Family Health Survey–3:[108]

- more than 48 percent of children under the age of five are stunted (low height for age, indicating chronic malnutrition);
- 43 percent are underweight (low weight for age, indicating both chronic and acute malnutrition);
- and about 20 percent have wasting (low weight for height, indicating acute malnutrition).

Clearly, the poverty and mal/under-nutrition levels in India are nothing less than a national emergency. But the Shylocks are unconcerned; they must have their pound of flesh. As a part of globalisation conditionalities, the World Bank has asked for a reduction in food subsidies. Successive Indian Governments have obsequiously been implementing its orders.

Targeted Public Distribution System

To reduce food subsidies, the Indian Government came up with the argument that the majority of the food subsidy is being siphoned off by the middle classes, and so the benefits are not really reaching the poor. It proposed that the ration system should identify the 'really needy', and only they should be provided subsidised foodgrains. It then began manipulating the definition of 'really needy', that is, the poor, to reduce its food subsidy bill.

As a first step, the government replaced the Universal Public Distribution System by the Targeted Public Distribution System in 1996, wherein it introduced two kinds of ration cards, one for those above the poverty line (called APL cards), and one for those it considered poor (Below Poverty Line or BPL cards). On the one hand, it gradually hiked the prices of foodgrains for APL households, bringing them closer to market prices, so that these households stopped buying grain from public distribution shops—more popularly called ration shops. And on the other, a majority of the poor were also pushed out of the public distribution system (PDS) by the simple stratagem of denying them BPL cards! This is admitted by NSS surveys, which show that 70.5 percent of rural households either possess no card or an APL card[109]—when three-quarters of the rural households do not earn enough to eat two full meals a day!

With a vast majority of the poor not buying foodgrains from the PDS, foodgrain stocks with the Government of India have soared. In July 2013, foodgrain stocks with the state-owned Food Corporation of India were more than 70 million tons, which is more than double the buffer stock and strategic reserve norm of 32 million tons.[110]

What has the government been doing with these mounting stocks? Exporting them, to earn foreign exchange needed to finance the luxury goods imports of the rich! In 2012–13, India exported 9.5 million tons of wheat and 10 million tons of rice—making India the world's biggest rice exporter, in a country with the largest number of malnourished people in the world.[111]

National Food Security Act

The mounting foodgrain stocks on the one hand, and rising malnutrition levels and starvation deaths on the other, led to an uproar across the country. Activist groups and NGOs started mounting pressure on the government to expand the scope of the public distribution system. The Supreme Court too intervened, and passed a series of orders ensuring a multitude of food rights, such as providing 35 kg subsidised rations per family, heavily subsidised rations for poor families (the Antyodaya Anna Yojana), security to pregnant and lactating women, and so on.[112]

The government was in a quandary. The increasingly vociferous people's movement and Supreme Court orders were becoming a huge embarrassment. But the World Bank and foreign investors were also equally firm—that the government should do nothing to increase its expenditures on the poor. A way out of the dilemma was found by the government's sorcerous bureaucrats. They conjured up a bill—the National Food Security Bill—that ostensibly aimed to provide food security to all the poor, but in effect, subverted the whole issue.

Elections to the 16th Lok Sabha (2014) were approaching. To exhibit its hurry to provide 'Right to Food' to the people, the government first promulgated the National Food Security Ordinance on July 5, 2013, and then introduced the National Food Security Bill in the Lok Sabha on August 7, 2013 to replace the ordinance. The Parliament passed the Bill and it was signed into law on September 12, 2013.

Under the National Food Security Act (NFSA), 75 percent of the rural population and 50 percent of the urban population (on the whole, roughly 67 percent of the total population) will be entitled to five kilograms of grains (rice/wheat/millets) per person per month at the price of Rs 3/2/1 per kg. The Act also provides for children in the age group of 6 months to 6 years to be given an age-appropriate meal, free of charge, through the local anganwadi, and children in the age group of 6 to 14 to be given one free cooked mid-day meal every day (except on school holidays) in all government and government-aided schools. Another provision is that all pregnant women and lactating mothers would be entitled to maternity benefit of Rs 1,000 per month for six months.[113]

While the chairperson of the UPA Government, Sonia Gandhi, claimed that the food bill was a "historic step" to weed out hunger from the country,[114] the reality is that the NFSA is actually a disgrace for a country that claims to be an emerging economic superpower:

- Firstly, the Act provides the poor only starvation foodgrains. While the Indian Council for Medical Research recommends that an adult requires 14 kg of foodgrains per month and children 7 kg, the bill restricts the entitlement to only 5 kg per person per month!
- Secondly, the Act provides only for cereals, with no entitlements to other basic food necessities such as pulses and edible oil—whose prices have soared in recent years—required to combat malnutrition. The Empowered Group of Ministers, set up by the Central government to draw up the framework for the Act, was very clear about it. It proposed that the definition of food security be "limited to the specific issue of foodgrains security (wheat and rice) and be delinked from the larger issue of nutrition security"—a stand which actually violates Article 47 of the Indian Constitution.[115] The aim of the Act is thus clear. People, including children, can

remain hungry/malnourished/anaemic, but shouldn't die of starvation because that makes bad publicity!

- Thirdly, the Act does not provide even this limited coverage to all the poor—it expands the percentage of the population that would be provided subsidised foodgrains through the PDS to 67 percent, but as we have discussed above, 75 percent of the rural population and 73 percent of the urban population are unable to access the minimum recommended 2,200/2,100 calories.
- Even states like Tamil Nadu and Chhattisgarh have better food security acts.[116] Thus, for instance, Tamil Nadu has a universal public distribution system, wherein each and every family, whether below the poverty line or not, is entitled to 20 kg rice free of cost. The PDS in Tamil Nadu also supplies other essentials like wheat, sugar, kerosene and tur dal at subsidised rates.[117]

Since the enactment of the National Food Security Act, there has been some increase in budget allocations for food security. The then Finance Minister P. Chidambaram increased the allocation from Rs 85,000 crore in 2012–13 to Rs 90,000 crore in 2013–14. He further increased it to Rs 1,15,000 crore in his interim budget for 2014–15.[118] But the reality is that even this increased allocation is inadequate for a full roll out of the Act. The Delhi-based advocacy organisation, Centre for Budget and Governance Accountability, estimates that for a genuine near universal PDS that provides 35 kg of cereals per month per household to 80 percent of the country's households, the total food subsidy needed per annum is Rs 1,70,618 crore.[119] Note that this amount is not very large—it is less than one-third of the total tax concessions given to the rich in the 2013–14 budget. Chidambaram's budget allocation for 2014–15 was only 67 percent of this. It is because of this inadequate allocation for food security that the NFSA is presently being implemented only in eleven states, and that too, only partially, even though the NFSA mandates that state governments should implement the Act within 365 days of its passage.[120]

When the National Food Security Bill was being debated in Parliament, BJP leaders had criticised it as being very inadequate.

Arun Jaitley had stated: "Are we substantially expanding the right over what existed prior to this Bill being brought in? Are we substantially increasing the outlay? The answer is 'no' . . ." Murli Manohar Joshi had even moved an amendment demanding that "every person . . . shall be entitled to ten kilograms of foodgrains, two and a half kilograms of pulses and nine hundred grams of cooking oil per person per month." The BJP election manifesto promised "universal food security", saying that it is integral to national security. Yet, in the BJP Government's first budget after being voted to power, Finance Minister Arun Jaitley made a complete U-turn and kept the overall food subsidy allocation at the same level as Chidambaram's interim budget. Not only that, he also stated that the government would soon take steps "to overhaul the subsidy regime, including food and petroleum subsidies, and make it more targeted . . ."[121] In World Bank diction, 'targeting' means that the government is soon going to reduce its food subsidy allocation.

The Humbug in Practice: A Recent Example

That all the talk about reducing the fiscal deficit is basically to provide a theoretical justification for the government to reduce its already low social security expenditures and transfer the savings to big corporations, is borne out even more starkly by an example from Chidambaram's interim budget for 2014–15.

Despite being given huge subsidies of tens of thousands of crores of rupees, by 2013, the automobile industry was in doldrums, with growth slowing down, and capacity utilisation in factories down to 63–68 percent. The Society of Indian Automobile Manufacturers wrote to the government that the automobile industry would not be able to meet the Automotive Mission Plan (AMP) targets for 2016, and asked that the deadline be pushed ahead to 2026. It also appealed to the government for additional concessions.[122] An obliging finance minister, even though he was only presenting an interim budget in 2014, announced generous across-the-board excise duty reductions ranging from four to six percentage-points on two-wheelers, trucks and cars, including big cars and sport-utility vehicles (SUVs). It made two-wheelers cheaper by Rs 1,100–3,000. Cars are favoured more:

Nano became cheaper by Rs 4,500, Maruti Alto by Rs 10,000–12,000, and mid-sized sedans by Rs 24,000–36,000. SUVs are favoured even more, and became Rs 34,000–76,000 cheaper. Upper-end Audis will cost Rs 2–4 lakh less.

With the finance minister firm about bringing down the fiscal deficit to 4.1 percent of GDP in 2014–15, obviously, this 'incentive' to the automobile industry needs to be compensated. The poor can do with a bit more of austerity, and so the axe once again fell on social sector expenditures. In his interim budget, Chidambaram announced a cut in the budget for sanitation by 46 percent, rural drinking water by 12 percent, the National Health Mission by 13 percent and school education by 7 percent.[123]

New BJP Government Racing Down the Same Road

Elections to the 16th Lok Sabha were held in April–May 2014. The BJP-led NDA coalition swept to power with a thumping majority. In his very first budget speech, the new Finance Minister Arun Jaitley declared that the government was planning to adhere to the fiscal deficit target set by his predecessor. Swaminathan S. Anklesaria Aiyar, the prominent journalist and consulting editor for the *Economic Times*, observed that Jaitley's budget speech was nothing "but a Chidambaram budget with saffron lipstick added"; the former Finance Minister P. Chidambaram commented that the "imprint of the UPA Government's policies" can be seen in the budget presented by Arun Jaitley; and even the former Prime Minister Manmohan Singh hailed the BJP Government's attempts to adhere to the fiscal deficit target set by his government for the current fiscal.[124]

Nay, the new BJP Government is not just seeking to go down the same path as the UPA, it is actually seeking to do so at an accelerated speed. On August 13, 2014, the government, in an official press release, announced the constitution of an Expenditure Management Commission to suggest ways to reduce food, fertiliser and oil subsidies to contain the fiscal deficit.[125]

While seeking to slash expenditures on the poor, the finance minister has announced a host of new infrastructural projects, all involving huge transfers of government funds to the private sector via the PPP route. These include:[126]

- Plans for new infrastructure projects such as port projects, airports in smaller cities and expressways, all to be set up through the PPP route;
- Revival of Special Economic Zones;
- Setting up 100 smart cities.

Apart from this, the finance minister has also announced:

- A slew of measures to fast-track PPP projects that have been held up for various reasons;
- Setting up of a National Industrial Corridor Authority to coordinate development of several new industrial corridors.

To accelerate the acquisition of the thousands of hectares of land that will be needed for all these projects, the government has passed an ordinance to modify the Land Acquisition Act, omitting for a wide range of projects the requirements of a social impact assessment study, and also the informed consent of a large number of families affected by the acquisition of land, so as to make land acquisition easier.[127]

Keeping step, the new Environment Minister Prakash Javadekar, soon after taking charge, promised to ensure "fast clearances" for infrastructural projects.[128]

All this within just six months! The corporates are delighted. They had invested heavily in the NDA election campaign;[129] their investments are paying off . . .

Secession of the Rich

There is little room for doubt.

India's westoxicated elite has abandoned all concern for the tribal child dying of malnutrition in Melghat, the farmer in Andhra Pradesh committing suicide because of his inability to pay his medical bills, the old man dying of cold on the streets of Patna because of lack of social security, the village beauty sold off to pay her father's debts in Bundelkhand . . .

The major political parties that dominate the Indian Parliament, and the corporate houses that control the reins of power from behind the scenes, have decided to secede from the people. They have decided to dump the vision of our nation's founding fathers embedded in the Directive Principles of our Constitution:

- ✍ to build an egalitarian society and a social order in which justice, social, economic and political, shall inform all the institutions of the national life [Article 38 (1)];
- ✍ to strive to minimise inequalities in income [Article 38 (2)];
- ✍ to direct policy towards ensuring that the operation of the economic system does not result in concentration of wealth [Article 39 (c)];
- ✍ to ensure that children are given opportunities and facilities to develop in a healthy manner and in conditions of freedom and dignity [Article 39 (f)];
- ✍ to make effective provision for securing the right to education and to public assistance in cases of unemployment, old age, sickness and disablement, and in other cases of undeserved want [Article 41];
- ✍ to regard raising the level of nutrition and the standard of living of its people and the improvement of public health as among the primary duties of the state [Article 47].

6. People Fight Back, Worldwide

Recolonisation of the Third World

During the last two decades of the twentieth century, the imperialist countries once again succeeded in re-establishing their hegemony over large parts of the Third World that they had once colonised. Taking advantage of the Third World debt crisis, they forced the countries of Asia, Africa and Latin America to dismantle their autonomous capitalist development models and open up their economies for inflow of imperialist capital and goods, and allow developed country corporations to once again plunder their raw material resources and markets—in what has euphemistically been labelled as globalisation of the world economy.

This model has had calamitous consequences for the people of the Third World countries. Davison Budhoo, an economist with the IMF, resigned from that institution in 1988 in protest against the impact of IMF conditionalities on the people of the countries of Latin America and Africa. In an article titled *IMF/World Bank Wreak Havoc on Third World*, he writes:[130]

> But the greatest failure of these programs is to be seen in their impact on the people. Using figures provided by the United Nations Children's Fund (UNICEF) and the UN Economic Commission for Africa, it has been estimated that at least six million children under five years of age have died each year since 1982 in Africa, Asia and Latin America because of the anti-people, even genocidal, focus of IMF–World Bank SAPs.
>
> And that is just the tip of the iceberg. Even more pervasively, these programs have created economic, social and cultural devastation whenever and wherever they are introduced. The prestigious and highly Northern-oriented UNDP has determined that some 1.2 billion people in the Third World now live in absolute poverty (almost twice the number ten years ago), over half of sub-Saharan children are starving or malnourished, 1.6 billion people in the Third World are without potable water and well over two billion are unemployed or underemployed. In some countries of Africa, infant mortality rates are double what they were ten years ago, before SAPs were widespread.
>
> Recently, UNDP reported (in its 1992 *Human Development Report*) that, mainly because of inherent inequities built into SAPs, the income gap between rich and poor in the Third World doubled in the course of the 1980s. Today, the richest fifth of the world (including most of Europe and North America) receives 150 times more in income than the poorest fifth (located almost exclusively in the South). "This [disparity] was a big shock to me," said the Chief Adviser to UNDP at a press conference. "I had never expected a ratio of 150 to 1; perhaps 40 to 1." In scathingly cynical terms, the Report concluded that "the World Bank and the IMF should be the buffer to protect developing countries, but their recent record shows that they have become institutions for recycling debt, not recycling resources."

Latin America Shows the Way

The people of the Third World countries have not been silent spectators to this orgy of plunder. From the factories of East Asia and the mines of South Africa to the cities of Brazil, the highlands of Ecuador and the farmlands of Mexico, the people are fighting back. The media has suppressed all news of these struggles—to create an impression that people everywhere are euphoric about globalisation. The most exhilarating developments have taken place in Latin America, where in several countries, powerful peoples' movements have led to revolutionary governments winning elections and coming to power. Trashing the WB–IMF imposed Structural Adjustment Programmes, these governments have actively intervened in the economy and massively increased their social sector expenditures—in just one decade, the average public social sector expenditures of the Latin American countries has gone up by four times, from an average of 4.8 percent of GDP in 2001–02 to 18.6 percent in 2009–10.

The Bolivarian Revolution

We give below a brief note on the numerous social programmes launched in Venezuela after Hugo Chavez, the leader of the Bolivarian movement, won the presidential elections in 1998. (Chavez unfortunately died in 2013 due to cancer. Despite the setback, the Bolivarian revolution has continued uninterrupted under the leadership of his successor, Nicolas Maduro.)[131]

Free and Universal Education

- In 2003, Chavez launched *Mission Robinson*, a literacy and primary education programme. In just two years, the programme was able to teach almost 1.5 million Venezuelans basic literacy skills, and in October 2005, the United Nations body UNESCO declared Venezuela to be an "Illiteracy Free Territory". In 2011, Mission Robinson was extended with a special focus on incorporating senior citizens, particularly those in remote or rural areas, into the programme.
- *Mission Ribas* was launched to provide remedial high school

level classes to Venezuelan high school drop-outs. Classes are held in the evenings, the aim being to enable everyone to get a high school diploma. By 2011, more than 6 lakh people had graduated from high school under this programme.

- As a part of a policy to provide free universal education at all levels to all Venezuelans, Chavez launched *Mission Sucre* to provide free higher education courses to all those graduating from Mission Ribas.

Free/Affordable Health Care for All

The Bolivarian Government has undertaken terrific new initiatives to provide free/affordable health care to all the Venezuelan people:

- With the help of Cuba, it set up health centres in the remotest and poorest areas of Venezuela; these are called *Barrio Adentro* (translates roughly as 'Into the heart of the neighbourhood') clinics, where today tens of thousands of Cuban and Venezuelan doctors, dentists and nurses work.
- Apart from these clinics, hundreds of community medical surgical centres, medical diagnostic centres, rehabilitation rooms and high technology centres have also been set up.
- *Mission Miracle* was launched with the help of Cuba to provide free eye operations not just for Venezuelans, but for the needy all over Latin America. This has performed more than 14 lakh eye surgeries since it was launched in 2004—restoring the eyesights of lakhs of poor from all over Latin America who couldn't afford eye surgery in their home countries.
- More recent initiatives include a law to regulate medicine prices and the setting up of a chain of medicine shops all across Venezuela to provide more than 1,000 essential medicines at prices 30–40 percent below market prices. These shops also provide health services like free vaccinations, medical information, etc.
- Since most Venezuelan doctors practising in the upper middle class areas of the cities were not willing to work on a fixed government salary in the free clinics started by the government in the slums, the Venezuelan Government launched a new

medical education programme to train young people imbued with a spirit of social concern as doctors. In 2011, the first batch of 8,200 students trained as community medicine doctors graduated from Venezuela's Bolivarian University. In this medical education programme, the emphasis is not on specialisation; students go out to communities right from first year onwards to treat patients, with emphasis on prevention of illnesses and promoting good health practices; they also learn to solve social problems. There is no fees for the programme, and the state in fact provides a stipend to students. Tens of thousands of students are currently enrolled in the 6 year course, which is actually more intense than the traditional course.

Healthy Food for All

- The government initiated *Mission Mercal* to provide healthy food to all at affordable rates, by setting up a chain of shops—these provide essential food items, including fresh produce, dairy products, grains, fruits and vegetable oils, to the poor at prices 60–80 percent below market rates. By 2011, the food programme had expanded and set up distribution centers throughout the nation's 23 states.
- It has even set up mobile high quality butcher shops to provide meat at less than half the price found in private outlets, and set up hundreds of restaurants to provide popular and healthy Venezuelan snacks like corn patties and juices and lunches at prices that are as low as 15–50 percent of market prices!

Housing for All

- In 2011, the government launched *Great Housing Mission* to provide housing to every Venezuelan. For this, research was done to build durable and good quality houses using locally available materials, factories have been set up to make these materials using which houses can be made in a matter of a few weeks, and land has been identified to build these houses. Entire new socialist cities are being set up under this plan.

Within two years (by 2013), more than 5 lakh houses had been built, and the Mission has set a target of building 3 million houses by 2019. Low income families receive heavy subsidies to help them buy these homes, and those earning below the minimum wage receive their new homes for free.

- To improve people's living standards, the government imposed price controls on several essential household items such as soaps, detergents, cleaning agents and sanitary napkins. It also launched *Mission My Well Equipped House* to provide household appliances like refrigerators and washing machines to people at cheap rates. The government signed an agreement with China to buy these supplies, with the eventual aim of setting up an appliance manufacturing unit in Venezuela.

Old Age Security for All

- To provide security to senior citizens, the government rolled out *Mission Greater Love* to provide a pension to every senior citizen in the country, wherein all men above the age of 60 and women above the age of 55 get a pension equal to the national minimum wage. Before the revolution, there were only 3.5 lakh people in the country who were receiving a pension, which was only 10 percent of the minimum wage. Now there are 19 lakh senior citizens enjoying a pension equivalent to the minimum wage; the government has even launched a drive to ensure that no one is left out. Senior citizens' committees have been formed to involve them in education, health and social security systems.

All this remarkable progress has taken place, despite continuous efforts by the US Government and its intelligence agencies, in association with the Venezuelan elites, to undermine and destabilise and ultimately overthrow the Venezuelan revolution, through economic sabotages, electoral interventions, assassination plots, psychological warfare, multimillion-dollar funding to extremist right-wing opposition groups in Venezuela and a plan to isolate Venezuela at the international level.

People are Beginning to Stir in India too

In India too, the people have not taken the ruling class offensive to roll back the welfare state and privatise essential services lying down. Just as flowers spring up with the onset of spring in every nook and corner, people are beginning to organise in small-small groups all over the country. Of late, these movements have also begun to come together on larger platforms. Some prominent examples:

☺ **All India Forum for Right to Education:** Several student and teacher organisations, peoples' organisations and many eminent educationists from all over the country have come together under the banner of 'All India Forum for Right to Education' (AIFRTE) to wage a united fight against the inequities of the present education system and the neoliberal assault on education under World Bank pressure. They have launched an all-India campaign to create awareness and mobilise the people to fight: (i) against the growing commercialisation of education in the country; and (ii) for a genuinely free, equitable and publicly funded common school system from the pre-primary stage to Class XII, and an affordable higher education system accessible to all those wanting to pursue higher education.

☺ **Right to Food Campaign:** This is an umbrella organisation of numerous organisations and individuals committed to fighting together for the fundamental right of all people of India to be free from hunger and undernutrition. Among its demands include: (i) a national Employment Guarantee Act; (ii) universal mid-day meals in primary schools; (iii) universalisation of Integrated Child Development Services for children under the age of six; (iv) universalisation of the public distribution system; (v) social security arrangements for those not able to work.

☺ **Pension Parishad:** More than 100 people's organisations and NGOs have come together under this banner to demand that the government implement a universal and non-contributory old-age pension scheme for all people above the age of 60 in the country. They are demanding a minimum amount of monthly pension not less than 50 percent of minimum wage or Rs 2,000 per month, whichever is higher.

☺ **Jaganyacha Hakkacha Andolan:** In another exciting experiment, people's organisations, trade unions and NGOs from all over the State of Maharashtra have joined hands to form the Jaganyachya Hakkachya Andolan (Movement for Dignified Right to Life). These organisations were earlier fighting separately against privatisation and for improved delivery of this or that social service, such as health/education/food/pensions. At a convention in Pune in August 2013, they decided to forge a joint front to demand that all essential social services—education, healthcare, food security, domestic water and sanitation, pension, employment security and transport—be recognised as people's basic rights by the government. They further raised the following important demands: (i) the government (Centre + states) should substantially increase its spending on social services to at least 15 percent of the GDP; (ii) privatisation of social services must be stopped, and public systems for delivery of social services must be strengthened; (iii) quality of social services must be improved, and people must be involved in monitoring the delivery of social services; (iv) targeting of social services must end, and they should be universalised.

Other Struggles

Apart from these struggles for better social services, all sections of the working people—farmers/unorganised workers/bank and insurance employees/government employees/factory workers/ traders—have also been organising across the country on various other aspects of globalisation. Globalisation has also worsened the conditions of the historically socially oppressed sections of society—the Dalits, the minorities, the women, the disabled and the adivasis—and their movements too have been growing in recent years.

However, these struggles have not prevented the ruling classes from going ahead with their sordid agenda of imperialist globalisation. Though the people's movement has been growing, it is at present still weak. It still has a long way to go before it can start achieving significant victories . . .

The People, United, Will Never Be Defeated

Alice: *There's no use trying, one can't believe impossible things.*
Queen: *I daresay you haven't had much practice. When I was your age, I always did it for half-an-hour a day. Why, sometimes I've believed as many as six impossible things before breakfast.*

– Lewis Carroll, *Alice in Wonderland*

Yet, there is no reason for despair. We are living in times that are so full of surprises, in a world that is changing so rapidly, that we can believe in the 'impossible'. Yes, indeed, what appeared to be impossible till a few decades ago is becoming a reality today. Who, for example, would have believed a 150, or 50, or even 20 years ago that Bolivia, a country that had been colonised by white colonialists from Europe for over 400 years and who had virtually decimated the indigenous population, would one day elect an indigenous president? Yet, that has happened, the people of Bolivia voted Evo Morales to power in 2006, and in elections held in October 2014, he won an unprecedented third term as Bolivia's president.

Revolutionary change is taking place not just in Bolivia, but all over Latin America, a continent that till just two decades ago was ruled by dictators and military juntas, by regimes that relied on the most brutal forms of torture and terror to repress people's movements. And then, the impossible started to happen. The people of Venezuela voted Hugo Chavez to power. And he stayed on as president, despite the best efforts of the USA to overthrow him. He even survived a military coup backed by the USA—so powerful is the people's movement there. Following in Venezuela's footsteps, in one country after another, the military dictatorships have been overthrown, and democratic governments, some more radical, some less, have been voted to power, and the continent is being transformed. Latin America, that former continent of carnage and fear, is now a beacon of hope for the rest of the world and many of its governments lead the global fight against corporate globalisation.

The song, *The people, united, will never be defeated*, was composed in Chile as the anthem for the socialist government of Salvador Allende in the early 1970s. However, soon after, the government was overthrown in a US–backed coup in September 1973 that brought the brutal regime of General Pinochet to power. Who would have believed during those depressing years that within just three decades, that song would echo not just all over the Latin American continent, but across the globe?

Let us also believe in the 'impossible', and begin our own small initiatives to organise the people, and join hands with the various movements taking place across the country. Like the tiny rivulets flowing down the Himalayas that ultimately unite to form the mighty Ganges, these movement will also grow with time, to transform the country and build a new society that will guarantee to all its citizens all the basic necessities required for people to live like human beings—healthy food, best possible health care, invigorating education, decent shelter, security in old age and clean pollution-free environment.

References

1. Computed from: *GDP at Factor Cost at 2004–05 Prices, Share to Total GDP and % Rate of Growth in GDP (31–05–2014)*, http://planningcommission.nic.in.
2. Tushar Dhara, "India to Top China as Fastest Growing Economy by 2015, Morgan Stanley Says", August 16, 2010, http://www.bloomberg.com.
3. *Indian Economy: Some Indicators at a Glance*, http://planningcommission.nic.in.
4. "India Displaces Japan to Become Third-Largest World Economy in Terms of PPP: World Bank", April 30, 2014, http://articles.economictimes.indiatimes.com.
5. "Riding the Bull Wave", November 2005, http://www.business-standard.com.
6. India's GDP for 2013–14 is estimated at Rs 113 lakh crore – see *Key Fiscal Indicators 2003–04 to 2014–15 BE (12/07/14)*, http://planningcommission.nic.in. Calculations done taking $1 = Rs 61 for 2014.
7. "List of Countries by the Number of US Dollar Billionaires", http://en.wikipedia.org; "Indian Billionaires 2014: Big Winners, Big Losers", March 3, 2014, http://www.forbes.com.

8. Saritha Rai, "Amid Economic Distress, India Gains the Most Uber-Wealthy Among BRICS", September 11, 2013, http://www.forbes.com. Calculations done assuming $1 = Rs 65; India's GDP = Rs 126 lakh crore.
9. Utsa Patnaik, "Number Games: India's Declining Poverty Figures Based on Flawed Estimation Method; Accurate Figures Show 75 Percent in Poverty", *World Poverty*, August 25, 2012, http://academicsstand.org; Utsa Patnaik, "Poverty Trends in India 2004–05 to 2009–10: Updating Poverty Estimates and Comparing Official Figures", *Economic and Political Weekly*, October 5, 2013, http://www.epw.in.
10. *Children in India 2012 – A Statistical Appraisal*, Ministry of Statistics and Programme Implementation, Government of India, 2012, http://mospi.nic.in; *India – Nutrition*, www.unicef.org.
11. Pramit Bhattacharya, "Government to Discontinue National Family Health Survey", April 11, 2012, http://www.livemint.com.
12. *Nutrition*, http://www.cini-india.org.
13. M. Abdul Salam, "Higher Education in India at a Glance", University of Calicut, http://www.slideshare.net; "Higher Education in India at a Glance", UGC, June 2013, http://www.ugc.ac.in.
14. *Twelfth Five Year Plan: 2012–17, Vol. III: Social Sectors*, Planning Commission, Government of India, p. 53, http://planningcommission.gov.in.
15. "Time for School Series – Interview: Amartya Sen", September 2, 2004, http://www.pbs.org.
16. Peter S. Goodman, "Emphasis on Growth is Called Misguided", September 22, 2009, http://www.nytimes.com; Vandana Shiva, "How Economic Growth has Become Anti-Life", November 1, 2013, http://www.theguardian.com; David Jolly, "G.D.P. Seen as Inadequate Measure of Economic Health", September 14, 2009, http://www.nytimes.com.
17. Aditya Mukherjee, *Imperialism, Nationalism and the Making of the Indian Capitalist Class*, Sage Publications, New Delhi, 2002, pp. 49–50, 358; see also: Neeraj Jain, *Globalisation or Recolonisation?* Chapter 1, published by Lokayat, Pune, 2006, available on internet at lokayat.org.in.
18. For more on this, see: Neeraj Jain, *Globalisation or Recolonisation?* ibid.
19. Dalip S. Swamy, *The World Bank and Globalisation of Indian Economy*, Public Interest Research Group, Delhi, 1994, pp. 5, 15, 19. For the relationship between World Bank–IMF and the developed countries, see: Eric Toussaint and Damien Millet, *Debt, the IMF, and the World*

Bank, Aakar Books, Delhi, 2011.

20. There are several articles available on the internet outlining these conditionalities. See for example: *Structural Adjustment in India*, World Bank, 2012, http://lnweb90.worldbank.org; Montek S. Ahluwalia, *Structural Adjustment and Reform in Developing Countries*, April 1994, www.planningcommission.nic.in; Ashwini Deshpande, Prabirjit Sarkar, "Structural Adjustment in India – A Critical Assessment", *Economic and Political Weekly*, December 9, 1995, http://www.epw.in; David Harvey, *A Brief History of Neoliberalism*, Oxford University Press, 2005, pp. 7–8, 29, 64–66.
21. "The Reality: Gaping Inequality", in "A Middle Class India", *Aspects of India's Economy*, No. 58, September 2014, http://www.rupe-india.org.
22. "India Could Revert to 8.5–9 Percent Growth in Two Years: Kaushik Basu", *PTI*, November 6, 2012, http://articles.economic times.indiatimes.com.
23. "More Effort Needed to Reduce Govt Subsidies: C. Rangarajan", *PTI*, December 26, 2013, http://archive.indianexpress.com.
24. "Govt Will Meet Its Fiscal Deficit Target: Raghuram Rajan", February 13, 2014, http://www.livemint.com.
25. "Fiscal Deficit Will Be Contained at 4.8% of GDP: Chidambaram", January 15, 2014, http://zeenews.india.com.
26. "Jaitley Terms Chidambaram's Fiscal Deficit Target of 4.1% as 'Daunting'", *Business Standard*, July 10, 2014, http://www.business-standard.com
27. "Priorities Cut out: Rajan Meets Jaitley, Talks Growth and Prices", *Hindustan Times*, May 28, 2014, http://www.hindustantimes.com.
28. "Jaitley Terms Chidambaram's Fiscal Deficit Target of 4.1% as 'Daunting'", op. cit.
29. *India – Macro-economic Summary: 1999–00 to 2013–14 (on August 2, 2014)*, http://planningcommission.nic.in.
30. Prabhat Patnaik, "The Humbug of Finance", April 5, 2000, www.macroscan.org; "Keynes, Capitalism, and the Crisis: John Bellamy Foster Interviewed by Brian Ashley", March 20, 2009, http://www.countercurrents.org.
31. Discussing this issue in detail is beyond the scope of this essay. This issue is discussed in detail in several articles published in the *Monthly Review*, the famed New York journal. See for example: John Bellamy Foster and Robert W. McChesney, "The Endless Crisis", *Monthly Review*, May 2012, http://monthlyreview.org.
32. Noam Chomsky, *Profit Over People*, Madhyam Books, Delhi, 1999,

pp. 66–68; Walden Bello, *The Global Collapse: A Non-Orthodox View*, 2009, http://mrzine.monthlyreview.org.

33. Discussing this important issue is beyond the scope of this essay. See for instance: Eduardo Galeano, *Open Veins of Latin America*, Monthly Review Press, New York, 1973.
34. All this is well documented. See for instance: David Harvey, *A Brief History of Neoliberalism*, op. cit., pp. 7–8, 29, 64–66; Paulo Nakatani and Rémy Herrera, "The South Has Already Repaid Its External Debt to the North: But the North Denies Its Debt to the South", *Monthly Review*, June 2007, http://monthlyreview.org; Walden Bello and David Kinley, *An Analysis of the International Monetary Fund's Role in the Third World Debt Crisis, Its Relation to Big Banks, and the Forces Influencing Its Decisions*, July 1983, http://multinationalmonitor.org; Walden Bello, *Structural Adjustment Programs: 'SUCCESS' for Whom?* http://www.converge.org.nz; Harry Magdoff and Paul Sweezy, *Stagnation and Financial Explosion*, Monthly Review Press, New York and Aakar Books, Delhi, pp. 176–195; Eric Toussaint and Damien Millet, *Debt, the IMF, and the World Bank*, op. cit.
35. For more on this, see: Neeraj Jain, *Globalisation or Recolonisation?* op.cit.
36. For a discussion on why the World Bank ordered India to replace budget deficit with fiscal deficit, see: Neeraj Jain, ibid., pp. 103–4.
37. World Bank, "India: Trends, Issues and Options", May 1990, p. 36, cited in *Aspects of India's Economy*, No. 2, Research Unit for Political Economy, Prabhadevi, Mumbai, p. 13.
38. "The 'Fiscal Deficit' Bogeyman and His Uses", *Aspects of India's Economy*, May 2013, http://www.rupe-india.org.
39. Ibid.
40. "P. Sainath on Corporate Bailout #Rs 36.5 Trillion #Budget 2014", July 13, 2014, http://www.indiaresists.com. For GDP for 2013–14, see endnote 6.
41. *Key Fiscal Indicators 2003–04 to 2014–15 BE (12/07/14)*, op. cit.
42. For GDP for 2013–14, see endnote 6.
43. P. Sainath, "The Feeding Frenzy of Kleptocracy", *The Hindu*, March 16, 2013, http://www.thehindu.com. Fiscal Deficit for 2013–14 was Rs 5.24 lakh crore – see *Key Fiscal Indicators 2003–04 to 2014–15 BE (12/07/14)*, op. cit.
44. "P. Sainath on Corporate Bailout #Rs 36.5 Trillion #Budget 2014", op. cit. To calculate 'Revenue Forgone as % of GDP', we have taken GDP figures from: *Key Fiscal Indicators 2003–04 to 2014–15 BE (12/07/14)*, ibid.

45. "P. Sainath on Corporate Bailout #Rs 36.5 Trillion #Budget 2014", ibid.; "The 'Fiscal Deficit' Bogeyman and His Uses", op. cit.; P. Sainath, "The Feeding Frenzy of Kleptocracy", op. cit.
46. Original source: *IMF WEO Database*, www.imf.org; taken from: "The 'Fiscal Deficit' Bogeyman and His Uses", ibid.
47. Cited in: "The 'Fiscal Deficit' Bogeyman and His Uses", ibid.
48. "High Tax Regime Makes the Economy Lethargic: Jaitley", http://www.moneycontrol.com; "More Tax Concessions When Economy Improves: Arun Jaitley", *PTI*, July 12, 2014, http://indianexpress.com.
49. Rahul Varman, *Cowboy Capitalism: The Curious Case of Reliance KG Basin Gas Business*, February 24, 2013, http://sanhati.com.
50. "A Modest Proposal Regarding Subsidies", *Aspects of India's Economy*, No. 51, August 2011, http://www.rupe-india.org.
51. "A Modest Proposal Regarding Subsidies", ibid.; Rahul Varman, *Cowboy Capitalism: The Curious Case of Reliance KG Basin Gas Business*, op. cit.
52. "A Modest Proposal Regarding Subsidies", ibid.; Rahul Varman, *Cowboy Capitalism: The Curious Case of Reliance KG Basin Gas Business*, ibid.
53. "A Modest Proposal Regarding Subsidies", ibid.
54. All facts given in this section taken from: *Iron and Steel: The POSCO–India Story*, Mining Zone Peoples' Solidarity Group, http://miningzone.org.
55. See, for instance: "A Modest Proposal Regarding Subsidies", op. cit.
56. G. Srinivasan, "Seeing a Sellout", *Frontline*, Sepember 8–21, 2012, http://www.frontline.in.
57. "Doing Big Business in Modi's Gujarat", *Forbes*, March 12, 2014, http://www.forbes.com; "State Govt Gifts Adani 5.78 cr sq mt of Land in Kutch for Peanuts", *DNA*, March 1, 2012, http://daily.bhaskar.com; "Thousands of Acres of Land Doled out to Adani by Modi Govt on Throwaway Prices", November 23, 2013, http://www.ummid.com.
58. "Foreign Investment and Land Acquisition: From Posco to Poena", *Aspects of India's Economy*, No. 51, August 2011, http://www.rupe-india.org; Sunil Jain, "7 Cities, 2,000 sq km, Rs 325,000 Crore", October 7, 2010, http://www.financialexpress.com.
59. All facts in this section summarised from: *Corporate Cronyism in 'Vibrant Gujarat'*, July 10, 2012, http://www.hardnewsmedia.com; Paranjoy Guha Thakurta, "India: Cheapest Car Rides on Govt Subsidies", *Inter Press Service*, May 23, 2009, http://www.globalissues.org; "Rs 30,000-Crore Sops for Nano Project: Document", *The Hindu*, November 12, 2008, http://www.hindu.com; "Modhwadia Blasts Modi Govt Over Nano Sops to Tatas", March 5, 2011, http://archive.indianexpress.com.

60. "PM to Release Auto Mission Plan on 29th", *TNN*, January 26, 2007, http://articles.economictimes.indiatimes.com; "Private Corporate Sector-Led Growth and Exclusion", *Aspects of India's Economy*, Nos. 44–46, April 2008, http://www.rupe-india.org; "Auto Sector to Contribute $145 Bln to GDP by 2016", January 29, 2007, http://news.oneindia.in.
61. "Behind the Attack on 'Subsidies'", *Aspects of India's Economy*, No. 49, August 2010, http://www.rupe-india.org; *FAQs – Public Private Partnership in India*, Ministry of Finance, Government of India, http://pppinindia.com.
62. *Draft Compendium of PPP Projects in Infrastructure, 2012,* Planning Commission, Government of India, January 2013, p. 14. www.infrastructure.gov.in.
63. "Yamuna Expressway to Become Operational This Month", *TNN*, April 7, 2012, http://articles.economictimes.indiatimes.com; Naazneen Karmali, "Road to Riches", April 12, 2010, http://www.forbes.com; Jyotika Sood, "Road to Disaster", June 15, 2011, http://www.downtoearth.org.in.
64. "Private Corporate Sector-Led Growth and Exclusion", *Aspects of India's Economy*, op. cit.; "CPM Trains Divest Gun on Govt", *The Telegraph*, March 24, 2004, http://www.telegraphindia.com.
65. Praful Bidwai, "Of Sleazy, Criminalised Capitalism", *Frontline*, May 12–25, 2001, http://www.frontline.in; V. Sridhar, "Battle Over Balco", *Frontline*, March 17–30, 2001, http://www.frontline.in.
66. Purnima S. Tripathi, "A Familiar Ring", *Frontline*, February 26–March 11, 2011, http://www.frontline.in; Tapan Sen, "Now, 'Post-Closing' Fraud!" *People's Democracy*, February 16, 2003, http://pd.cpim.org.
67. "Why Do Credit Rating Agencies Press India to Reduce Government Spending?" *Aspects of India's Economy*, No. 53, May 2013, http://www.rupe-india.org.
68. K.C. Chakrabarty, *Two Decades of Credit Management in Banks*, Bancon 2013, http://www.slideshare.net; Mayur Shetty, "Rs 1 Lakh Crore Bad Loans of Corporates Written Off: RBI", November 17, 2013, http://timesofindia.indiatimes.com.
69. "Corporate Debt Restructuring", *The Economic Times*, http://economictimes.indiatimes.com; "Corporate Debt Restructuring News", http://profit.ndtv.com; Samar Halarnkar, "Serve the Rich: Banks Go Easy on India's Big Loan Defaulters", November 28, 2013, http://www.hindustantimes.com.
70. "Need to Revamp Corporate Debt Restructuring Mechanism: Report",

PTI, August 12, 2013, http://articles.economictimes.indiatimes.com; *Report on Trend and Progress of Banking in India 2012–13*, Reserve Bank of India, 2013, p. 67, http://rbidocs.rbi.org.in.

71. Megha Bahree, "Top Indian Companies Burdened with Debt", August 19, 2013, http://www.forbes.com; Anand Adhikari, "India on Sale", October 13, 2013, http://businesstoday.intoday.in.
72. Sarita C. Singh, "Power Companies like Tata Power, Adani Power, Reliance Power and Others Breathe Easy as Government Plans Loan Recast", December 2, 2013, http://articles.economictimes.indiatimes.com.
73. *Report on Trend and Progress of Banking in India 2012–13*, op. cit., p. 65.
74. "A Modest Proposal Regarding Subsidies", *Aspects of India's Economy*, op. cit.
75. "Modi Orders Inquiry into Nano MoU Note", *The Financial Express*, November 11, 2008, http://m.financialexpress.com.
76. "A Modest Proposal Regarding Subsidies", *Aspects of India's Economy*, op. cit.; *Perspectives on Poverty in India : Stylized Facts from Survey Data*, World Bank, April 2011, https://openknowledge.worldbank.org.
77. "Crony Capitalism a Big Threat to Countries like India, RBI Chief Raghuram Rajan Says", August 12, 2014, http://timesofindia.indiatimes.com; Bharadwaj Sharma, "Crony Capitalism Leads to Decline in Economic Growth: Raghuram Rajan", August 12, 2014, http://www.ibtimes.co.in.
78. Noam Chomsky, *Neoliberalism and Global Order*, 1996, http://strategema.narod.ru.
79. For OECD: *Government Social Spending: Total Public Social Expenditure as a Percentage of GDP*, OECD iLibrary, December 20, 2013, http://www.oecd-ilibrary.org; For EU-27: "Chapter 3 – Social Protection Systems Confronting the Crisis", in *Employment and Social Developments in Europe 2012*, European Commission, Brussels, January 2013, www.europarl.europa.eu; For Latin America: *Sustainable Development in Latin America and the Caribbean: Regional Perspective Towards the Post-2015 Development Agenda*, United Nations ECLAC, July 2013, www.eclac.org.
80. See endnotes 79 and 81.
81. *SAARC Development Goals: India Country Report 2013*, Ministry of Statistics and Programme Implementation, Government of India, p. 36, http://mospi.nic.in.
82. "The 'Fiscal Deficit' Bogeyman and His Uses", *Aspects of India's Economy*,

op. cit.; "India Ranks 135 in Human Development Index: UNDP", *TNN*, July 24, 2014, http://timesofindia.indiatimes.com.

83. David Coady et al. (edited), *The Economics of Public Health Care Reform in Advanced and Emerging Economies*, International Monetary Fund, 2012, pp. 23–34, http://books.google.co.in.
84. "Policy Brief: Save Public Health – Ensure Health for ALL NOW!" Cehat, www.cehat.org; Sakti Golder, "Public Expenditure for Healthcare", 2011, http://www.theindiaeconomyreview.org.
85. *SAARC Development Goals: India Country Report 2013*, op. cit., p. 36; *Reclaiming Public Provisioning Priorities for the 12th Five Year Plan*, 2011, Centre for Budget and Governance Accountability, New Delhi, www.cbgaindia.org.
86. David Coady et al. (edited), *The Economics of Public Health Care Reform in Advanced and Emerging Economies*, op. cit., p. 288; Kounteya Sinha, "Health Spend Set to Double in 12th Plan", *TNN*, November 19, 2011, http://timesofindia.indiatimes.com.
87. *World Health Statistics 2013*, World Health Organisation, 2013, Switzerland.
88. P. Sainath, "Health as Someone Else's Wealth", *The Hindu*, July 1, 2005, http://www.hindu.com.
89. *Reclaiming Public Provisioning Priorities for the 12th Five Year Plan*, op. cit.
90. Richard Horton, Pam Das, "Indian Health: The Path from Crisis to Progress", *Lancet*, January 11, 2011, http://www.thelancet.com.
91. T.J. John, L. Dandona, V.P. Sharma, M. Kakkar, "Continuing Challenge of Infectious Diseases in India", *Lancet*, January 12, 2011, http://www.thelancet.com; N. Dhingra, P. Jha, V.P. Sharma et al., "Adult and Child Malaria Mortality in India", *Lancet*, November 20, 2010, http://www.thelancet.com.
92. "Tuberculosis in India", *Wikipedia*, http://en.wikipedia.org; *Global Tuberculosis Report 2012*, World Health Organisation, 2012, http://who.int.
93. David Coady et al. (edited), *The Economics of Public Health Care Reform in Advanced and Emerging Economies*, op. cit., p. 288.
94. V.K. Paul, H.S. Sachdev, D. Mavalankar et al., "Reproductive Health, and Child Health and Nutrition in India: Meeting the Challenge", *Lancet*, January 12, 2011, http://www.thelancet.com; *UNICEF – Goal: Reduce Child Mortality*, www.unicef.org; "India Tops in Rate of Maternal Deaths Worldwide", *DNA*, May 16, 2012, http://www.dnaindia.com.
95. M. Govinda Rao, Mita Choudhary, *Health Care Financing Reforms in*

India, National Institute of Public Finance and Policy, March 2012, https://www.nipfp.org.in.

96. V. Patel, S. Chatterji, D. Chisholm et al., "Chronic Diseases and Injuries in India", *Lancet*, January 12, 2011, http://www.thelancet.com.
97. T.J. John, L. Dandona, V.P. Sharma, M. Kakkar, "Continuing Challenge of Infectious Diseases in India", *Lancet*, January 12, 2011, http://www.thelancet.com.
98. Nikhila M. Vijay, "Medical Tourism – Subsidising Health Care for Developed Countries", *Third World Resurgence*, November/December 2007, http://www.twnside.org.sg; Ravi Duggal, *The Uncharitable Trust Hospitals*, June 17, 2012, http://righttohealthcare.blogspot.in; Jyoti Shelar and Lata Mishra, "One-Sided Deal: Hospitals Get but Don't Give Back", April 26, 2012, https://kractivist.wordpress.com.
99. *Medical Tourism – Incredible India*, http://www.incredibleindia.org
100. "International Medical Tourism Industry Pegged at $ 40 Billion a Year", *Bloomberg*, June 27, 2013, http://articles.economictimes.indiatimes.com; Vinay Grover, "India Seems to be the Most Promising Medical Tourism Destination", October 22, 2013, http://healthandcare.in.
101. "Poverty Dips to 29.8% in 2009–10: Planning Commission", March 19, 2012, http://www.dnaindia.com.
102. "'Let Them Eat Fat'", *Aspects of India's Economy*, No. 55, March 2014, http://www.rupe-india.org; C.P. Chandrasekhar, "Chronic Famishment", *The Hindu*, April 15, 2012, http://www.thehindu.com.
103. Utsa Patnaik, "Poverty Trends in India 2004–05 to 2009–10: Updating Poverty Estimates and Comparing Official Figures", op. cit.
104. Utsa Patnaik, "Number Games: India's Declining Poverty Figures Based on Flawed Estimation Method; Accurate Figures Show 75 Percent in Poverty", op. cit.
105. "'Let Them Eat Fat'", *Aspects of India's Economy*, op. cit.; C.P. Chandrasekhar, "Chronic Famishment", op. cit.
106. "'Let Them Eat Fat'", ibid.; C.P. Chandrasekhar, "Chronic Famishment", ibid.
107. Utsa Patnaik, "Number Games: India's Declining Poverty Figures Based on Flawed Estimation Method; Accurate Figures Show 75 Percent in Poverty", op. cit.; Utsa Patnaik, "Poverty Trends in India 2004–05 to 2009–10: Updating Poverty Estimates and Comparing Official Figures", op. cit.
108. *Children in India 2012 – A Statistical Appraisal*, Ministry of Statistics and Programme Implementation, op. cit.; *India – Nutrition*,

www.unicef.org.

109. Madura Swaminathan, "Public Distribution System and Social Exclusion", *The Hindu*, May 7, 2008, http://www.thehindu.com.
110. "Foodgrain Stocks Fall Below 70 Mt, Exceed Reserve Norms by a Margin", August 9, 2013, http://www.financialexpress.com.
111. "India's Food Crisis: Rotting Food-Grains, Hungry People", April 1, 2013, http://www.rediff.com.
112. Sachin Kumar Jain, *India's National Food Security Act: Entitlement of Hunger*, Asian Human Rights Commission, April 2010, http://www.humanrights.asia.
113. "National Food Security Act, 2013", *Wikipedia*, http://en.wikipedia.org; "Summary of the National Food Security Bill 2013", *Tehelka Bureau*, March 22, 2013, http://www.tehelka.com.
114. "Parliament Approves Food Security Bill with Amendments", *IANS*, September 3, 2013, http://indiatoday.intoday.in.
115. Ravi S. Jha, "India's Food Security Bill: An Inadequate Remedy?" *Guardian Professional*, July 15, 2013, http://www.theguardian.com; Sachin Kumar Jain, *India's National Food Security Act: Entitlement of Hunger*, op. cit.
116. Jean Dreze, "The Food Security Debate in India", July 9, 2013, http://india.blogs.nytimes.com.
117. *Ration Card Types and Commodity Entitlements*, Civil Supplies and Consumer Protection Department, http://www.consumer.tn.gov.in; S. Vydhianathan, R.K. Radhakrishnan, "Behind the Success Story of Universal PDS in Tamil Nadu", August 11, 2010, http://www.thehindu.com.
118. "Major Cut in Fuel, Food, Fertilizer Subsidies", February 28, 2013, http://www.thehindu.com; "Interim Budget 2014: Subsidy Bill Pegged Marginally Higher at Rs 2.5 lakh crore", *PTI*, February 17, 2014, http://profit.ndtv.com; *Union Budget 2015–2016*, http://indiabudget.nic.in.
119. *Has the Tide Turned: Response to Union Budget 2014–15*, Centre for Budget and Governance Accountability, 2014, p. 48, http://www.cbgaindia.org.
120. Ibid., p. 47.
121. Sanjeeb Mukherjee, "Outlay Shows States May Go Slow on Food Security Plan", July 12, 2014, http://www.business-standard.com; "Right to Food Campaign orr Budget 14", July 12, 2014, http://www.indiaresists.com.
122. "Car Sales May Barely Grow This Fiscal", January 9, 2013, http://

www.thehindu.com; Amrit Raj, Shally Seth Mohile, "Auto Industry: Running out of Gas?" July 18, 2013, http://www.livemint.com.

123. Praful Bidwai, "Courting a Four-Wheel Disaster", March 1, 2014, http://www.thenews.com.pk.
124. "Budget 2014 Lacks in Specifics, Says Manmohan Singh", July 10, 2014, http://profit.ndtv.com; Swaminathan S. Anklesaria Aiyar, "Arun Jaitley's Maiden Budget is like Chidambaram's with a Saffron Lipstick", *ET Bureau*, July 11, 2014, http://articles.economictimes.indiatimes.com; "Chidambaram Says Jaitley's Budget Has UPA Imprint", July 10, 2014, http://www.livemint.com.
125. "Bimal Jalan to Head Expenditure Commission", August 13, 2014, http://www.thehindubusinessline.com.
126. "PPP is New Mantra for Infra in Jaitley's Maiden Budget", July 10, 2014, http://zeenews.india.com; "Budget 2014–15: PPP is the New Mantra for Infrastructure", July 10, 2014, http://www.outlookindia.com; *Institution for Mainstreaming PPPS Will Be Set-Up: Shipping, Inland Navigation, Airports and Roads Sector Given Priority*, Press Information Bureau, Government of India, Ministry of Finance, July 10, 2014, http://pib.nic.in; "Big-Ticket Infrastructure Projects in Sight, All Roads Lead to PPPs", July 11, 2014, http://www.indiantollways.com; M. Rajendran, "Revival of SEZs on the Cards", *Hindustan Times*, July 11, 2014, http://www.hindustantimes.com.
127. Mahendra K. Singh, "Consent Clause in Land Acquisition Law May be Eased", *TNN*, July 15, 2014, http://timesofindia.indiatimes.com.
128. "Prakash Javadekar Promises Fast Clearances to Infrastructure Projects", *PTI*, May 29, 2014, http://articles.economictimes.indiatimes.com.
129. "Black Money Power", May 4, 2014, http://www.economist.com; Siddharth Varadarajan, "The Cult of Cronyism", *Seminar*, April 2014, http://svaradarajan.com; "Corporate Sector Lauds Narendra Modi Government's Maiden Union Budget", July 10, 2014, http://www.newswala.com; "Budget 2014–15: Scores High on Infra and Highways Building", July 11, 2014, http://www.nbmcw.com.
130. Davison Budhoo, "IMF/World Bank Wreak Havoc on Third World", *Third World Traveler*, http://www.thirdworldtraveler.com.
131. All the facts given below are taken from various articles available on the independent US-based non-profit website, http://venezuelanalysis.com.

II

UNION BUDGET 2015–16: WHAT IS IN IT FOR THE PEOPLE?

The union budget, which is a yearly affair, is a comprehensive display of the government's revenues and expenditures. It makes an estimate of the revenues from all sources for the following fiscal year, and outlines the expenditures that the government proposes to make in the coming fiscal year under various heads.

Therefore, an analysis of the union budget reveals the basic orientation of the government, what are its priorities and how concerned is it about the welfare of the common people.

Most media intellectuals who commented on the BJP Government's Budget 2015–16 praised the budget, saying it was "reformist and growth-oriented", "pragmatic", "balanced", "reflects clear intent to put the economy on the path of double digit growth", contained "path-breaking proposals", and so on.

Let us analyse more closely to see what it really contains. But before we go ahead with analysing the budget, let us first understand an economic concept, fiscal deficit, because it has come to play an important role in the making of the budget.

Fiscal Deficit

Fiscal deficit is just another term for government borrowings of various types. The government borrows when its expenditures exceed its receipts of all types.

- Fiscal Deficit = Government Expenditures – Receipts
- Receipts = Tax Revenues (Net to Centre) + Non-Tax Revenues + Non-Debt Capital Receipts

> **Box 2.1: Some Economic Terms**
>
> **Direct Taxes:** Taxes levied on the income of individuals or organisations (e.g. income tax, corporation tax, inheritance tax).
>
> **Indirect Taxes:** Taxes paid by consumers when they buy goods and services (e.g. sales tax, customs duties, excise duties).
>
> **Custom Duties:** Levies on goods imported to or exported from the country.
>
> **Excise Duties:** Duties imposed on goods manufactured within the country.

Receipts include tax revenues (Centre's share), non-tax revenues and non-debt capital receipts. Tax revenues include direct taxes (income tax, corporation tax, etc.) and indirect taxes (customs duties, excise duties, sales tax, etc.). Of the total (or gross) tax revenues of the Central government, it transfers a portion of it to the states; the remaining is what is included here. Non-tax revenues include profits of public sector enterprises, interest receipts on loans given by the government (to public sector enterprises, state governments, etc.), and income such as sale of spectrum. Non-debt capital receipts include disinvestment income and return of loans. (See Box 2.1 and Box 2.3 for an explanation of the various economic terms used here.)

Jaitley Vows to Bring Down the Fiscal Deficit

As discussed in the previous essay, ever since India's rulers decided to accept World Bank conditionalities and begin globalisation of the Indian economy, reduction of the fiscal deficit has become a key aspect of budget making of the Government of India. All the finance ministers of all the governments that have come to power at the Centre since 1991, irrespective of the colour of the government, have focussed on 'reducing government expenditures' and bringing down the fiscal deficit to 'sustainable levels'.

The finance minister of the new BJP Government that came to power in May 2014 is also walking down this same path. Soon after taking over the reins of the Finance Ministry in May last year (2014), Arun Jaitley declared that reducing the fiscal deficit would be one of his top priorities.[1] His predecessor, P. Chidambaram, had brought down the fiscal deficit from 4.8 percent of GDP in 2012–13 to 4.5 percent in 2013–14; and had set a target for further reducing it to 4.1

percent for the year 2014–15 in his interim budget presented just before the 2014 Lok Sabha elections. Jaitley, in his first budget speech in July 2014, vowed to adhere to this "daunting" fiscal deficit target.[2]

> **Box 2.2: Gross Domestic Product (GDP)**
>
> GDP measures the monetary value of final goods and services—that is, those that are bought by the final user—produced in a country in a given period of time (usually a year). GDP also includes some non-market production, such as defence or education services provided by the government.

While presenting the first full budget of the new government on February 28, 2015, the finance minister proudly announced that the government had succeeded in sticking to the fiscal deficit target of 4.1 percent of GDP for the year 2014–15. He further declared that in the financial year 2015–16, the fiscal deficit would be brought down to 3.9 percent, and then further to 3.6 percent and finally to 3 percent in 2016–17 and 2017–18, respectively.[3]

Humbug of Finance

The fact is, the economic theory that the government must balance its expenditure with its income, that is, must bring down its fiscal deficit to near zero, is plain humbug. John Maynard Keynes, one of the most influential economists of the twentieth century, had demonstrated way back in the 1930s that in an economy where there is poverty and unemployment, the government can, and in fact should, expand public works and generate employment by borrowing, that is, enlarging the fiscal deficit; such government expenditure would also stimulate private expenditure through the "multiplier" effect.[4] Even the governments of the developed countries like the United States and Japan, when faced with recessionary conditions, have resorted to huge levels of public spending and high fiscal deficits. To give a latest example, following the financial crash of 2008, the US Government poured in billions of dollars into the economy and its fiscal deficit zoomed to over a trillion dollars![5]

Keynes had castigated economists for arguing against increasing government spending to reduce unemployment and poverty in the name of fiscal deficit reduction—he called it "humbug of finance". Then why have all our finance ministers—from Manmohan Singh and P. Chidambaram to Arun Jaitley now—been harping on the necessity of reducing the government's fiscal deficit?

Box 2.3: Understanding Some Budget Terms

i) Union Budget = Total Receipts = Total Expenditure

- Union Budget for 2015–16 = Rs 1,777,477 crore

ii) Gross Tax Revenues

- Gross Tax Revenues include direct taxes (income tax, corporation tax, etc.) and indirect taxes (customs duties, excise duties, sales tax, etc.).
- Total Gross Tax Revenues, 2015–16 = Rs 1,449,500 crore

Of the total gross tax revenues of the Central government, a portion is transferred to the states. The remaining is what shows in the Union Budget (Centre's Net Tax Revenue).

- Gross Tax Revenues = Tax Revenue (Net to Centre) + States' Share of Central Tax Revenues + Transfer to National Calamity Fund
- Centre's Net Tax Revenue, 2015–16 = Rs 919,842 crore
- States' Share of Central Tax Revenues, 2015–16 = Rs 523,958 crore

iii) Total Receipts (in Union Budget) = Total Revenue Receipts + Total Capital Receipts

- Revenue Receipts = Tax Revenue (Net to Centre) + Non-Tax Revenue
  - Non-tax revenues include profits of public sector enterprises, interest receipts on loans given by the government (to public sector enterprises, state governments, etc.), and income such as sale of spectrum.
- Capital Receipts = Non-Debt Capital Receipts + Debt Receipts
  - Non-debt capital receipts include disinvestment income and return of loans.
  - Debt receipts are government borrowings. The government borrows when its total expenditures exceed its receipts (revenue receipts + non-debt capital receipts). These borrowings are also called the fiscal deficit.

iv) Total Expenditure (in Union Budget): Two different sets of classifications are used:

- Revenue vs Capital Expenditure
  - *Capital Expenditure*: Expenditure used to create assets or to reduce liabilities, e.g. building a road, or paying back a loan.

- *Revenue Expenditure:* Expenditure that does not create assets, e.g. expenses on salaries or other administrative costs.

▪ Plan vs Non-Plan Expenditure

- *Plan Expenditure:* Expenditure on schemes and projects covered by the Five Year Plans. These Plans are developed by the Planning Commission after consulting individual ministries. Plan expenditure can have both revenue and capital components. For instance, under the Sarva Shiksha Abhiyan, salaries of teachers could be classified as revenue expenditure, while expenditure on building a school may be classified as capital expenditure.
- Plan Expenditure can also be classified as:
  Plan Expenditure = Total Budget Support for Central Plan + Central Assistance for State and Union Territory (UT) Plans
- *Non-Plan Expenditure:* Ongoing expenditure by the government not covered by the Plans. These include interest payments on government debt, expenditure on organs of the state such as the judiciary and the police and even expenditure on the maintenance of existing government establishments such as schools and hospitals. Non-plan expenditure too, has revenue and capital components.

v) Union Budget 2015–16

▪ Plan Expenditure, 2015–16 = Rs 465,277 crore
  - Total Budget Support for Central Plan = Rs 260,493 crore
  - Central Assistance for State and UT Plans = Rs 204,784 crore

▪ Non-Plan Expenditure, 2015–16 = Rs 1,312,200 crore

vi) Central Plan Outlay: This year's instalment of the Five Year Plan. The funding for this is raised through:

▪ Central Plan Outlay = Total Budget Support for Central Plan + Internal and Extra Budgetary Resources (IEBR) of Public Enterprises

▪ IEBR, 2015–16 = Rs 317,889 crore

▪ Central Plan Outlay, 2015–16 = Rs 578,382 crore

Source for all figures: Union Budget documents, 2015–16.

As we have discussed in several of our writings (and also the previous essay in this book), ever since India began globalisation in 1991, the country's mainstream political parties have been running the economy solely for the benefit of giant foreign and Indian corporations. The fiscal deficit reduction gospel serves as a 'theoretical facade' to hide the government's anti-people policies. On the one hand, the finance ministers have been doling out lakhs of crores of rupees as 'incentives' to business houses in the name of promoting growth–development–entrepreneurism. And on the other hand, in the name of reducing the government's fiscal deficit, they have been slashing the government's already low social sector expenditures meant to provide essential services—such as education, health, food and even drinking water—to the poor at affordable rates.

But then why are all the top economic advisors of the government—from Raghuram Rajan to Arvind Panagariya—and all the leading management gurus giving interviews to news channels every other day about the importance of reducing the fiscal deficit of the government? They have unfortunately all become prize fighters for big business!

All this will sound amazing to many of our readers. But that is indeed the stupefying truth about the propaganda regarding the need to reduce the government's fiscal deficit. A closer look at the Modi–Jaitley Government's 2015–16 budget figures will prove our argument. But before that, let us also take a brief look at Jaitley's 2014–15 budget. The 2014–15 budget sets the orientation, and the 2015–16 budget is an acceleration down this path.

1. Union Budget 2014–15

Tax Concessions to the Rich

Every year, for the past several years, the budget documents have included a statement on the estimated revenue forgone by the government due to exemptions in major taxes levied by the Centre.

The 2015–16 budget documents[6] reveal that in 2014–15, the Modi Government gave away Rs 5.49 lakh crore* in tax exemptions/ deductions/ incentives to the very rich.[7] These major write-offs are in corporate income tax, customs duties and excise duties.

* *The write-offs as mentioned in the budget are actually Rs 5.89 lakh crore. From that, we have deducted the Rs 40,434 crore forgone on personal income tax, since this write-off benefits a wider group of people.*

To put this amount in perspective, these tax concessions to the country's rich equal nearly one-third of the union budget. They actually exceed our fiscal deficit for 2014–15 of Rs 5.13 lakh crore (see Table 2.1)! Had Jaitley really been concerned about reducing the fiscal deficit, he could have reduced these concessions given to India's richie rich.

Table 2.1: Comparison of Tax Concessions to the Rich in 2014–15 with Other Budget Figures

Tax Concessions to Rich, 2014–15	Rs 5.49 lakh crore
Fiscal Deficit, 2014–15 RE*	Rs 5.13 lakh crore
Size of Union Budget, 2014–15 RE	Rs 16.81 lakh crore
Tax Concessions to Rich, 2014–15, as % of Union Budget, 2014–15 RE	32.7%
Gross Tax Revenues, 2014–15 RE	Rs 12.51 lakh crore
Tax Concessions to Rich, 2014–15, as % of Gross Tax Revenues, 2014–15 RE	43.9%

* RE – Revised Estimate; see Box 2.4 for explanation.

Box 2.4: Some More Definitions: Budget Estimate (BE), Revised Estimate (RE) and Actual

The 'budget estimate' for any ministry or scheme is the amount allocated to it in the budget papers for the following year. For instance, in his budget speech of February 2015, the finance minister presented 'budget estimates' for the financial year 2015–16 which runs from April 2015 to March 2016. Once the financial year gets underway, some ministries may need more funds than was actually allocated to them under the 'budget estimates'. The government approaches Parliament with such 'supplementary' requests for funds during the course of the financial year. These supplementary demands are reflected in the 'revised estimates' for the current year. Thus along with 'budget estimates' for 2015–16, the finance minister also presented the 'revised estimates' for 2014–15. 'Actual' expenditures are the final amounts spent under different heads and may exceed (or fall short of) the 'revised estimates'. Since the 'actual' expenditure can only be assessed once the financial year is over and final accounts have been prepared, the 'actual' expenditures presented in the budget papers of 2015–16 are for the earlier financial year, i.e. for 2013–14.

These tax concessions are being given to some of the richest people in the world. *Forbes*, the renowned American business magazine, puts out a list of the world's billionaires every year. Its 2014 list included the names of 56 Indians, with a collective net worth of $191.5 billion.[8] That is equivalent to Rs 11.8 lakh crore, more than double our fiscal deficit for 2014–15 (calculated assuming $1 = Rs 62).

These super tax concessions are obscene and totally unjustified. A single statistic is enough to prove this: in 2014–15, the single biggest chunk of customs duties forgone was on diamonds and gold, accounting for Rs 75,592 crore.[9]

It is because of these huge tax concessions to the rich that the government's gross tax revenues for the year 2014–15 have fallen short of target. Jaitley had set a target of collecting gross tax revenues amounting to 10.6 percent of the GDP for the year 2014–15 (itself a huge fall from the peak of 11.71 percent reached in 2007–08). The revised estimates for 2014–15 show that there has been a shortfall in tax revenues to the tune of Rs 1.13 lakh crore, and hence the gross tax revenues as a percentage of the GDP have been revised downward in 2014–15 RE to 9.9 percent.[10]

Yet, Fiscal Deficit Target Achieved!

Despite this fall in gross tax revenues, how has the government succeeded in achieving the fiscal deficit target of 4.1 percent of the GDP for 2014–15?

Table 2.2: Union Budget, 2014–15 and 2015–16: Reduction in Expenditures on Vulnerable Sections[11] (*Rs crore*)

	2014–15 BE (1)*	*2014–15 RE (2)*	*Reduction: 1 – 2 (%)*	*2015–16 BE (3)*	*Reduction: 1 – 3 (%)*
Scheduled Caste Sub Plan	50,548	33,638	33	30,851	39
Tribal Sub Plan	32,387	20,536	37	19,980	38
Schemes for Welfare of Children	81,075	69,888	14	57,919	29
Gender Budget	98,030	81,984	16	79,258	19

*BE – Budget Estimate: See Box 2.4 for explanation.

It has achieved this mainly by making huge cuts in its expenditure. For 2014–15, the total government expenditure was budgeted at Rs 1,794,892 crore. However, the revised estimates show that there was a decline in both Plan and Non-plan expenditure, and hence the revised budget expenditure was less than the budgeted estimate by Rs 113,734 crore (see Table 2.3, p. 108).[11]

Where were these cuts made? The revised estimates for 2014–15 show that the Central government made huge cuts in its spending on social sectors. The government slashed its budgetary spending on schemes for the most vulnerable and marginalised sections of the Indian society by as much as 14 to 37 percent, to meet its fiscal deficit target! (See Table 2.2, fourth column; the various heads are explained later in this essay.)

2. Analysing Budget 2015–16

Yet More Tax Concessions to the Rich

In the run-up to the budget, Finance Minister Arun Jaitley repeatedly asserted that the economy is constrained by "fiscal deficit in revenue."[13] But as we have seen above, this has not prevented him from giving lakhs of crores of rupees of tax concessions and other sops to corporate houses.

Consequently, despite the fact that the tax-to-GDP ratio of the country is amongst the lowest in the world (see Essay I in this book, Chart 1.2), the combined Centre and states tax-to-GDP ratio has fallen further to 17.9 percent of GDP for 2013–14 BE,[14] and to about 15–16 percent more recently.[15]

Notwithstanding such low level of tax revenues, in the 2015–16 budget, Jaitley has announced a reduction in corporate tax rates from 30 percent to 25 percent over the next four years, starting from the next financial year. This is expected to provide corporates a total tax relief bonanza of Rs 2 lakh crore: Rs 20,000 crore in the first year, Rs 40,000 crore in the second year, Rs 60,000 crore in the third year and Rs 80,000 crore in fourth year.[16] The finance minister has stated that this reduction in tax rates would be matched by removal of tax exemptions and incentives for corporate tax payers—these exemptions/

concessions led to a total revenue loss of Rs 62,399 crore in 2014–15.[17] But whether this will actually take place is to be seen—in all probability, given the absolute pro-corporate nature of the government, nothing of this sort is going to take place.

Treading on the footsteps of Chidambaram, Jaitley has further deferred the implementation of the General Anti-Avoidance Rules (GAAR) for two more years. GAAR is meant to address important issues such as abuse of tax treaties, use of tax havens for the purpose of reducing tax bills and other clever tax avoidance arrangements resorted to by multinational corporations (MNCs) that are draining the country's resources. The first time GAAR was attempted to be introduced was in 2012; since then, first the UPA Government and now the BJP Government have been postponing its implementation. Several other countries around the world, including the BRICS nations of Brazil, South Africa and China, have introduced GAAR; but the Indian Government is not willing to put in place legal mechanisms to check the widespread tax evasion that MNCs indulge in. This is yet another proof of the absolute surrender of the Indian Government before giant foreign corporations.[18]

Public–Private–Partnership

Budget 2015–16 announces several more sops for corporate houses:

- A significant increase of Rs 70,000 crore in investment in infrastructure in 2015–16 over 2014–15. A special focus is on building highways. The Budget increased the total Plan expenditure of the Ministry of Road Transport and Highways from Rs 28,881 crore in 2014–15 BE to Rs 42,913 crore in 2015–16, an increase of Rs 14,032 crore.[19]
- The formation of a National Investment and Infrastructure Fund (NIIF) and tax-free bonds for raising funds for investment in rail, roads and irrigation. The finance minister stated that the government will ensure an annual flow of Rs 20,000 crore to the NIIF.[20]
- The finance minister also emphasised the need for a revamp of the public–private–partnership or PPP model. Calling the

> present model "weak", he stated that the government would need to further protect the private sector against investment risks in the infrastructure sector, and that "the sovereign will have to bear a major part of the risk."[21]

This last statement is absolutely amazing, given that the government has already been transferring mind-boggling sums to the private sector in the name of PPP (for a more detailed discussion of these transfers, see Essay I, p. 54).

Increase in Indirect Taxes

To compensate for this loss in revenue, the finance minister has announced an increase in the service tax rate from 12.36 percent (including cess and surcharge) to a flat 14 percent. This is a very regressive way of increasing tax revenues.

There are two types of taxes, direct taxes and indirect taxes. Direct taxes are levied on incomes, such as wages, profits and property, and so fall directly on the rich; while indirect taxes are imposed on goods and impersonal services, and so fall on all, both the rich and the poor. An equitable system of taxation taxes individuals and corporations according to their ability to pay, which in practice means that in such a system, the government collects its tax revenues more from direct taxes than indirect taxes.

Leave aside the more progressive countries like Venezuela, even in unabashedly capitalist countries across the world, be it the developing countries of South Africa and Brazil, or be it the developed countries of the OECD, the direct tax revenue as a percentage of total revenues varies from 55 percent to 65 percent and more. But in India, for every Rs 100 collected by the government as tax revenues, only around Rs 30 comes from direct taxes (and the rest, Rs 70, from indirect taxes).[22] The latest taxation proposals of the finance minister that augment indirect tax revenues while giving yet more direct tax concessions only further increase the regressivity of the tax structure in the country. According to the finance minister, his tax proposals will result in a direct tax loss of Rs 8,315 crore, and an indirect tax gain of Rs 23,383 crore, resulting in a net revenue gain of Rs 15,068 crore.[23]

Reduction in Government Spending

The low revenue collections (as shown by the low tax-to-GDP ratio), combined with the keenness of the finance minister to reduce the fiscal deficit, has made him reduce the total budget outlay for 2015–16 to even less than the budget estimates for 2014–15. In real terms, this implies that the government has reduced its total budgetary spending quite sharply (Table 2.3).

Table 2.3: India's Budget, 2014–15 and 2015–16: Reduction in Total Budget Expenditure and Plan Expenditure[24] (*Rs crore*)

	2014–15 BE (1)	*2014–15 RE (2)*	*Reduction 1 – 2 (%)*	*2015–16 BE (3)*	*Reduction 1 – 3 (%)*
Budget Outlay	1,794,892	1,681,158	6.3	1,777,477	1
Plan Expenditure	575,000	467,934	18.6	465,277	19.1
GDP at Current Market Prices (2011–12 series)	12,653,762*			14,108,945	
Budget as % of GDP	14.1	13.3		12.6	

* Advance Estimate (for definition, see Box 2.5)

As a proportion of the size of the Indian economy, the magnitude of the union budget for 2015–16 (estimated size Rs 1,777,477 crore) has declined to 12.6 percent of the GDP. This figure was 13.3 percent for 2014–15 RE and 14.1 percent for 2014–15 BE.[25]

Worse, the government's projected Plan expenditure has declined by a whopping 19 percent over the budget estimates for 2014–15. This is the first time that the Plan budget has been reduced.[26]

Sharp Cuts in Social Sector Investments

With total budgetary spending reduced below last year's level, and the government continuing to provide huge subsidies to corporate houses, obviously, the brunt of the cuts in government spending have been borne by the social sectors in Jaitley's 2015–16 budget.

As it is, the total public social sector expenditure of the Government of India is abysmally low! Jaitley is lying through his

Box 2.5: GDP Statistics: Advance Estimate and Revised Estimate

The annual estimate of GDP for a financial year is first brought out two months before the end of the financial year, on February 7. This GDP figure is called Advance Estimate. This figure is later revised at least three times, on January 31 of the succeeding years. After the release of the Third Revised Estimate (RE), which is done two years and ten months after the completion of a financial year, the data more or less stabilises. (Thus, the first RE for GDP data for 2011–12 was released on January 31, 2013, and the third RE was released on January 31, 2015—this last figure can be considered to be the final GDP figure for 2011–12.)

teeth when he claims that the subsidy burden of the government is very high.[27] The total social sector expenditure of the Government of India (Central government only) is barely 1.7 percent of GDP.[28] In contrast, the developed countries spend as much as a quarter of their GDP on public social support, with public social spending-to-GDP ratios above 30 percent for Denmark, Finland, France and Belgium.[29] The actual difference in social sector spending on the people between the developed countries and India is much higher than that suggested by these percentages, as the per capita GDP of the developed countries is several times more than India (the average per capita GDP of the countries of the European Union is $32,000, while the per capita GDP for India is only $1,688[30]).

Most developed countries have a very elaborate social security network for their citizens. The people in these countries consider government spending on social services to be their right, and therefore there are huge protests, with millions coming out on the streets, whenever the governments of these countries attempt to raise school and college fees, or cut their spending on health or pensions. In contrast, in India, due to the low political consciousness of the people, they do not consider government spending on social services to be their right. Due to the false propaganda dished out by the intellectuals–politicians–bureaucrats and the media, people have come to believe that the government really does not have the money to provide good quality health and education facilities and good quality rations, including pulses and edible oil, to all the people at cheap/affordable rates. Therefore, there are no mass protests when school/college fees rise, health care costs go through the roof, or bus fares skyrocket.

It is because of India's low spending on providing basic human needs to all citizens that it is at the bottom in the Social Progress Index compiled by the US-based non-profit group Social Progress Imperative. The index aims to measure quality of life throughout the globe, using 54 indicators in the areas of basic human needs, foundations of well-being and opportunity to progress. The Social Progress Index 2014 ranks India at a lowly 102 out of 132 countries.[31]

Table 2.4: Social Sector Expenditures by Union Government[32]

(*Rs crore*)

	2013–14	*2014–15 BE*	*2014–15 RE*	*2015–16 BE*
Total Exp. under Social Sector Ministries/ Deptts. (excluding Food Subsidy)	218,206	286,534	235,991	237,297
Total Exp. under Social Sector Ministries/ Deptts. (including Food Subsidy)	311,122	402,191	359,061	362,509
GDP at Current Market Prices (2011–12 series)	11,345,056	12,653,762	12,653,762	14,108,945
Social Sector Exp. (excluding Food Subsidy) as % of GDP	1.92	2.26	1.86	1.68
Social Sector Exp. (including Food Subsidy) as % of GDP	2.74	3.18	2.84	2.57

And yet Delhi's badshahs are further reducing the government's social sector expenditures. In his Budget 2015–16, Arun Jaitley has further reduced the government's already low expenditures on social services. As shown in Table 2.2 (p. 104), government spending on the vulnerable and disadvantaged sections—women, scheduled castes and tribes, and children—has taken a big hit in 2015–16, by as much as 20–40 percent over the budget estimates for 2014–15. Consequently, Central government spending on social services has fallen from an already low 2.26 percent of the GDP (excluding food subsidy) in 2014–15 BE to 1.68 percent of the GDP in 2015–16. Including food subsidy, it has fallen from 3.18 percent of the GDP to 2.57 percent of the GDP (Table 2.4).

The government is claiming that actual social sector expenditures are not going to fall as these cuts would be more than compensated by an increase in the states' share in Central taxes. The Centre has accepted the recommendation of the 14th Finance Commission to increase the share of the states in the divisible pool of Central taxes from 32 percent previously to 42 percent. But simultaneously, the Centre has reduced its funding for Central Assistance for State and Union Territory Plans by a whopping 40 percent (see Box 2.6A).

Therefore, the net increase in spending capacity of the state governments is very modest, by just 5.9 percent! (And for some states, like for instance Maharashtra, the net transfer of Central funds to them has actually fallen—see Box 2.6B)! As we discuss in detail below, the Centre has cut its social sector spending by as much as 20 to 40 percent in most sectors, with the cuts going up to as much as 50–70 percent for the Ministry of Water Resources, River Development and Ganga Rejuvenation, the Ministry of Drinking Water and Sanitation, the Department of Land Resources and the Ministry of Panchayati Raj. The net increase in Central funding to the states is simply not enough to compensate for the huge cuts made in Central government spending on social sectors.

Furthermore, the class nature of the various state governments and the Central government is the same. In all likelihood, the state governments are going to utilise this small increase in Central funding to increase the subsidies given by them to corporate houses, instead of increasing their social sector expenditures. As we have discussed elsewhere, various state governments have been competing with each other to give subsidies to corporate houses for setting up projects in their states![33]

Box 2.6
A: Increased Devolution to States: A Gigantic Fraud

The government is claiming that it has not reduced its expenditure on social sectors in actuality, as its cuts in social sector expenditures would be more than compensated by the increase in states' share of Central taxes.

But the Centre, while increasing the states' share in Central taxes, has, in a deft sleight of hand, managed to keep the total transfers to the states at nearly the same level as previous years by drastically cutting its spending on Central Assistance for State and Union Territory Plans! The Centre has unbundled the schemes for which it provides assistance to states into three categories. It will continue to fully fund those schemes which are mandated by legal obligations (e.g. MGNREGA) or are backed by Cess collection (e.g. funds for Sarva Shiksha Abhiyan from the Prarambhik Shiksha Kosh), and also some schemes targeted at poverty alleviation. But for other Centrally sponsored schemes, some of them will be implemented with a changed pattern of sharing of resources, with states contributing a higher share; and for some schemes, the Centre has decided to stop Central funding altogether; if the states want to continue these schemes, they will have to do so entirely from their own resources.

As a result of this jugglery, the net increase in spending capacity of the states (combined for all states) in 2015–16 (as compared to 2014–15 BE) is projected to go up by only 5.91 percent or Rs 46,729 crore (see Table below).

Table: Transfer of Resources to States (*Rs crore*)

	2014-15 BE	*2015-16 BE*	*Change (%)*
States Share of Taxes and Duties (1)	382,216	523,958	+ 37.1
Non-Plan Grants and Loans to States (2)	70,019	108,630	+ 55.1
Central Assistance for State and UT Plans (3)	338,408	204,784	– 39.5
Total Union Resources Transferred to States (1+2+3)	790,643	837,372	+ 5.9
GDP at Current Market Prices (2011–12 series)	12,653,762	14,108,945	
Total Union Resources Transferred to States as % of GDP	6.25%	5.94%	

Sources: "Of Bold Strokes and Fine Prints: Analysis of Union Budget 2015–16", CBGA, March 2015, p. 9, http://www.cbgaindia.org; Union Budget documents, 2015–16.

B: Total Central Transfers to the State of Maharashtra, 2015–16

According to figures given in the Maharashtra State budget for 2015–16, despite the increase in the state's share in Central tax revenues, the total transfers from the Centre to Maharashtra State for 2015–16 have actually fallen.

Table: Maharashtra: Devolution of Funds from Centre (*Rs crore*)

	2014-15 BE	*2015-16 BE*	*Change (%)*
State's Share of Central Tax Revenues	20,213	29,062	+ 43.8
Grant-in-Aid from Central Government to Maharashtra	27,958	17,869	– 36.1
Total Transfer of Central Funds to Maharashtra	48,171	46,931	– 2.6

Source: Maharashtra State, Budget 2015–16 documents. (Unfortunately, budget documents not available online, taken directly from MLAs.)

Therefore, it is obvious that combined Central and state government spending on various social sectors is going to take a big hit in this financial year.

Actual Cuts to be More

Additionally, as several analysts have pointed out, the government projection for its tax revenues is much inflated. The Centre expects the gross tax revenues to go up by 15.8 percent in 2015–16 BE as compared to an actual increase of 9.9 percent in 2014–15 (see Table 2.5), even though it expects the GDP to go up by 11.5 percent in 2015–16, the same as in 2014–15. That is highly improbable; in all likelihood, the Centre's gross tax revenues in 2015–16 are going to be below the target set for the year.[34] If that happens, then obviously, the Centre will have to further cut its overall budgetary spending below the budget estimate for this year; since cuts in subsidies to the rich are a no-no, the axe is obviously going to fall on social sector spending. Therefore, in all probability, the actual spending on social sectors this year is going to be much below the already low spending levels planned for this fiscal.

Table 2.5: Trends in Tax Revenues, 2013–14 to 2015–16[35] *(Rs crore)*

	2013–14 (1)	*2014–15 RE* (2)	*Change 2 – 1* (%)	*2015–16 BE* (3)	*Change 3 – 2* (%)
Gross Tax Revenues	1,138,734	1,251,391	9.89%	1,449,490	15.83%

Sector-Wise Analysis of Cuts in Social Sector Spending

Let us take a closer look at the cuts faced by the various sectors/ministries related to the social sectors.

Budgetary Resources Earmarked for Women

This is also known as the Gender Budget. The Gender Budget Statement (GBS), first introduced in Union Budget 2005–06, captures the quantum of budgetary resources earmarked for women by various departments and ministries.

India is one of the world's worst places to be a woman. She may be killed even before being born, or as an infant or a little girl. If she survives, there is every possibility that as she grows up, she may be molested/raped/tortured by her husband. In India, a crime against a woman is committed every 100 seconds: a woman is molested every 7 minutes, raped every 15 minutes (reported cases only, actual are obviously much more), a case of cruelty committed by either the husband or his relatives occurs every 5 minutes, and a dowry death occurs every 65 minutes (all figures for 2013).[36]

Table 2.6: Budgetary Allocations Earmarked for Women, 2014–15 and 2015–16[37] *(Rs crore)*

	2014–15 BE	*2015–16 BE*	*Reduction (%)*
Ministry of Women and Child Development	21,194	10,382	51
Gender Budget	98,030	79,258	19
of which:			
Department of School Education and Literacy	16,208	12,472	23

And yet, an insensitive government has slashed the Gender Budget by a whopping 19 percent this year as compared to the budget estimate for 2014–15. The total allocation under the GBS as a proportion of the union budget has in fact been going down over the last several years; this year, it is only 0.94 percent of the union budget, as against 1.04 percent last year and 1.55 percent in 2011–12.

As far as specific schemes go, although the list of schemes in the GBS is very long, the reality is, most of these interventions are only on paper, as reflected in the fact that they are very meagrely funded—of the 59 schemes meant exclusively for women, as many as 54 schemes have allocations of less than Rs 100 crore! Thus, soon after coming to power, the Modi Government had announced the setting up of 'One Stop Crisis Centres' for women across the country to provide assistance to victims of sexual assault—one in each district, 660 in all. One year later, this scheme has virtually been scrapped, with only two crore rupees being allocated for this scheme in Budget 2015–16. The allocation for a 24-hour Women's Helpline to assist women in distress is a princely one crore! The allocation for construction of shelter homes for single women and destitutes, and for the Scheme for Assistance to States for Implementation of Protection of Women from Domestic Violence Act, 2005, has been totally withdrawn. And there is only a meagre allocation of Rs 30 crore for hostels for working women.

Prime Minister Modi himself launched the 'Beti Bachao Beti Padhao Abhiyan' in January this year (2015) whose declared aim is to end discrimination against the girl child and educate her. However, the scheme gets only Rs 100 crore in this year's budget, which is a mockery of this important slogan.

The key ministry that looks after women's welfare is the Ministry of Women and Child Development. The allocation for this ministry in the Union Budget 2015–16 has been slashed by more than 50 percent over the budget estimate of 2014–15.[38]

Budgetary Outlays for Schemes for Welfare of Children

A nation can be judged by the way it treats its children. On that count, India metes out suffering, neglect and insecurity to millions of its very young. Indeed, India is one of the most dangerous places to be a child:

- We have the highest under-five child mortality rate in the world, with 12 lakh such deaths in 2015. A majority of these deaths are from preventable causes such as diarrhoea and malaria.[39]
- Around 48 percent of all children below the age of five are stunted, 43 percent are underweight and about 20 percent are wasted.[40]
- India has the largest number of child labourers in the world. While official figures put the number of child workers in the country at around 13 million, a 2011 UNICEF report says that more than 28 million children in India between the ages 5–14 are engaged in child labour.[41]
- More than 8 crore children drop out of school without completing even basic schooling (that is, education up to Class VIII).[42]
- And as for the girl child, it's a miracle that she survives at all! For all the reasons given briefly in the previous section, the child sex ratio in India (number of girls to a thousand boys) declined from 945 to 914 over the period 1991–2011. The 2011 Census reveals that there are about 7 million fewer girls than boys in the age-group 0–6 in the country, implying that millions of female foetuses have been aborted and young girls killed during the past decade.[43]

Appalling figures! And yet, the government has reduced the total allocation for child oriented schemes sharply by 30 percent in this year's budget, as compared to last year's budget estimate (Table 2.7).

Table 2.7: Budgetary Allocations for Welfare of Children, 2014–15 and 2015–16[44] (*Rs crore*)

	2014–15 BE	*2015–16 BE*	*Reduction (%)*
Schemes for Welfare of Children	81,075	57,919	29
of which:			
Department of School Education and Literacy	54,101	40,757	25
Integrated Child Development Scheme	18,391	8,449	54

The largest component of the Child Budget is for education of children; that has been slashed by 25 percent. From the point of view of child health, the most important scheme is the Integrated Child Development Scheme. As the budget itself puts it, it is meant to be "an integrated package of health, supplementary nutrition and educational services to children up to six years of age, pregnant women and nursing mothers." Despite the terrible state of India's children, the government has cut the allocation for this salient programme by as much as 54 percent as compared to 2014–15 BE![45]

Resources Earmarked for Dalits and Adivasis

More than six decades after the Constitution outlawed the practice of untouchability and discrimination on the basis of caste, and guaranteed that every citizen shall have equality of status and opportunity, the scheduled castes and scheduled tribes continue to face many forms of untouchability practices as well as social, economic and institutional deprivations. Not only that, they are also subjected to enormous atrocities, ranging from abuse on caste name, murders, rapes, arson, social and economic boycotts, to naked parading of SC/ST women, and being forced to drink urine and eat human excreta.

Table 2.8: Scheduled Caste Sub Plan and Tribal Sub Plan, 2014–15 and 2015–16[46] (*Rs crore*)

	2014–15 BE (1)	*Allocation as % of Total Plan Exp.*	*2015–16 BE (2)*	*Allocation as % of Total Plan Exp.*	*Reduction 1–2 (%)*
Scheduled Caste Sub Plan	50,548	8.8	30,851	6.6	39
Tribal Sub Plan	32,387	5.6	19,980	4.3	38

In the 1970s, the government launched the Scheduled Caste Sub Plan (SCSP) and Tribal Sub Plan (TSP) to ensure the flow of targeted funds from the general sectors in the Central ministries towards the development of the Dalits and Adivasis. The guidelines under these two programmes clearly state that the allocations for them as a proportion of the Plan outlay should be at least in proportion to their share in the total population.[47] The population share for the Dalits is 16.6 percent and for Adivasis is 8.6 percent, according to the 2011 Census. However, the allocations for SCSP and TSP have never reached the stipulated norm of 16 percent and 8 percent of the Plan outlay respectively. In this year's budget estimates, the allocations for SCSP and TSP have been sharply reduced, by as much as 38–39 percent over 2014–15 BE. Consequently, the allocation for SCSP has fallen to just 6.6 percent and for TSP to a lowly 4.3 percent of the total Plan expenditure for 2015–16 (Table 2.8)![48]

Abandoning the Health Sector to God

India is the disease capital of the world. Malaria kills two lakh people every year, while tuberculosis kills three lakh. India accounts for one-fourth of the deaths in the world due to diarrhoea, one-third of the deaths due to leprosy, and more than half the deaths due to Japanese encephalitis. It holds the record for the highest number of maternal deaths in the world: 56,000 mothers die every year from pregnancy or childbirth related causes. India also has the highest number of child deaths in the world: 12 lakh children under the age of five die in India every year, with pneumonia and diarrhoea accounting for one-third of these deaths. India is in the grip of an epidemic of chronic diseases like cardiovascular diseases and diabetes. More than 50 percent of the deaths in India occur due to chronic diseases, with cardiovascular diseases being a major contributor.[49]

India is actually faced with a 'health emergency'. The reason is India's low level of public health spending. Public health expenditure in India (Centre and states combined) is only about 1 percent of GDP, as compared to 5–7 percent for the advanced economies and 3–5 percent of GDP for several emerging economies.[50] According to the WHO, India ranks 171 out of 175 countries in public health spending, and is ranked even below the sub-Saharan countries.[51] An article in the *Lancet*, the world's most revered health journal, points out that it is possible for India to address these health challenges, there are many inexpensive strategies available, but their implementation would require increased public investment in health and strengthening of the public health system.[52]

During the 2014 Lok Sabha election campaign, Modi had promised to make health a top priority and roll out universal health coverage. However, after coming to power, he has made a complete U-turn on this promise. The Union Budget 2015–16 has actually reduced the already low allocations for the Ministry of Health and Family Welfare by 16 percent, or about Rs 6,000 crore (from Rs 37,965.7 crore in 2014–15 BE to Rs 32,068.2 crore in 2015–16 BE) (Table 2.9). This has pushed India's health system to the edge, and forced the normally reticent editor-in-chief of *Lancet*, Richard Horton, to lambast Prime Minister Narendra Modi for ignoring India's health sector. He stated that before Modi, even though health was not high on the agenda of the government, at least it was on the agenda. But since the coming of Modi to power, "health has completely vanished from the government's focus." He went on to warn that India is on the verge of collapse under the weight of its own ill health. He further stated that ignoring health will see epidemics sweeping across the country, "creating an unsustainable future and destroying national security."[53]

How can a country that allows so many of its mothers and children to die due to inadequate provision of health care claim to be a world leader? It is only an indication of the utter insensitivity of India's upper classes and political leaders. They have totally divorced themselves from the people of the country, they have actually become anti-people.

Table 2.9: Budgetary Allocations for Health, 2014–15 and 2015–16[54] (*Rs crore*)

	2014–15 BE	*2015–16 BE*	*Reduction (%)*
Ministry of Health and Family Welfare	**37,966**	**32,068**	**15.5**
of which			
Dept. of Health and Family Welfare	35,163	29,653	19.9
Dept. of Health Research	1,018	1,018	0
Dept. of AIDS Control	1,785	1,397	21.7
Ministry of AYUSH*	1,272	1,214	4.6

*Ayurveda, Yoga and Naturopathy, Unani, Siddha and Homoeopathy

Accelerating Commercialisation of Education

The state of India's education system is alarming, to put it mildly. The Twelfth Plan (2012–17) admits that even after three years of the passage of the Right to Education Act which is supposed to guarantee free and compulsory education to all children in the age group 6–14, the drop-out rate at the elementary level is still as high as 42.39 percent![55]

But this is just one aspect of the terrible state of education in the country. Seven decades after independence, the conditions in a majority of the schools are so bad that it is a "national shame". More than 50 percent of the 8.4 lakh primary schools in the country are single, or at best, two teacher schools. And a staggering 70 percent schools have three or less than three teachers. More than one lakh primary schools in the country are single classroom schools (or function in the open, without any classrooms), and a whopping 64 percent of the primary schools (5.3 lakh schools) function with three classrooms or less. What must be the quality of education being imparted to students in schools where a single teacher is teaching two or more than two different classes in a single room!

An official survey of 2011 found that: 21 percent of all elementary schools did not have functional drinking water facilities; 40 percent of the schools did not have usable toilet facilities; nearly 60 percent elementary schools were not electrified; 49 percent schools did not have libraries; and so on.[56]

Table 2.10: Budgetary Allocations for Education, 2014–15 and 2015–16[57] (*Rs crore*)

	2014–15 BE	*2015–16 BE*	*Reduction (%)*
Ministry of Human Resource Development	82,771	69,075	16.6
Department of School Education and Literacy	55,115	42,220	23.4
of which:			
Sarva Shiksha Abhiyan	28,258	22,000	22.1
Mid-Day Meal Scheme	13,152	9,236	29.8
Department of Higher Education	27,656	26,855	2.9

And yet the allocation for education in Budget 2015–16 has been slashed by as much as 16.5 percent as compared to the 2014–15 estimate! The Sarva Shiksha Abhiyan is the main scheme of the Central government for implementing the Right to Education (RTE) Act and universalising education. This scheme is to be fully funded by the Central government. The allocation for this scheme has been cut by 22 percent—implying that the government is not interested in implementing the RTE Act and putting all out-of-school children in school! The Mid-Day Meal Scheme is another very important scheme for elementary education that is supposed to be fully funded by the Central government. The allocation for this too has been chopped, by 30 percent. The country's ruling classes are not willing to spend money even on providing a decent nutritious meal once a day to the country's children!

Drinking Water and Sanitation: Swachh Bharat Mission

The Swachh Bharat Mission (SBM) is one of the most heavily publicised programmes of the Central government, endorsed by Prime Minister Modi himself. It includes both the National Rural Drinking Water Programme (NRDWP) and Swachh Bharat Abhiyan (SBA). It has both a rural and an urban component.

While the entire BJP political leadership, from the prime minister to the finance minister, have been harping on 'Clean India', the government is simply not willing to fund the Swachh Bharat Mission. It has cut the budget for the SBM by more than half (Table 2.11)![58]

Table 2.11: Budgetary Allocations for Swachh Bharat Mission, 2014–15 and 2015–16[59] (*Rs crore*)

	2014–15 BE	*2015–16 BE*	*Reduction (%)*
Ministry of Drinking Water and Sanitation	15,267	6,244	59.1
of which:			
National Rural Drinking Water Programme	11,000	2,611	76.3
Swachh Bharat Abhiyan	4,260	3,625	14.9

Rural Development

As per Census 2011, nearly 83 crore people in India are living in rural areas, and constitute about 69 percent of the total population of the country. Therefore, all-encompassing development of rural areas is crucial for development of the country.

The BJP had declared in its election manifesto for the 16th Lok Sabha elections that it would focus on improving village infrastructure if voted to power. But like its other promises, this too has been buried and forgotten. The finance minister has in fact reduced the total allocation for the Ministry of Rural Development (MoRD) by 12.5 percent.

The most important programmes under the MoRD are the Indira Awas Yojna (IAY), the National Rural Livelihood Mission (NRLM), Pradhan Mantri Gram Sadak Yojna (PMGSY) and the Mahatma Gandhi National Rural Employment Guarantee Scheme (MNREGS). The Union government is seeking to transfer the IAY and the NRLM to state governments, and so allocation for both these schemes has been slashed by nearly 40 percent.

Table 2.12: Budgetary Allocations for Ministry of Rural Development, 2014–15 and 2015–16[60] (*Rs crore*)

	2014–15 BE	*2015–16 BE*	*Change (%)*
Ministry of Rural Development	83,852	73,333	– 12.5
Department of Rural Development	80,093	71,695	– 10.5
of which:			
National Rural Livelihood Mission	3,859	2,383	– 38.2
Indira Awas Yojna	16,000	10,025	– 37.3
Pradhan Mantri Gram Sadak Yojna	14,391	14,291	– 0.7
Mahatma Gandhi National Rural Employment Guarantee Scheme	34,000	34,699	+ 2
Department of Land Resources	3,759	1,638	– 56.4

The flagship programme of the MoRD is the MNREGS. On paper at least this programme, that is legislatively supposed to be fully funded by the Centre, has escaped the steep cuts that have been made in social sector spending of the Central government in the 2015–16 budget. The outlay for this programme in Budget 2015–16 has been pegged at Rs 34,699 crore, 2 percent more than the allocation for 2014–15 (a decline in real terms).

However, the fact of the matter is, even in 2014–15, the fund allocation for MNREGS was inadequate to meet the declared objectives of the MNREGA. The states had projected an estimated 278 crore person-days of work for 2014–15, amounting to an estimated cost of Rs 66,000 crore. The Ministry of Rural Development too had accepted this figure. But the finance minister allocated only Rs 34,000 crore in the budget for 2014–15.[61] Consequently, in 2014–15, MNREGS was able to generate only 165.1 crore person-days of jobs for the poor, compared with 220.4 crore person-day jobs generated in 2013–14.[62] This works out to an average wage employment per household of only 39 days per year in 2014–15—significantly lower than the figure of 46 days reached in 2013–14. This was the scheme's worst performance since its introduction nine years ago. It is another matter that in all the nine years so far, the scheme has never been able to provide the 100 days of employment guaranteed under the MNREGA.[63] The government has continued to violate the Act in other ways too. Though the Act guarantees employment to all rural households seeking work, there are a very large number of households—probably around 20 percent of rural households—who desire work but are unable to get employment under this Act. (NSS data show that around 19 percent of rural households sought work but did not get employment under the MNREGS in 2011–12—that year MNREGS provided 211.4 crore person-days of employment to 5 crore households.)[64]

Secondly, even for providing this low level of person-days of employment, the funds provided by the Centre proved inadequate and the states paid out Rs 6,000 crore from their own funds in 2014–15. Therefore, even if the Centre wants to maintain MNREGS at the same (inadequate) level as last year, the minimum outlay it should have provided is Rs 46,000 crore (consisting of Rs 34,000 crore plus Rs 6,000 crore arrears plus Rs 6,000 crore shortfall that caused the arrears in the first place); the fact that it has not done so, but kept the provision at roughly the same level as last year therefore implies, in actuality, a huge cut of 32 percent![65]

Allocations for Food Security

This important programme's allocation has also not been cut by the Central government in Budget 2015–16, at least on paper (Table 2.13).

Table 2.13: Budgetary Allocations for Food Security, 2014–15 and 2015–16[66] (*Rs crore*)

	2014–15 BE	*2014–15 RE*	*2015–16 BE*
Ministry of Consumer Affairs, Food and Public Distribution:			
Food Subsidy	115,000	122,676	124,419
GDP at Current Market Prices (2011–12 series)	12,653,762		14,108,945
Food Subsidy as % of GDP	0.91	0.97	0.88

As discussed in the previous essay in this book, the National Food Security Act is actually a very inadequate act, and only partially addresses the huge problem of mal/under-nutrition in the country. But even if we ignore this important issue and consider the allocation for food security only from the perspective of full implementation of the National Food Security Act as it stands today, this allocation is not enough. Because of this inadequate allocation, the Act is presently being implemented only in 11 states, that too partially. A full roll-out of the Act would require considerable more budgetary support as compared to the food subsidy bill in 2014–15. However, Jaitley has increased the food subsidy budget by only Rs 2,000 crore for this year (over 2014–15 RE), implying that the government is not anticipating any increase in the quantum of grain to be distributed through the PDS this year (and is assuming that grain would be procured at the same prices as last year).[67]

Other Cuts in Social Sector Expenditures

Other social sectors have had to bear even sharper cuts in their budgetary outlays (Table 2.14).

The Minister for Panchayati Raj has virtually been made jobless, with allocations for this ministry reduced to near zero. The allocation for the Ministry of Water Resources and River Development—that looks after another of Prime Minister Modi's pet themes, river rejuvenation—has also been reduced by two-thirds. The only river that the government is interested in is the Ganga. However, even this has not been given an allocation from the budget; instead, Rs 2,100 crore from the National Clean Energy Fund has been diverted for the 'National Ganga Plan'. Other rivers can continue to die . . .

Table 2.14: Reduction in Budget Expenditure of Other Social Sector Related Ministries, 2014–15 and 2015–16[68] (*Rs crore*)

	2014–15 BE	*2015–16 BE*	*Change (%)*
Ministry of Water Resources, River Development and Ganga Rejuvenation	13,837	4,232	– 69.4
within this:			
National Ganga Plan (funds from National Clean Energy Fund)	1,500	2,100	40
Ministry of Agriculture:			
Dept. of Agriculture and Cooperation	22,652	17,004	– 24.9
Dept. of Agricultural Research and Education	6,144	6,320	2.9
Dept. of Animal Husbandry, Dairying and Fisheries	2,266	1,585	– 30.1
Ministry of Panchayati Raj	7,001	95	– 98.6
Ministry of Urban Development:			
Dept. of Urban Development	17,629	16,832	– 4.5
Ministry of Housing and Urban Poverty Alleviation	6,009	5,634	– 6.2

Yet, No Cuts in Defence and Police Expenditures

The squeeze in Central government spending has not affected

the government's spending on the military and police—they have remained at the same high level as last year in real terms. While the total social sector expenditures of the Central government fell by 15.6 percent in 2015–16 over the previous year's budget estimates, the military expenditure rose by 8.7 percent and expenditure on the police by 4.5 percent (Table 2.15).

The official military expenditure of the Government of India is projected at Rs 3.1 lakh crore for 2015–16 (includes pensions). The actual military budget, or the unofficial military budget, is more than this, as a significant part of the budgets of the Department of Atomic Energy and the Department of Space (the former is responsible for making nuclear weapons, the latter for the missile programme, but no separate provision is made for either of these two expensive programmes) too should be included while calculating the country's total military expenditure. Just the official military budget for 2015–16 (Rs 310,080 crore) is 17.4 percent of the total government expenditure, and is 31 percent more than the Centre's combined spending on all social services (excluding food subsidy)—Rs 236,722 crore.

Table 2.15: Budgetary Allocations for Military and Police, 2014–15 and 2015–16[69] *(Rs crore)*

	2014–15 BE	*2015–16 BE*	*Increase (%)*
Ministry of Defence	285,203	310,080	8.7
Ministry of Home Affairs: Police	59,451	62,125	4.5

Likewise, the Centre's outlay on internal security, that is, police, is Rs 62,125 crore. Add this to the military budget, and the total—Rs 372,205 crore—is more than the total Central spending on all social services, including food subsidy—Rs 362,195 crore.

Police is also a state subject, and the states too spend heavily on the police.

One can debate whether this or that head of expenditure that is included within the broad categories of defence and police should be called as expenditure on external security or internal security. For instance, a large part of the army is now deployed within the country, for internal security; while the Border Security Force, included in police expenditure, is also used to defend the country's borders. But one fact is noticeable. The protests within the country against the pro-corporate and anti-people policies of the government are increasing, and the government is increasingly deploying the police and even the military to repress these protests. While the government claims shortage of funds for meeting the legitimate demands of people for improved welfare services, there seems to be no shortage of funds for repressing these protests.

BJP: Twin Brother of UPA

To conclude, Budget 2015–16 of the BJP Government is not only a continuation, but also an acceleration of the neo-liberal policies of the previous UPA Government. Since 1991, ever since India began globalisation and opened up the economy to foreign multinationals, successive governments at the Centre have been offering the most lucrative concessions to foreign investors to entice them to invest in the country. The divisive, communal agenda being pursued by the Modi Government is actually only a cover, to disguise its real economic agenda of running the economy solely for the profiteering of big corporate houses:

- transferring public money and resources to the tune of lakhs of crores of rupees to foreign and Indian business houses in the name of promoting GDP growth;
- cutting welfare expenditures on the poor—whose aim is to provide the bare means of sustenance to the poor at affordable rates—in the name of containing the fiscal deficit, and privatising and handing over these services to private corporations for their naked profiteering.

In pursuing this neoliberal agenda, the country's ruling political class—that is, the political parties that dominate the Indian Parliament, the bureaucrats, the country's leading intellectuals, and the big corporate houses—are actually wilfully and deliberately trashing the socialist vision of our nation's founding fathers embedded in the

Directive Principles of the Constitution of India, which direct the state to:

- strive to build an egalitarian society and reduce inequalities in income;
- implement policies to ensure good quality education and health facilities for all people, and raise their level of nutrition and standard of living.

Let Us Join Hands, to Build a New India...

There is no doubt, the country is being ruled by the corporate houses. They control and fund the mainstream political parties. During election time, these parties come up with attractive slogans like 'Garibi Hatao' or 'Achhe Din Aayenge' and launch a media blitz with the help of a corporate-controlled media to sell us dreams of a better future; once the elections are over, whoever wins forgets all the promises made and goes about implementing the very same policies as the previous governments.

We need to see through this hoax, and build our own movements and organisations that will, in the years to come, grow and democratically take over the reins of power in the country and build a new society that is oriented not towards maximising the profits of the big corporations, but a society whose basic priority would be the well-being and happiness of the ordinary working people. This is not a utopian dream; it is possible. If people in Venezuela and Bolivia and Ecuador are doing it, so can we!

References

1. "Checking Inflation, Fiscal Deficit Top Priority: Arun Jaitley", *Indian Express*, May 27, 2014, http://www.indianexpress.com.
2. "Jaitley Terms Chidambaram's Fiscal Deficit Target of 4.1% as 'Daunting'", *Business Standard*, July 10, 2014, http://www.business-standard.com.
3. "Jaitley Goes for Growth, Delays Cut in Fiscal Deficit", February 28, 2015, http://www.thehindubusinessline.com.

4. We have discussed this in greater detail in the previous essay in this book, *Is the Government Really Poor?*
5. *US Government Spending in Recent Decades*, http://www.usgovernmentspending.com; *US Federal Defict Definition – Plus Charts and Analysis*, http://www.usgovernmentspending.com.
6. All figures related to the union budget taken from Union Budget documents available at *Union Budget 2015–2016*, http://indiabudget.nic.in.
7. "Budget 2015–16 in Eight Charts", March 3, 2015, http://www.thehindu.com.
8. "India's Billionaires List Rises to All Time High of 56: Forbes", March 4, 2014, http://www.vccircle.com.
9. *Statement of Revenue Impact of Tax Incentives Under the Central Tax System: Financial Years 2013–14 and 2014–15*, http://exactuscorp.co.in.
10. P. Ramakumar, *Seek Truth from Facts: Jaitley's Budget Sharply Cuts Spending for the Poor*, February 28, 2015, http://ramakumarr.blogspot.in; *The Medium Term Fiscal Policy Statement – Union Budget*, http://www.indiabudget.nic.in; *Government of India Budget 2015–16*, ICRA Research Services, February 2015, http://www.icra.in; "3 Reasons Why India's Tax–GDP Ratio Has Fallen", March 7, 2015, http://www.rediff.com.
11. Union Budget documents, 2015–16, op. cit.
12. Union Budget documents, 2015–16, ibid.
13. See, for example: "Arun Jaitley Hints at Special Steps to Boost Public Spending", January 19, 2015, http://indianexpress.com.
14. *Of Bold Strokes and Fine Prints: Analysis of Union Budget 2015–16*, Centre for Budget and Governance Accountability, March 2015, p. 11, http://www.cbgaindia.org.
15. "India Has Among Lowest Tax/GDP Ratios, No Room for Sops", March 4, http://www.daijiworld.com.
16. "Jaitley Gave Bonanza to Corporates: Chidambaram", *The Hindu Business Line*, March 1, 2015, http://www.thehindubusinessline.com.
17. R. Jagannathan, "Budget 2015: Chidu Is Wrong to Claim Corporates Are Main Gainers", March 1, 2015, http://www.firstpost.com.
18. *Of Bold Strokes and Fine Prints: Analysis of Union Budget 2015–16*, op. cit., pp. 16–17.
19. Union Budget documents, 2015–16, op. cit.
20. "Budget 2015: Infrastructure Investment to be Raised by Rs 70,000 Crore", February 28, 2015, http://www.livemint.com.
21. Ibid.

22. *Of Bold Strokes and Fine Prints: Analysis of Union Budget 2015–16*, op. cit., pp. 18–19; Jorge Martinez-Vazquez, *Taxation in Asia*, Asian Development Bank, 2011, p. 4, http://www.adb.org.
23. *Of Bold Strokes and Fine Prints: Analysis of Union Budget 2015–16*, ibid., p. 18.
24. Union Budget documents, 2015–16, op. cit.
25. According to the budget documents, GDP for 2014–15 was Rs 12,653,762 crore (Advance Estimate); and GDP for 2015–16 has been projected at Rs 14,108,945 crore.
26. *Budget 2015–16: Analyzing the Estimated Budget: Where Is the Plan for Most Marginalised?* A Short Review by Delhi Forum, available on the internet at: https://groups.google.com.
27. "Subsidy Burden Is Very High: Arun Jaitley", *NDTV Profit*, July 18, 2014, https://profit.ndtv.com; "Jaitley for Subsidy Rationalisation, Against High Taxation", August 17, 2014, http://archive.financialexpress.com.
28. "Four Charts That Show Why India Must Change Its Spending Priorities", August 7, 2014, http://www.livemint.com.
29. *Social Expenditure Update*, OECD, November 2014, http://www.oecd.org.
30. "List of Countries by GDP (Nominal) Per Capita", https://en.wikipedia.org.
31. "India Ranks 102 on Social Progress", *The Hindu Business Line*, April 4, 2015, http://www.thehindubusinessline.com.
32. *Of Bold Strokes and Fine Prints: Analysis of Union Budget 2015–16*, op. cit., p. 9; Union Budget documents, 2015–16, op. cit.
33. We have given examples for this in the previous essay in this book, *Is the Government Really Poor?*
34. "Budget Lays Down Multiple Goals, but Fails on Fiscal Consolidation Front: C Rangarajan", March 4, 2015, http://www.rediff.com.
35. Union Budget documents, 2015–16, op. cit.
36. *Crime Against Women – National Crime Records Bureau*, http://ncrb.gov.in.
37. Calculated from: Union Budget documents, 2015–16, op. cit.
38. *Of Bold Strokes and Fine Prints: Analysis of Union Budget 2015–16*, op. cit., pp. 21–24; "Gender Budgeting? Central Allocation for 2015–16 Lowest in Five Years", March 8, 2015, http://www.counterview.net; Union Budget documents, 2015–16, ibid.; Piyasree Dasgupta, "All Hype, Zero Delivery: Modi Govt to Build Just 36 of the 660 Promised Rape Crisis Centres", February 26, 2015, http://www.firstpost.com;

"Save Girl Child, Educate Her, Pleads Modi", January 23, 2015, http://www.thehindu.com.

39. "20% of World's Under-5 Deaths Occur in India", September 9, 2015, http://timesofindia.indiatimes.com.
40. *Children in India 2012 – A Statistical Appraisal*, Ministry of Statistics and Programme Implementation, Government of India, 2012, http://mospi.nic.in; *India – Nutrition*, www.unicef.org.
41. Nelson Vinod Moses, "5 Reasons Why India Remains One of the Most 'Dangerous' Places to Be a Child", November 21, 2013, http://social.yourstory.com.
42. *Twelfth Five Year Plan: 2012–17, Vol. III: Social Sectors*, Planning Commission, Government of India, p. 53, http://planningcommission.nic.in.
43. "India Loses 3 Million Girls in Infanticide", October 9, 2012, http://www.thehindu.com; Rita Banerji, "Census Reveals 17 Million Girls Killed in India in Age Group 1–15 years!" October 2, 2013, https://genderbytes.wordpress.com.
44. Calculated from: Union Budget documents, 2015–16, op. cit.
45. Union Budget documents, 2015–16, ibid.
46. Calculated from: Union Budget documents, 2015–16, ibid.
47. "Union Budget 2015–16 Reduces Funds for SCs and STs", March 5, 2015, http://www.downtoearth.org.in.
48. See Table 2.2; *Of Bold Strokes and Fine Prints: Analysis of Union Budget 2015–16*, op. cit., pp. 31–34.
49. All statistics taken from Essay I of this book, *Is the Government Really Poor?* and endnote 39.
50. David Coady et al. (ed.), *The Economics of Public Health Care Reform in Advanced and Emerging Economies*, International Monetary Fund, 2012, pp. 23–34, 288, http://books.google.co.in; Mita Choudhury, H.K. Amar Nath, *An Estimate of Public Expenditure on Health in India*, National Institute of Public Finance and Policy, New Delhi, May 2012, http://www.nipfp.org.in.
51. Nirmala M. Nagaraj, "India Ranks 171 out of 175 in Public Health Spending, Says WHO Study", *TNN*, August 11, 2009, http://timesofindia.indiatimes.com.
52. V. Patel, S. Chatterji, D. Chisholm et al., "Chronic Diseases and Injuries in India", *Lancet*, January 12, 2011, http://www.thelancet.com.
53. Kounteya Sinha, "British Medical Journal Lancet to Take Modi to Task for Ignoring Health Sector", *TNN*, October 21, 2015, http://timesofindia.indiatimes.com; "Health's Vanished from Modi Govt

Focus: Lancet", October 22, 2015, http://health.economictimes.indiatimes.com.

54. Calculated from: Union Budget documents, 2015–16, op. cit.
55. *Twelfth Five Year Plan: 2012–17, Vol. III: Social Sectors*, op. cit., p. 53.
56. "DISE Survey, 2010–11", NUEPA, New Delhi, taken from: *An Overview of Status of Drinking Water and Sanitation in Schools in India*, http://www.dise.in; *Elementary Education in Urban India: Analytical Reports, 2011–12*, and *Elementary Education in Rural India: Analytical Reports, 2011–12*, NUEPA, http://www.dise.in; *Elementary Education in India: Progress Towards UEE: Analytical Tables 2011–12*, http://www.dise.in.
57. Calculated from: Union Budget documents, 2015–16, op. cit.
58. Ibid.; *Of Bold Strokes and Fine Prints: Analysis of Union Budget 2015–16*, op. cit., pp. 60–62.
59. Calculated from: Union Budget documents, 2015–16, ibid.
60. Ibid.
61. Mridula Chari, "Economists Fear Changes to NREGA but Fund Squeeze Is Already Curtailing Its Operations", October 15, 2014, http://www.scroll.in.
62. "It's Not Rural India Alone; Job Scheme Also in Distress", *Business Standard*, April 28, 2015, http://www.business-standard.com.
63. "NREGA: Each Household Got Only 39 Job Days Last Year", April 6, 2015, http://indianexpress.com.
64. *Of Bold Strokes and Fine Prints: Analysis of Union Budget 2015–16*, op. cit., pp. 64–65.
65. [(46,000 – 34,699)/34,699 x 100]. Source: "Budget 2015–16: Bonanza for the Corporates", *People's Democracy*, March 15, 2015, http://peoplesdemocracy.in.
66. Union Budget documents, 2015–16, op. cit.
67. "Food Security, Elimination of Hunger Low Priority of Modi Govt", http://www.maeeshat.in; *Budget 2015–16: Food Security, Malnutrition and Eliminating Hunger Low Priority for the Modi Government*, Right to Food Campaign, New Delhi, March 3, 2015, https://groups.yahoo.com.
68. Union Budget documents, 2015–16, op. cit.
69. Ibid.

III

INSURANCE PRIVATISATION: MYTHS AND REALITIES

Introduction

After failing to get the Insurance Laws (Amendment) Bill passed during the winter session of Parliament, the ruling BJP–NDA Government decided to take the ordinance route to pass this bill. On December 26, 2014, the President of India signed into law the Insurance Laws (Amendment) Ordinance 2014.

The Insurance Laws (Amendment) Ordinance increases the foreign direct investment (FDI) limit in private sector insurance companies from the earlier 26 percent to 49 percent. It also allows public sector insurance companies to mobilise money from the capital market, thus diluting the government's shareholding.

The Insurance Laws (Amendment) Bill had initially been introduced in Parliament by the previous UPA–Congress Government in 2008. The BJP had then opposed the passage of the bill, and together with other opposition parties, thwarted the Manmohan Singh Government from getting Parliamentary approval for the bill. After the UPA was defeated in the 2014 Lok Sabha elections and the BJP–NDA Government came to power, in a complete reversal of roles, the BJP now attempted to get the Parliament to pass the very same bill; however, a united opposition, which included the Congress, prevented the Rajya Sabha from taking up the bill for discussion and approval.*

* *The BJP finally got Parliamentary approval for the Insurance Laws (Amendment) Bill in March 2015, after the Congress decided to support the Bill.*

Some History

Ever since India began globalisation two decades ago, successive governments at the Centre have been attempting to gradually privatise the public sector insurance companies, which are amongst the best insurance companies in the world. These companies include the Life Insurance Corporation of India (LIC), General Insurance Corporation of India (GIC) and its former subsidiaries, the Oriental Insurance Company, New India Assurance, United India Insurance and National Insurance Company. The first step was taken in 1994 when the government set up a rubber stamp committee, the Malhotra Committee, to examine the problems afflicting the insurance industry. It duly recommended the entry of domestic and foreign private entities in the insurance sector and denationalisation of the public sector insurance companies. Based on these recommendations, in 1999, the government permitted private sector firms to enter both life and non-life insurance business, with a cap of 26 percent on ownership by foreign firms. In 2000, the four subsidiaries of the GIC were made into independent companies (and GIC was converted into a national re-insurer)—so that they could be privatised piecemeal. In 2008, the UPA Government introduced the above mentioned Insurance Laws (Amendment) Bill to hike foreign holding in insurance joint ventures to 49 percent; however, all its attempts to get the Bill passed by Parliament failed due to opposition from several political parties, including the BJP.

The partial opening up of the insurance sector has led to the entry of a stream of private players into the business. Presently (2015), including the public sector insurance companies, there are 24 life insurance companies and 28 non-life insurance companies (including two specialised state-owned firms, the Export Credit Guarantee Corporation of India and Agricultural Insurance Corporation of India) populating the industry.

Government Claims

Defending the Bill, Finance Minister Arun Jaitley claimed that it would help mobilise much needed investment in the "suffering" insurance sector and also mobilise much needed investments for India's infrastructure needs. He also claimed that insurance penetration and density in the country are very low, and FDI would enable expansion of insurance and enable its benefits to reach large sections of the people.[1] Precisely the very same points had been made by P. Chidambaram when he was the finance minister and was attempting to get the Parliament to approve the very same Bill: "At present, the penetration of insurance, measured by total premium as proportion of GDP, is only 4.4 percent in the life insurance segment and 0.76 percent in the non-life insurance segment. In a population of 120-crore plus, a very small number of people have insurance. The FDI cap of 26 percent must be raised and additional capital brought in to facilitate the faster spread of insurance. The insurance companies are in need of additional capital to expand their operations."[2]

Jaitley (like his predecessor Chidambaram) is lying through his teeth. Inviting private players, including foreign ones, into the domestic insurance sector is not going to lead to an increase in penetration of insurance in the country, neither is it going to result in increased investments in infrastructure. On the other hand, what is definitely going to happen is that frauds are going to increase, as private insurance companies are infamous for swindling policy holders. Let us examine these issues in greater detail.

1. Privatisation Myths

Will FDI Increase Insurance Penetration?

Insurance penetration is defined as the ratio of total premium income to the gross domestic product (GDP) of the country. Actually, insurance penetration in India is bound to be low; comparing it to countries with much higher per capita incomes is totally meaningless. As the Swiss Reinsurance Company points out in one of its reports (called *Sigma*), "Demand for insurance depends on disposable income."[3] The amount of income a person would be willing to spend on insurance depends on his/her income level. In a country where more than 70 percent of the population lives at or below subsistence levels, obviously the percentage of population with savings to spare for spending on insurance is going to be very small.

Despite this constraint, the performance of India's public sector insurance companies in mobilising premiums has been remarkable. Life insurance penetration in India at 4.4 percent is actually higher than the global average of 4 percent! Astonishingly, this figure is also higher than the United States' 3.5 percent and Germany's 3.3 percent![4] This high level of insurance penetration is all the more remarkable, given that these countries have a per capita income many times that of India. In fact, even the IMF, in its 2013 *Country Report* on insurance sector in India, admitted: "India is a clear outperformer in terms of expected life insurance penetration and is broadly in line with expectations in the non-life sector."[5] In another commendation of the performance of India's insurance industry, the World Economic Forum's *Financial Development Report 2012* placed India at the top of global rankings in terms of life insurance density (measured as ratio of direct premium to per capita GDP), and third in terms of non-life insurance density.[6]

This outstanding performance of India's public sector life and non-life insurance companies has got nothing to do with the entry of private players into the insurance sector. Even during the years when LIC had complete monopoly over life insurance, because of its painstaking efforts, life insurance penetration in the country had steadily increased—from 0.7 percent in 1985–86, it had doubled to 1.4 percent in 1997–98. Data put out by the *Sigma* report of May 1999 clearly reveals that even during those years, LIC had outperformed the life insurance industry of far more developed countries by a huge margin. Post-liberalisation, the growth of the life insurance industry has continued to be driven by LIC. Even after 12 years of competition, LIC retains a market share of 71 percent in premium income and 83 percent in the number of policies (as on March 31, 2013). In the non-life sector, the market share of the four PSUs was more than that of all the other private players combined and stood at 58 percent.[7]

The reason for this creditable performance is that LIC has gone far beyond what can be called a profitable market (that is, those households who can afford insurance comfortably) into low profit areas. Since nationalisation, LIC has spread out its branches to rural and semi-urban areas in a big way. Through numerous socially purposive schemes, it has helped provide insurance cover to millions of low income households. This is why the *IMF Country Report* quoted earlier admits: "Insurance sector in India has a relatively large footprint relative to other forms of financial intermediation given India's income levels."[8]

Will FDI Lead to Increased Investments?

Insurance is one of the means of channelising domestic savings for meeting infrastructural and social investment needs according to national priorities. This in fact was one of the most important reasons for nationalising the insurance industry. At the time of nationalisation of the life insurance industry in 1956, there were 245 private insurers in the life insurance business. Explaining the reasons for nationalising this industry, the then Finance Minister C.D. Deshmukh stated on January 19, 1956 in a radio broadcast:

> The nationalisation of life insurance is a further step in the direction of more effective mobilisation of people's savings. It is a truism which nevertheless cannot too often be repeated, that a nation's savings are the prime mover of its economic development.[9]

LIC has fully justified the faith reposed in it. In its very first year of operation, it sold 794,585 policies, which was nearly 30 percent more than the number of policies sold by all the 245 private players combined prior to their nationalisation.[10]

Ever since then, the public sector insurance companies have contributed huge amounts to successive Five Year Plans. Thus, LIC provided more than Rs 7 lakh crore to the Eleventh Plan (2007–2012) while the four general insurance companies and GIC contributed about Rs 1 lakh crore. A significant part of the investments made by LIC are in socially purposive schemes, such as housing, roads, rural electrification, municipal sewerage schemes and the like. Many of these schemes have been granted funds at lower than market rate.[11]

What is even more amazing, around 25 percent of the internal borrowings of the Central government are met by LIC every year.[12]

The Government of India invested Rs 5 crore by way of equity in LIC in 1956. On this initial investment, LIC paid out a dividend of Rs 1,436 crore to the government for the year 2012–13. And yet the government wants to privatise the LIC!

The government is claiming that the private sector insurance companies would be even more successful than public sector companies in mobilising people's savings for investment in infrastructure. Even assuming that the private sector insurance companies are successful in mobilising a larger portion of domestic savings as compared to the public sector companies (which of course they can never do, for reasons discussed below), why will they invest according to national priorities of development? They would be more interested in investing in sectors where they get the maximum returns. Allowing foreign insurance companies to take control of our domestic savings by privatising public sector insurance companies is even more stupid!

This is borne out by the government's own reports. Over the four-year period 2005–09, of the total investment of Rs 57,103 crore made by insurance companies in the infrastructural sector, nearly 90 percent of the investment was made by public sector companies; the share of the private sector companies was just 10 percent, despite the fact that they had a market share of 30–35 percent in new premium incomes. This was admitted to even by the *Economic Survey 2009–10*: "Private-sector insurance companies are yet to make large-scale investments in the infrastructure sector."[13] The *Economic Survey* admitted that meeting the infrastructure investment target of 9 percent of GDP during the Eleventh Plan period would be an extremely challenging task.[14]

The huge difference in the approach of public sector and private sector insurance companies towards the funds mobilised by them (in the form of premium incomes) is also apparent from their Operating Expense Ratio (salaries and other management expenses as a percentage of premium income). The IMF study quoted above notes that the Operating Expense Ratio in the LIC was just 6.6 percent in 2010, as compared to 20.9 percent in the private sector.[15] This implies that the public sector companies behave much more responsibly towards their policy holders and the country, while the private sector companies are more interested in siphoning off money under various guises.

2. Sterling Performance of LIC–GIC

Insurance: Risky Business

The performance indicators of the Indian public sector insurance companies given above clearly reveal that they have outperformed the insurance industry of far more developed countries by a huge margin. Why have the public sector insurance companies been able to achieve such a high insurance penetration ratio?

The answer is simple: their *public sector* nature. Because of this, people are willing to entrust their hard-earned savings to them; they know that these public sector companies will not swindle them or run away with their savings.

Insurance is a risky business. The insured (policy holder) pays a sum in advance (called premium) to the insurance company in lieu of a promise that the company will fully or partially meet the costs of some future event (such as an accident, fire, theft or sickness or provide for dependents in case of death), the occurrence of which is uncertain. The insurer deploys the funds in investments that offer returns that ensure the availability of adequate funds in case that event actually occurs and the insured person files a claim.

There are huge risks here. The insurance company will have to make an estimate of what percentage of the insured people will file claims, and will have to price the policy such that the sums collected and invested yield sufficient and stable returns to cover the claims. The insurance company may underestimate the probability of claims arising. Or it may make wrong investment choices—like for example invest in risky instruments that promise higher returns, but have higher risks, like shares or derivatives. In either case, it can run into huge losses.

There is also another possibility. Since insurance is only a promise by the insurance company to pay the costs for some future event, it makes the insurance business particularly susceptible to fraud and malpractice. On a small equity base, massive funds can be mobilised (in the form of premium incomes), and then the insurance company can just declare bankruptcy and vanish—making it an ideal hunting ground for fly-by-night operators.

And So, Nationalisation

This is precisely the reason why the insurance sector in India was nationalised in the first place. The insurance industry in India, from its beginnings in the last quarter of the nineteenth century till the initial years after independence, was in the private sector. In 1956, life insurance was nationalised; 245 Indian and foreign companies were taken over and amalgamated to establish the LIC. In 1971–72, general insurance was nationalised, and four general insurance companies took over the business of 107 private companies, with the GIC as the holding company.[16] These decisions to nationalise were taken because the private insurance companies were indulging in innumerable malpractices and even outright swindling. Companies would simply declare bankruptcy and vanish, depriving lakhs of policy holders of their life savings. Most of the big private insurance companies were controlled by India's big business houses; the list included some of India's best known industrialists—the Birlas, Tatas, Singhanias and Dalmias—and they would often siphon off the resources raised from policy holders into other enterprises. Legislation had proved totally ineffective in checking these frauds, and eventually the government was left with no alternative but to nationalise the insurance sector.[17]

During the debate in Parliament in February–March 1956 on nationalisation of life insurance, the then finance minister, C.D. Deshmukh, had made the following observation on the ingenuity displayed by the private insurance companies in circumventing legislation to defraud policy holders:

> The number of ways in which fraud can be practised which was 42 in Kautilya's days has risen to astronomical figures these days.[18]

Foreign Insurance Companies: Crooks, Scoundrels . . .

Such swindling in the insurance sector is actually a global phenomenon. In the US, insurance companies routinely pay people 40–70 percent less than what their policies promise when they suffer tragedies like fires destroying their homes or car accidents. Thousands of complaints have been filed with state insurance departments and courts. Being economically very strong and politically very powerful, the insurance companies use all kinds of legal tricks to keep the cases dragging on for years, till the plaintiffs tire out and accept what the insurers offer. To give another example of the manipulative power of US insurance companies, they have been successful in preventing the US Government from providing universal health care to its citizens. With health care in the US being very costly, the insurance companies have being shamelessly fleecing US citizens by keeping health insurance premiums very high, and indiscriminately hiking them—they rose by a whopping 159 percent between 1990 and 2010. The result is that an increasing number of Americans simply cannot afford health insurance—the number of non-elderly uninsured Americans increased from 41 million in 2004 to 49 million in 2010.[19]

Worse, several insurance companies in the developed countries have been driven into bankruptcy, because of speculative investments and unethical practices.[20] Lloyd's of London, Britain's fabled insurance market, ran up billions of dollars of losses in the late-1980s and early-1990s that left thousands of its individual investors in financial ruin. According to the British Broadcasting Corporation (BBC), underwriting 'errors' was a major cause for its mounting losses, which is a euphemism for recklessness and lack of principles.[21]

In the US, the number of failures reached such scandalous proportions that the US House of Representatives set up a sub-committee to investigate insurance companies' insolvencies. In its report titled *Failed Promises* submitted in February 1990, the committee found the US insurance industry to be marked by "scandalous mismanagement and rascality by certain persons entrusted with operating insurance companies, along with an appalling lack of regulatory controls to detect, prevent and punish such activities." The report went on to say:

> Relatively few crooks, scoundrels and incompetents are capable of bankrupting huge companies and possibly the entire industry. ... Fast operators in the industry are ignoring the rules, creating new schemes to enrich themselves, and walking away unscathed.[22]

That was more than two decades ago. Things have not changed much since then, as is borne out by the failure and $150 billion bailout of the global insurance major American International Group (AIG) in September 2008. AIG is the world's biggest insurer in terms of market capitalisation. It failed because it made huge investments in exotic financial instruments in search of high returns. So long as the going was good, no one asked any questions; but when the stock market collapsed in 2008, the investments became worthless and AIG verged on bankruptcy. The US Government was forced to step in and pour in taxpayer dollars to bail out the company as its collapse could have triggered a chain of bankruptcies, threatening the stability of the entire financial sector.[23]

LIC: World Record in Claims Settlement

In contrast to this huge global insurance scam, the Indian public sector insurance companies have been beacons of stability. The performance figures for LIC speak for themselves (See Table 3.1).

Table 3.1: LIC Performance Indicators[24]

	31–12–1957 (Just after nationalisation)	*31–03–2013*
Premium Income	89	208,589
Life Fund*	410	1,433,103

* Sum total of premiums and interest earnings less expenses of management and claims.

The public sector insurance companies have conscientiously kept their promise to their policy holders. One of the best ways to measure the reliability of an insurance company is its claims settlement record. While the (average) international claim settlement ratio is an abysmal 40 percent, the figure for LIC for 2011–12 was an incredible 97.42

percent, a world record (and for the GIC, it was 74 percent). The percentage of claims repudiated was a mere 1.3 percent. [It is probably because of the LIC that the private life insurance companies in India are also forced to settle a high percentage of claims, much higher than their global counterparts, but lower than the LIC—in 2011–12, their claims settlement record was 89.34 percent, and percentage of repudiations was 7.82 percent.][25]

To Conclude

This then is the secret behind the fantastic performance of the public sector insurance companies in India in mobilising such huge amounts of domestic savings—their reliability due to their public sector nature.

3. Entire Financial Sector on Sale

The government is seeking to privatise not just the public sector insurance companies, but also public sector banks, the workers' provident fund corpus and the pension fund corpus.

Just like the insurance companies, the public sector banks and provident funds/pension funds have played a crucial role in India's development plans. They have mobilised the savings of the common people to the tune of hundreds of thousands of crores of rupees, and put them at the disposal of the government for investment in national priorities like agriculture, small industries, housing, rural electrification, development of backward areas, infrastructure, and the like. Once the control of these institutions and funds passes into the hands of private sector corporations, they will utilise this capital for furthering their interests of profit accumulation rather than for national interests. One of the most common practices of private financial corporations (insurance, banks and pension funds) the world over is to invest in the stock markets for quick and high returns. So long as the stock market is booming, the profits are huge and everyone (including the customers) is happy. But sooner or later, the stock market is bound to collapse, and when that happens, the financial companies go broke and people find that their hard-earned savings have vanished overnight.

BJP Begins Privatisation of Public Sector Banks

In his very first budget speech in July 2014, Finance Minister Arun Jaitley made a major policy announcement that is actually going to sound the death knell for India's public sector banks. He announced that Indian banks need to be strengthened in accordance with international standards, or what are known as Basel III standards (a set of standards and practices created to ensure that international banks have enough capital to sustain themselves during periods of economic strain). These standards are actually voluntary and are more meant for private sector banks, but the Indian Government is treating them as compulsory for public sector banks too. To adhere to these standards, India's public sector banks require vast sums—to maintain the stipulated ratio between their core capital and the loans they have made. Jaitley in his budget speech estimated that the banks would need a total capital infusion of Rs 2.4 lakh crore by 2018 to meet Basel III norms.[26]

There are two ways in which banks can raise these vast sums. One is that the government pumps in the required money. The other is that they raise money from the market, which means that government stake in these banks would fall, from its present shareholding of between 65 to 80 percent.

Jaitley declared that the government does not have the huge sums needed to enable the banks to attain Basel III standards. But that is actually a lie! As we have explained in detail in Essay I of this book, the Indian Government has been giving away lakhs of crores of rupees in subsidies and tax write-offs to corporate houses; just the tax concessions given in 2014–15 to India's rich total a whopping Rs 5.49 lakh crore. So, even if the government wants the public sector banks to adhere to Basel III standards, which is actually not necessary, without reducing the public shareholding of the banks, it has enough money for this; all that it has to do is reduce some of the tax concessions to India's richie rich. But then, the finance minister is not really interested in strengthening public sector banks; the issue of Basel III standards is only a bogey, an excuse in whose name the government is seeking to gradually privatise the banks.

In December 2014, the Union Cabinet issued a communique stating: "Capital requirements of banks have increased under Basel-III. The quantum of capital support needed by banks is huge, which cannot be funded by budgetary support alone. If the public sector banks are permitted to bring down government holding to 52 percent in a phased manner, they can raise up to Rs 160,825 crore from the market."[27]

The deposits mobilised by the public sector banks had crossed Rs 58 lakh crore as on March 31, 2014.[28] Once the public sector banks are de-nationalised, there is no guarantee that their private owners will not indulge in speculative trading, resulting in a possible financial collapse sometime in the future. Or they may indulge in financial mismanagement or outright cheating and declare bankruptcy. The East Asian financial crisis of 1997 saw numerous private financial institutions going into liquidation. Some of the biggest private sector banks in the developed countries have collapsed in recent years, especially after the 2008 financial crisis—they were engaged in risky financial dealings in the stock markets with people's savings.[29] In India, during the past many years, numerous cooperative sector banks have gone bankrupt because of fraud by their directors, resulting in lakhs of ordinary people losing their hard-earned life savings. However, because of government controls, no public sector bank in India has ever closed down. This guarantee will end, once these banks are privatised. Imagine what will happen if say the Bank of Maharashtra declares bankruptcy and downs its shutters all of a sudden one day!

We are not indulging in fear mongering. A committee set up by the RBI, the Nayak Committee, has not only recommended that the government should speedily bring down its stake in public sector banks, even more breathtakingly, it has recommended that the government should permit speculative capitalists to invest in public sector banks! The committee's proposed list includes nearly all manner of casino capitalists: pension funds, long-only mutual funds, long-short hedge funds, exchange-traded funds and private equity funds (including sovereign wealth funds).[30] In other words, it wishes to invite into India's public sector banks the very speculative forces who precipitated the global financial crash of 2008, that led to the collapse of numerous financial institutions and compelled unprecedented state bail-out of banks throughout the world. The committee proposes to place such speculators and hot-money managers on the boards of (privatised) public sector banks. India escaped from being singed by the 2008 financial crash because the dominant institutions in India's financial sector are in the public sector. Had the LIC/GIC/Bank of Maharashtra/Canara Bank/Punjab National Bank . . . been in the private sector, several of them would definitely have collapsed. Once the government goes ahead and implements the Nayak Committee recommendations, it will not be long before this actually happens.

Pension Funds Also Being Privatised

The government has also taken the first steps to privatise pension funds, allow foreign players to gradually take control of these funds, end government guarantee on pensions and allow pension funds to be invested in stock markets in the name of higher returns. For this, in 2013, the UPA which was then in power and the BJP which was then in the opposition joined hands to pass the New Pension Fund Development and Regulatory Authority (NPFDRA) Act. This Act introduced a New Pension Scheme; all Central government employees joining service on or after January 1, 2004 (except the armed forces) and employees of all state governments who have joined the New Pension Scheme (NPS) have to mandatorily join this pension scheme. Under this scheme, while all its subscribers will have to give a defined contribution to the Pension Fund created by the Act, they will not get an assured pension upon their retirement. The pension they will get will depend upon the earnings of the Pension Fund from its investments in the stock market. The Fund will be managed by a private insurance company. The government will not contribute anything to the Fund, and will bear no liability.

By early 2015, 94 lakh employees had been brought under the NPS fold, and the NPS corpus had risen to Rs 87,000 crore. Of this corpus, 13 percent had been invested in the stock market.

Likewise, the government has also taken the first steps to privatise the management of the workers' provident fund corpus, which had by 2014 grown to a huge Rs 6.5 lakh crore, and allow the private fund managers to invest a part of these funds in the stock markets.[31]

What happens when the stock market collapses? The stock market collapse of 2008 led to the disappearance of billions of dollars from pension plans of workers around the world (wherever they were privatised). In the USA, state and local governments' pension funds support some 27 million Americans, and many lost a fifth of their value when the stock markets collapsed in 2008.[32] The California Public Employees' Retirement System (CalPERS), the largest pension fund in the US and fourth largest in the world, suffered one of its worst annual declines since the fund's inception in 1932. In October 2007, it had $260 billion in assets, comparable to the GDP of Poland, Indonesia or Denmark; just a year later, the worth of CalPERS was down to $186 billion! Tens of thousands of retiring state employees now face the stark choice of accepting much reduced pension checks or working past their retirement age.[33]

4. Why Privatisation?

Why is the government seeking to privatise the financial sector, and hand over control of the country's domestic savings to foreign and Indian private corporations?

To return to the subject matter of this essay, why is the government hell-bent on privatising the public sector insurance companies—

- which are amongst the best run, most trustworthy and reliable insurance companies in the world;
- which have mobilised huge amounts of domestic savings, to the tune of lakhs of crores of rupees, and made them available to the government for investment according to national development priorities;
- which paid out a dividend of more than Rs 1,400 crore to the government in 2012–13 on its initial investment of just Rs 5 crore?

Once the government fully implements the Malhotra Committee recommendations, privatises the public sector insurance companies and removes the cap on FDI inflows into the insurance sector, the control of the Indian insurance industry will gradually pass into the hands of the foreign insurance companies, as they are gigantic and far bigger than the Indian private sector insurance companies. That would mean:

i) control over Indian savings will pass into the hands of foreign investors (and their Indian collaborators);
ii) they will not invest the premium incomes mobilised by them in infrastructural and socially oriented sectors;
iii) instead, these 'crooks, scoundrels and fast operators' (epithets used by US Senators to describe the US insurance companies) will resort to all kinds of cheatings and loot these hard earned savings of the Indian people, like they have done all over the globe.

Why are our country's rulers mortgaging the interests of the people of the country, and the future development of our country, to benefit big foreign corporations?

Globalisation

It has actually been happening for the last two decades, ever since 1991, when the Indian Government decided to accept the conditions of the World Bank–IMF and begin the globalisation of the Indian economy. By the late 1980s, the Indian economy was entrapped in an external debt crisis, and was on the verge of external account bankruptcy. India's foreign creditors, that is, the USA and other developed countries—also known as the imperialist countries—were looking for just such an opportunity. Ever since India and other Third World countries had become independent in the decades after the Second World War, they had been looking for alternate ways to bring these countries back under their hegemony, so that they could once again control their raw material resources and exploit their markets. They now took advantage of India's external debt crisis to force the Government of India to agree to a 'restructuring' of the Indian economy. The basic elements of this so-called 'Structural Adjustment Programme' were:

- Removal of all controls on import of foreign goods;
- Removal of all restrictions on foreign investment in all sectors of the economy;
- Privatisation of the public sector, including financial sector; and no interference by the government in operation of free markets;
- Privatisation of welfare services, including drinking water, food, education and health, and removal of all controls placed on profiteering.

This is the reality about 'globalisation'—the restructuring of the economy at the behest of India's foreign creditors.

In the nineteenth century, the imperial powers had attempted to justify their genocidal colonial conquests as a mission to 'civilise' the 'natives'. The new colonisation—actually economic colonisation—at the turn of the twenty first century is being glorified as 'globalisation'. Leading intellectuals of the imperialist countries are glorifying the foreign capital flows to India and other Third World countries, also called 'foreign direct investment' or FDI, as "the best means of improving the human condition throughout the world."[34] Parroting this imperialist propaganda, prominent Indian academicians–economists–media intellectuals are also euphoric about globalisation and the benefits of FDI flows into the Indian economy, and are claiming that it will help propel India to the league of the developed nations. Every economics text book today teaches students the benefits of foreign capital flows (that is, FDI) for the Indian economy—in a country that has itself been the victim of two centuries of colonial rule and plunder by British capital, that so badly crippled the country that we continue to suffer from its consequences more than six decades after winning independence!

Despite whatever our economics textbooks may teach about globalisation, Henry Kissinger, US Secretary of State under Presidents Nixon and Ford, summed up its essence in a memorably arrogant phrase:

Globalisation is only another word for American domination.[35]

Since then (that is, 1991), even though coalition governments of a variety of colours have come to power at the Centre, globalisation of the economy has continued unabated. It is in fact accelerating under the newest 'Swadeshi' government of Narendra Modi. The country's major political parties, top bureaucrats, leading intellectuals—who together control political power in the country—have given up all concern for the people, and have been running the economy solely for the profit maximisation of giant foreign corporations and their junior partners, India's big business houses. Here is a brief sampling of the policies being implemented in the country over the past more than two decades:

- Giant corporations have launched a ferocious assault to dispossess the poor of their agricultural lands and forests. So that they can commandeer the resources—bauxite, iron ore, coal, water, etc., or set up special economic zones, infrastructural projects, etc., or build resorts, golf courses, villas, etc. Laws are being modified to facilitate this displacement and plunder.
- Indian agriculture is being deliberately strangulated, so that it can be taken over by giant agribusiness corporations. The consequence: more than three lakh farmers have committed suicide since the 'reforms' began—something that did not happen even during the British Raj.
- All reservations for small scale industries are being removed; consequently, lakhs of small businesses have downed their shutters.
- Government expenditure on welfare services is being reduced, and they are being privatised and transformed into instruments of naked profiteering:
    - government hospitals and municipal schools are being privatised; medicine prices have zoomed; school and college fees have gone through the roof; electricity prices are rising; bus fares are rising; the ration system designed to make available foodgrains and other essential items to the poor at affordable rates is being eliminated.

- Labour laws are being modified to make it easier for companies to hire and fire workers at will.
- The country is heading towards an ecological catastrophe: corporations are being allowed to cut down entire forests, destroy coastal lands in the name of aquaculture, over-exploit groundwater, pollute our seas–rivers–soil–groundwater–air, damage the health of not just the living but also of those yet to be born . . .

Heading into Financial Collapse

India began globalisation because it was entrapped in an external accounts and foreign exchange crisis. More than two decades later, because of the very consequences of opening up the economy to unrestricted inflows of foreign capital and goods, India's external accounts are in a far worse state as compared to 1991. Before we give the statistics, we first need to explain some terms.

Balance of Payments on Current Account

Of a country's financial transactions with the outside world, the balance of payments on current account covers its day-to-day transactions with other nations.

- *Balance of Payments on Current Account = Merchandise Trade (i.e., visible trade) Account + Invisibles Account*
    - **Merchandise Trade Account:** This is trade in visible commodities—things you can see, such as agricultural goods, petroleum, textiles, motor cars, and machinery. India earns less on merchandise exports than it spends on merchandise imports; therefore, it has a merchandise trade deficit, or, trade deficit for short.
    - **Invisibles Account:** This includes three other types of current receipts from, and payments to, those abroad:
        - **Services:** This includes components like: receipts from travel to India by foreigners and payments for travel abroad by Indians; earnings on IT-enabled services such as software and call centres, and payments for import of software; and so on.

- **Remittances:** Remittances to India by Indian workers abroad and remittances out of India by foreign individuals in India.
- **Investment Income:** This includes receipts on Indian investment (including loans) abroad and payments on foreign investments (including debt) in India.

Because these three types of receipts/payments are not for visible commodities, they are all part of the 'invisibles' account. India receives much more on the invisibles account than it pays out, due to its earnings from export of software and software workers, and remittances from Indian workers working in Gulf countries. Hence, in the net, India enjoys an invisibles account surplus.

- For India, our merchandise trade deficit is much larger than its invisibles surplus; hence India runs what is called a current account deficit (CAD).

Some Statistics

(i) Trade Deficit

Import liberalisation has led to a sharp rise in our trade deficit. Even though the government has made desperate attempts to promote exports—because of which our exports have shot up from $18 billion in 1991–92 to more than $300 billion in 2012–13—due to a huge rise in imports, our trade deficit for 2012–13 had gone up to $190 billion, a rise of 60 times over our trade deficit of $2.8 billion in 1991–92 (See Chart 3.1).[36]

A desperate government imposed controls on gold imports; because of this and other reasons, the trade deficit contracted to $147.6 billion for the year 2013–14.[37] Bowing to pressure from the gold import lobby, the government removed gold import controls in November 2014, because of which gold imports surged 20 percent in 2014–15 over the previous fiscal.[38] However, a lower oil import bill due to falling oil prices—the global benchmark Brent crude dropped by about 60 percent between June 2014 and January 2015—offset the rise in gold imports, and the trade deficit for 2014–15 slightly narrowed to $144.2 billion.[39]

Chart 3.1: Trade Deficit, 1991–92 to 2014–15[40]
(in $ billion)

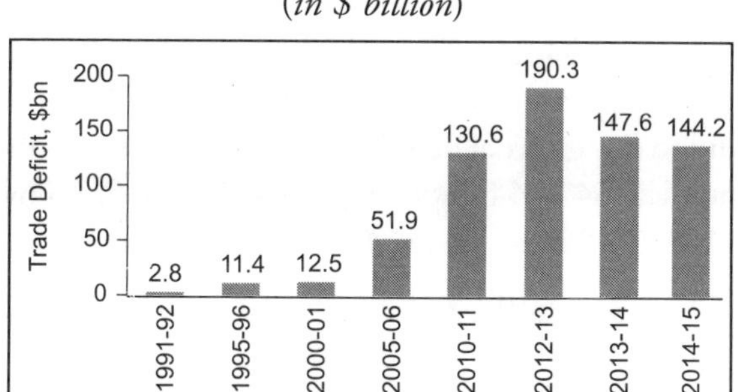

(ii) Current Account Deficit

The sharp rise in trade deficit for 2012–13 saw our current account deficit (CAD) zooming to $87.8 billion in 2012–13, from 1.2 billion in 1991–92. India's CAD to GDP ratio was 4.8 percent in 2012–13, the highest ever, even more than its value in 1990–91 when it was 3 percent.[41] Curbs on gold imports led to a contraction in the trade deficit, and hence the CAD too eased to $32.4 billion or 1.7 percent of GDP for the financial year 2013–14.[42] Falling oil prices led to a further reduction of the trade deficit and hence the CAD shrank further to $27.5 billion (1.3 percent of GDP) in 2014–15.[43]

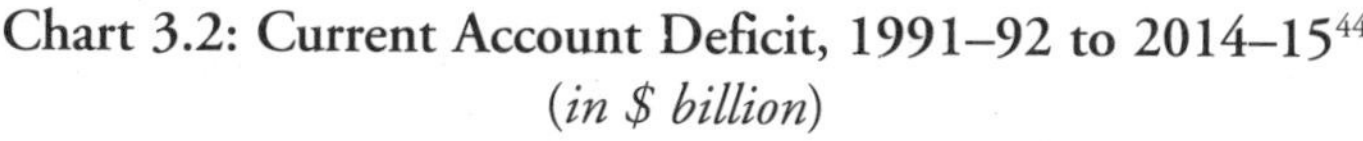
Chart 3.2: Current Account Deficit, 1991–92 to 2014–15[44]
(in $ billion)

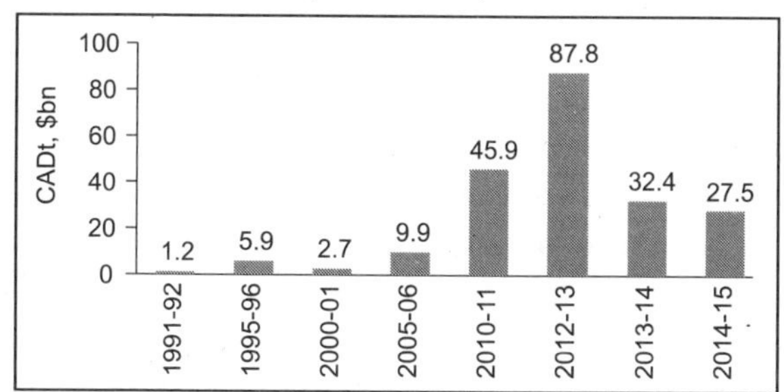

What Next

When a country like India runs up a current account deficit, it needs to attract foreign capital flows to bridge the deficit. These can be either in the form of foreign debt, or in the form of capital investment flows.

(i) External Debt: With India running up historically unprecedented current account deficits, we have been borrowing hugely, and so our external debt has gone through the roof! It stood at an astronomical $474.4 billion in end-March 2015, up by nearly six times from $83.8 billion in end-March 1991 (Chart 3.3).[45]

Chart 3.3: India: External Debt*, 1991 to 2015[46]
(in $ billion)

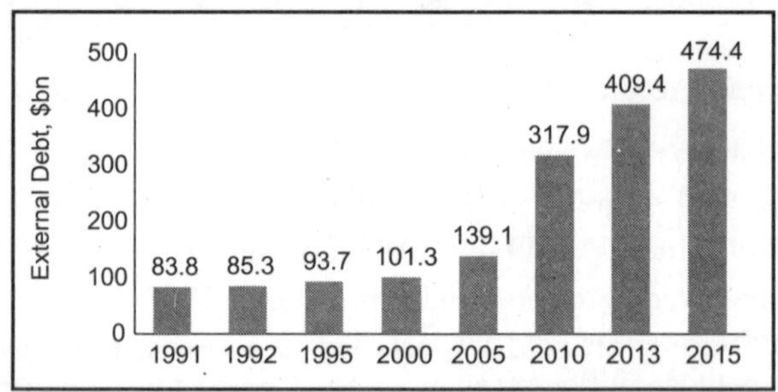

*All figures for end-March.

(ii) Capital Investment Flows: These investment flows can be of two types: (a) FDI (Foreign Direct Investment) flows—these are investments in setting up new companies, or investments in existing companies of at least 10 percent of the paid up capital of a company; (b) FII (Foreign Institutional Investment) or FPI (Foreign Portfolio Investment) flows—investment in securities, that is, shares, bonds, debentures, options, etc. in the primary and secondary markets. (Note: So far as investment in shares is concerned, where an investor has a stake of 10 percent or less in a company, it is treated as FII and, where an investor has a stake of more than 10 percent, it is treated as FDI.)

According to official statistics, cumulative FDI inflows into India (including 'equity flows' and 'other capital', and excluding 'reinvested earnings') over the period April 2000 to March 2014 totalled $242.7 billion.[47] And cumulative net investment by FIIs in shares in India since 1992, when the government allowed them to invest in the Indian market, up to March 2014, totalled $117.8 billion.[48]

External 'Debt' Trap

Interest has to be paid on foreign debt, and capital investment inflows result in profit outflows. Both these lead to a rise in the current account deficit in the subsequent years, implying that in the coming years, the country will need even more external debt/capital investment flows. It is a kind of debt trap!

Foreign Exchange Reserves vs. Short-Term Liabilities

Despite our rising current account deficit, and so the need for greater foreign debt and capital inflows, our finance ministers and official economists are telling us not to worry, as the country's external accounts situation is much better than it was in 1991. Their argument for this is that we have much more foreign exchange reserves than in 1990–91. .For instance, in December 2014, newsreports quoted Finance Minister Arun Jaitley as saying that the increase in India's current account deficit recorded in the period July–September 2014 was "not a cause for concern" as India's forex reserves are at a comfortable level.[49]

Foreign exchange reserves of a country are the total foreign assets held by the government and central bank of a country. These assets are in various international reserve currencies, mostly the US dollar, and to a lesser extent the euro, the pound sterling and the yen. They also include gold reserves and special drawing rights (SDRs). At one point, in end-1990, India's foreign exchange reserves had fallen to less than $1 billion and the country's policy makers had to resort to all kinds of measures, including secretly shipping out some of the country's gold reserves, to raise a few billion dollars.[50] In contrast, today we have a vast sum in the kitty: as of March 31, 2014, India's foreign exchange reserves stood at $304.2 billion.[51] Therefore, on the face of it, this argument about our external accounts situation being better than in 1991 seems plausible.

However, foreign exchange reserves do not only represent foreign exchange earnings of a country, they include all the foreign capital inflows that have come into the country too. This implies that if foreign investors start withdrawing their money from the country, the reserves will fall. This in fact was candidly admitted by the then RBI Governor at a Governors' Meeting in Kyoto, Japan in January 2011: "Our reserves comprise essentially borrowed resources, and we are therefore more vulnerable to sudden stops and reversals, as compared with countries with current account surpluses." And he made this statement at a time when our reserves totalled $299.4 billion, just $5 billion less than our present reserves level.[52]

Of course, not all the foreign investment can be taken out at short notice. Therefore, to get an idea of the actual safety buffer provided by the country's foreign exchange reserves, they should be compared with what can be called the 'short-notice' liabilities of the country. These are our potentially volatile foreign exchange liabilities, that is, foreign capital that has come into the country that can leave the country very quickly. These 'vulnerable external liabilities' or 'short-notice' external liabilities include: (i) short-term debt (i.e., debt repayable within a year); (ii) portfolio investments (i.e., FII investments in the share markets and in debt instruments), which can be withdrawn at any time; and (iii) those NRI deposits which are fully repatriable at any time (Foreign Currency Non-Resident deposits and Non-Resident External Rupee Account deposits). Let us take a look at the volume of these short-notice liabilities:

i) **Short-term debt:** Here we are referring to short-term debt by 'residual maturity', i.e., it includes not only debt that was originally contracted as short-term debt, but also that portion of long-term debt which falls due within a year from the reference date. According to RBI figures, India's total short-term debt (residual maturity) in end-March 2014 was $174.6 billion.[53]
ii) **Portfolio investments** by FIIs as of end-March 2014 stood at $193 billion.[54] [There is a need for two qualifications here. Firstly, this is only the historical value of portfolio investments, that is, it is only the original value of all the amounts that came in at different times in the past; their present value would be much more than this original historical value. Secondly, much of what is classified as 'FDI' may be hardly

different from FII capital. 'FDI' is supposedly more stable than FII capital, since it is not merely financial investment, but is a long-term stake in Indian assets, associated with management control. However, a recent comprehensive study has found that, because of changed official definitions as well as official eagerness to project a larger figure of FDI, more than half of what is being classified as 'FDI' is of the nature of purely financial investment, such as by private equity firms, venture capital funds and hedge funds.[55] While it can be argued that such investments are not as unstable as FII investments in the share market, they certainly cannot be considered to be stable investments. Both these factors imply that the actual value of total portfolio investments by FIIs is much more than the figure of $193 billion given above.]

iii) The outstanding sum in **Foreign Currency Non-Resident (FCNR) deposits and Non-Resident External Rupee Account (NRERA) deposits** (excluding the NRI deposits included in short-term debt of residual maturity) was $47.5 billion in end-March 2014. [Note: RBI gives total FCNR deposits as $52.9 billion and total NRERA deposits as $41.8 billion. Total (52.9 + 41.8) = $94.7 billion. Of this, $47.2 billion is included in its definition of short-term debt of residual maturity. Therefore, only the remainder, that is, 94.7 – 47.2 = $47.5 billion is included here.][56]

Total Short-Term Liabilities

- Total short-term liabilities (in end-March 2014)
  = Short-term debt (residual maturity) + Total portfolio investments + Outstanding sum in FCNR deposits and NRERA deposits
  = $174.6 billion + $193 billion + $47.5 billion
  = $415.1 billion
- Total foreign exchange reserves (in end-March 2014)
  = $304.2 billion

India on 'Sale'

It is thus clear that if the foreign investors decide to pull out their money, our foreign exchange reserves are simply insufficient to prevent the economy from once again plunging into foreign exchange bankruptcy, similar to what happened in 1990–91.

All this makes nonsense of the claim of our finance ministers that India is on its way to becoming an 'economic superpower'. The reality is the exact opposite. India's rulers have brought the Indian economy to the brink of an economic collapse, like that which has taken place in several Third World countries ever since they began globalisation in the 1980s (a famous example being the collapse of the 'East Asian Tigers' in 1997).[57] All that the international speculators have to do is start withdrawing their investments in India—which they can do at the tap of a computer key—and this superpower will meltdown.

This is the reason why India's finance ministers and prime ministers have been travelling to the capitals of the developed countries with a begging bowl, enticing foreign investors to invest in India and promising them all kinds of incentives and concessions. Prime Minister Narendra Modi, in just his first six months in office, has made more foreign trips than any other prime minister in the history of independent India.[58] When he returned from Japan with promises of Japanese investment worth 35 billion dollars, it was greeted with huge applause in the Indian corporate media.[59]

Delhi's new Moghuls are bending backwards to address concerns raised by US corporations in order to speeden up US FDI flows into India. Throwing all democratic norms to the winds, the Modi Government amended the Land Acquisition Act (LAA)—that had been passed by the Parliament just a year ago after much debate and discussion—through an ordinance promulgated on December 31, 2014. The amendment trashes whatever limited protection had been offered by the LAA-2013 to farmers and urban and rural poor communities. For five categories of projects, the amendment does away with the 'consent' clause that made the consent of 80 percent and 70 percent of the affected land holders mandatory before their land could be acquired for private and public–private–partnership projects respectively. These five categories are so broad that virtually every kind of project—including roads, railways, ports, airports, mines, electricity, oil and gas pipelines, telecom towers, dams, canals, sewage, hospitals, schools, colleges, markets, cold stores, agricultural facilities and tourism—comes under them.[60] Pleased, the High Priest of White House condescended to be the chief guest for India's 2015 Republic Day celebrations.

While in Delhi, Obama and Modi announced that they had reached a "breakthrough understanding" with regard to US objections to India's nuclear liability law—meaning that a way had been found to protect American reactor suppliers from the consequences of accidents caused by design defects in reactors supplied by them. The Civil Liability for Nuclear Damage Act passed by the Indian Parliament in 2010 was itself a weak law and a complete betrayal of the interests of the Indian people. It capped the liability for a nuclear accident at a mere Rs 1,500 crore—which is probably a thousand times smaller than the possible damages in case of a major nuclear accident. Worse, it channelled all the liability to the operator, that is, the public sector Nuclear Power Corporation of India, thus freeing the supplier of the reactor from all liabilities—except for a minor clause: the operator could recoup this compensation from the supplier of the reactor in case the accident took place due to design defects. The US reactor suppliers want this clause to be deleted too! Newsreports indicate that the Modi Government has agreed to create an insurance pool of Rs 1,500 crore to be financed by India's public sector insurance companies and the Government of India to meet supplier liability in case of design defects—thus transferring the limited liability of the supplier to the Indian people.[61]

This is inviting disaster! As it is, nuclear reactors are inherently accident prone; by providing legal indemnities to foreign nuclear reactor suppliers, the Modi Government is only encouraging them to supply risky equipment. A nuclear accident can destroy a nation—to quote Mikhail Gorbachev, former President of the USSR, where the Chernobyl nuclear accident took place in 1986.[62] Because of the Chernobyl catastrophe, it is estimated that nearly 10 lakh additional deaths have taken place over the period 1986–2004; and these deaths will continue to take place at the same rate in the coming decades and centuries because the accident has radioactively contaminated huge regions in the entire Northern Hemisphere with radionuclides that have half lives of thousands of years.[63] The Fukushima accident has similarly condemned the Japanese people to suffer epidemics of cancer, leukaemia and genetic defects for the rest of time.[64] If a major nuclear accident occurs in Mithivirdi (in Gujarat) where the US corporation Westinghouse is to supply the AP1000 reactor, at the minimum, Gujarat will be radioactively contaminated; and if it occurs in Kovvada (in Andhra Pradesh), where the US conglomerate GE is to supply the ESBW reactor, at the minimum, Andhra Pradesh will be radioactively contaminated—for 20–30 thousand years. Its consequences will cripple India for . . .

It is because of these dangers that even countries like Germany and Switzerland that had significant nuclear power programmes have decided to completely phase out all their nuclear power plants. In its bid to appease foreign investors and entice them to bring in their dollars, the Modi Government is putting at risk the very future of the country.

FDI in Insurance: Continuation of Globalisation

Taking control of the financial sector is crucial to the designs of foreign corporations and their governments if they are to transform this country into their economic colony. Economic colonies must not develop according to their own priorities; they must develop according to the priorities of their masters sitting far away in Washington, Paris, Bonn and London. And so, ever since India began globalisation in 1991, the World Bank, the IMF, and the imperialist governments have been demanding that the government end its control over the country's financial sector, in other words, privatise it, and allow foreign investors to enter and take it over. The Indian Government has been more than willing; the Malhotra Committee that recommended the privatisation of the insurance sector was essentially a rubber stamp committee that only echoed the wishes of India's foreign creditors. If the government has proceeded slowly to implement its recommendations, it is not because of any resistance on its part, but because of the strong resistance put up by the insurance sector employees.

Two decades of globalisation have pushed the Indian economy further into the clutches of India's foreign creditors. India's debt has reached record levels, making the country one of the most indebted countries in the world. In order to show to the country's foreign investors its commitment to economic reforms and globalisation, the new Modi Government, after failing to get the Parliament to pass the Insurance Laws Amendment bill, promulgated an ordinance hiking the ceiling on foreign equity ownership in the private sector insurance industry from 26 percent to 49 percent.

Requeim for Swaraj

We are at a loss for words to describe the treachery of our country's rulers. They have buried Swaraj in just 60 years. In his final address to the Constituent Assembly (November 25, 1949), Dr. Ambedkar had expressed his concern regarding India's future:

> On 26th January, 1950, India will be an independent country. What would happen to her independence? Will she maintain her independence or will she lose it again? . . . The point is that she once lost the independence she had. Will she lose it a second time? It is this thought which makes me most anxious for the future. What perturbs me greatly is the fact that not only has India once before lost her independence, but she lost it by the infidelity and treachery of some of her own people.

Unfortunately, the apprehension of the father of the Indian Constitution is proving to be prophetic!

5. We Must Advance Our Struggle!

Friends, our intense struggle for the past many years has not prevented the Indian Government from hiking the FDI limit in the private insurance sector to 49 percent. This is but another step towards its goal of eventually privatising India's public sector insurance companies and handing them over to foreign corporations.

Therefore, we need to deepen and expand our struggle. We need to reach out to the common people and involve them in our struggle. There are a very large number of common people who have been hoodwinked by the intense government and media propaganda and believe that privatisation of insurance will indeed benefit the country and the people. It is therefore important to continue with our campaign to educate the common people about the disastrous effects of this policy.

Of course, just increasing consciousness is not enough. Even amongst the many people who agree with us, many are hesitant to come out on the streets and protest, out of a sense of despondency. We will need to inspire them, and organise various forms of creative protests and motivate people to join them in increasing numbers. Ultimately, our struggle is a part of the growing nationwide movement against globalisation, against the sell-out of our country to foreign and Indian big business houses by India's ruling classes. As more and more people join this struggle, it will strengthen and become a powerful force to transform society, and build a new India, where development will not mean profit maximisation of a few big corporations, but fulfilment of the basic needs of all human beings—a job, steady income, a home, education and health care, and security in old age.

This may appear to be a utopia, but it is not so. The collective strength of the common people is huge; it can build heaven on earth. But because we are so disunited today, we have lost faith in our collective strength. Of course, it is going to be a long and arduous struggle, but it can be won. Every end needs a beginning, only if there is a beginning will there be an end. We therefore need to make a beginning somewhere, we need to take our own small initiatives. Let us make a beginning by trying to build a unity of employees, development officers, insurance agents and policy holders in and around our city, as the first step towards building a nationwide people's struggle to defeat the attempt of the Indian ruling classes to hand over control of the country's insurance sector to foreign brigands.

If we don't fight,
If we don't continue the fight,
Then the enemy bayonets,
Will finish us off,
And later,
Pointing towards our bones,
They'll say:
They are bones of slaves,
Of slaves.

References

1. "Raising FDI Will Benefit 'Struggling' Insurance Sector, Says BJP", December 11, 2014, https://in.news.yahoo.com; "Pending Insurance Laws (Amendment) Bill to be Tabled in Parliament Soon: FM", July 10, 2014, http://www.indiainfoline.com.
2. C.P. Chandrasekhar, "Importing Risk into Insurance", *Frontline*, November 2, 2012, p. 5, available online at: http://www.frontline.in.
3. *Aspects of India's Economy*, No. 28, published by RUPE, Prabhadevi, Mumbai, p. 22.
4. Amanulla Khan, "FDI Hike in Insurance Harmful", *People's Democracy*, October 28, 2012; "Life Insurance 2020: Competing for a Future", PwC, www.pwc.com.
5. Cited in: *Insurance Worker*, November 2013, Monthly Journal of the All India Insurance Employees Association (AIIEA), Bangalore, p. 4.
6. "WEF Report Puts India First in Life Insurance Density", http://www.lifebroker.com.au.
7. M.S.R.A. Srihari, "Yes, Insurance Needs Better Cover but Not with Foreign Capital", February 26, 2013, http://www.thehindu.com; Amanulla Khan, "Ten Years of Liberalisation of Insurance Sector", available online at http://indiantradeunion.blogspot.in; *Aspects of India's Economy*, No. 28, op. cit., p. 18.
8. Cited in: *Insurance Worker*, November 2013, op. cit., p. 4.
9. H.D. Malviya, *Insurance Business in India*, All India Congress Committee, New Delhi, 1956, p. 72.
10. Amanulla Khan, "Ten Years of Liberalisation of Insurance Sector", op. cit.
11. "Yes, Insurance Needs Better Cover but Not with Foreign Capital", op. cit.; *Aspects of India's Economy*, Nos. 26–27, op. cit., p. 148.

12. Sagnik Dutta, "Premium on Trust", *Frontline*, November 2, 2012, op. cit., p. 12.
13. "Energy, Infrastructure and Communications", *Economic Survey 2009–10*, Chapter 10, p. 265, http://indiabudget.nic.in.
14. Cited in: "More Insurance, Pension Funds Needed in Core", *Times of India*, lite.epaper.timesofindia.com.
15. Cited in: *Insurance Worker*, November 2013, op. cit., p. 4.
16. C.P. Chandrasekhar, "Importing Risk into Insurance", op. cit.
17. Jayati Ghosh, *The Indian Economy: 1998–99, An Alternative Survey*, Delhi Science Forum, New Delhi, p. 80; R. Padmanabhan, *Frontline*, April 22, 1994, Kasturi and Sons Ltd., Chennai, pp. 111–12; *In Defence of Nationalised LIC and GIC, Part I*, All India Insurance Employees Association Pamphlet, 1994, All India Insurance Employees' Association, Chennai, pp. 70–76.
18. *In Defence of Nationalised LIC and GIC, Part I*, ibid., p. 72.
19. David Dietz and Darrell Preston, "The Insurance Hoax", September 2007, http://www.bloomberg.com; Maureen Farrell, "Top Health-Insurance Scams", http://www.forbes.com; R. Ramakumar, "Hardly a Model", *Frontline*, November 2, 2012, op. cit., pp. 16–17.
20. Jayati Ghosh, *The Indian Economy: 1998–99, An Alternative Surve*y, op. cit., p. 79.
21. *In Defence of Nationalised LIC and GIC, Part II*, All India Insurance Employees Association Pamphlet, 1994, All India Insurance Employees' Association, Chennai, p. 10; Richard W. Stevenson, "Lloyd's Tries to Insure Its Future", April 30, 1993, http://www.nytimes.com.
22. *In Defence of Nationalised LIC and GIC, Part I*, op. cit., pp. 45–46.
23. C.P. Chandrasekhar, "Importing Risk into Insurance", op. cit.
24. Source: "The Life Insurance Business in Force in India (Statistics)", http://www.preservearticles.com; "LIC – The Jewel of India", http://geevee-rajahmundry.blogspot.in.
25. "Claims Record Better in LIC than Private Insurers, Says IRDA Report", December 24, 2012, http://www.thehindu.com; "Life Insurers Settle 8.22 Lakh Claims in FY12", December 24, 2012, http://www.indiainfoline.com; V. Sridhar, "For a Second Phase of Resistance", *Frontline*, January 20–February 2, 2001, op. cit.
26. "Public Sector Banks: Reform by Death", *Aspects of India's Economy*, No. 61, June 2015, http://rupe-india.org; Prabhat Patnaik, "Specious Macroeconomics", *Frontline*, August 8, 2014, http://www.frontline.in.
27. "Public Sector Banks: Reform by Death", ibid.
28. "Led by SBI Group, Public Sector Banks Dominate Credits, Deposits

Space", *PTI*, May 10, 2015, http://articles.economictimes.india times.com.

29. C.R. Sridhar, "Wall Street – Cold, Flat, and Broke", *MRZine*, October 10, 2008, http://www.monthlyreview.org/mrzine.
30. "Bank Board Bureau: Another Step Toward Privatisation and Foreign Takeover", *Aspects of India's Economy*, No. 61, June 2015, http://rupe-india.org.
31. "NPS Investment into Equities Touch 13% in FY15: PFRDA", June 29, 2015, http://www.firstpost.com; T.K. Rajalakshmi, "Social Security at Stake", *Frontline*, March 12–25, 2005, http://www.frontline.in; P.V.V. Murthi, "New Pension Scheme's Drawbacks Draw Flak", July 21, 2014, http://www.thehindu.com; T.K. Rajalakshmi, "A Private Party", *Frontline*, August 16–29, 2008, http://www.frontline.in; "Pension, Gratuity and PFs May Get to Invest Big Chunk in Equity and Debt MFs", June 25, 2014, http://articles.economictimes.indiatimes.com.
32. Jeremy Kaplan, "Pension Funds Weakened by Stock-Market Decline", *Time*, October 31, 2008, http://www.time.com.
33. Kevin Martinez, "California Pension Funds Close to Bankruptcy", January 30, 2009, https://www.wsws.org.
34. Michel Camdessus, Managing Director, IMF, speech at UNCTAD–X, February 13, 2000, available on internet at: *Development and Poverty Reduction: A Multilateral Approach*, https://www.imf.org.
35. Samir Amin, "The Political Economy of the Twentieth Century", *Monthly Review*, June 2000, http://monthlyreview.org.
36. *India's Foreign Trade: 2013–14*, August 11, 2014, http://rbi.org.in; *Balance of Payments*, http://indiabudget.nic.in/es98–99/chap62.pdf.
37. "What the Fall in the Current Account Deficit Reveals", *Aspects of India's Economy*, No. 55, March 2014, http://rupe-india.org; *Developments in India's Balance of Payments During the Fourth Quarter (January–March) of 2014–15*, Reserve Bank of India, Press Release, June 10, 2015, https://www.rbi.org.in.
38. Siddhartha Singh, Swansy Afonso, "India Eases Gold Import Restrictions to Remove Trade Distortions", November 29, 2014, http://www.bloomberg.com; "Gold Imports Up 19.5 % at $34.32 Bn in 2014–15", May 4, 2015, http://www.thehindu.com.
39. *Developments in India's Balance of Payments During the Fourth Quarter (January–March) of 2014–15*, op. cit.
40. C. Rangarajan, Prachi Mishra, "India's External Sector: Do We Need to Worry?" *Economic and Political Weekly*, February 16, 2013, http://www.epw.in; *Balance of Payments*, http://indiabudget.nic.in/es98–99/

chap62.pdf; *India's Foreign Trade: 2013–14*, op. cit.; *Developments in India's Balance of Payments During the Fourth Quarter (January–March) of 2014–15*, ibid.

41. "The External Crisis", *Aspects of India's Economy*, op. cit.; "Current Account Deficit Widens to Record 4.8%", June 27, 2013, http://www.business-standard.com; *Balance of Payments*, indiabudget.nic.in/es97–98/chap61.pdf.
42. "Current Account Gap Falls Further on Lower Gold Imports", *PTI*, May 26, 2014, http://articles.economictimes.indiatimes.com.
43. *Developments in India's Balance of Payments During the Fourth Quarter (January–March) of 2014–15*, op. cit.
44. C. Rangarajan, Prachi Mishra, "India's External Sector: Do We Need to Worry?", op. cit.; *Developments in India's Balance of Payments during 2013–14*, July 10, 2014, http://rbi.org.in; *Balance of Payments*, http://indiabudget.nic.in/es98–99/chap62.pdf; *The External Sector*, January 28, 2014, http://rbi.org.in; *Developments in India's Balance of Payments during the Fourth Quarter (January–March) of 2014–15*, op. cit.
45. *India's External Debt as at the End of June 2015*, Foreign Exchange Management – Reserve Bank of India, September 30, 2015, https://rbi.org.in; *India's External Debt: A Status Report*, Ministry of Finance, Government of India, June 2003, http://finmin.nic.in.
46. *India's External Debt: A Status Report, 2014–15*, http://www.finmin.nic.in. Figure for 2015 taken from: *India's External Debt as at the End of June 2015*, ibid.
47. *Fact Sheet on Foreign Direct Investment (FDI)*, Department of Industrial Policy and Promotion, Government of India, http://dipp.nic.in; *Advantage India – India: An Attractive Destination for FDI*, Ministry of External Affairs, Government of India, http://indiainbusiness.nic.in.
48. *Advantage India – Foreign Institutional Investment (FII) in India*, Ministry of External Affairs, ibid.
49. "Comfortable Forex Reserves to Ease CAD Worries, Says Jaitley", *ENS Economic Bureau*, December 10, 2014, http://www.newindianexpress.com.
50. "The External Crisis", *Aspects of India's Economy*, op. cit.; *Balance of Payments – Union Budget*, indiabudget.nic.in/es1992–93/5%20Balance%20of%20Payments.pdf.
51. *India's International Investment Position (IIP), March 2014*, RBI Press Release, June 30, 2014, http://rbi.org.in.
52. "India Vulnerable to Sudden Outflow of Forex: RBI", January 31, 2011, http://www.thehindu.com.

53. *India's External Debt at End - March 2014*, RBI Bulletin, September 10, 2014, http://rbi.org.in.
54. *India's International Investment Position (IIP), March 2014*, op. cit.
55. "The External Crisis", *Aspects of India's Economy*, op. cit.; K.S. Chalapati Rao, Biswajit Dhar, "India's FDI Inflows: Trends and Concepts", ISID Working Paper, 2011, http://mpra.ub.uni-muenchen.de.
56. *India's External Debt at End - March 2014*, RBI Bulletin, op. cit.
57. For more on the East Asian financial crisis, see: Neeraj Jain, *Globalisation or Recolonisation?* Lokayat publication, Pune; available online at www.lokayat.org.in.
58. Archis Mohan, "PM's Foreign Visits May Be a Record of Sorts", November 7, 2014, http://www.business-standard.com.
59. "Modi Welcomes Japan's $35 Billion Push for India's Inclusive Growth", September 1, 2014, http://indiatoday.intoday.in.
60. "Exclusive! Medha Patkar: Land Acquisition Ordinance Will Destroy Poor", January 14, 2015, http://www.rediff.com; Sam Rajappa, "Why Land Ordinance of Modi Government is Anti-People", February 2, 2015, http://www.theweekendleader.com; Yogendra Yadav, "Land Acquisition Ordinance is Worse than We Thought", January 1, 2015, https://www.facebook.com.
61. Suvrat Raju, M.V. Ramana, "Nuclear Deal No Cause for Celebration", January 31, 2015, http://www.thehindu.com; Suhasini Haidar, "N-Deal Logjam Cleared: Modi, Obama Agree Not to Dilute Liability Law", January 26, 2015, http://www.thehindu.com.
62. "Gorbachev: Chernobyl, Not Perestroika, Caused Soviet Union Collapse", April 29, 2006, http://economistsview.typepad.com.
63. *Chernobyl Radiation Killed Nearly One Million People: New Book*, April 26, 2010, http://www.ens-newswire.com; Alexey V. Yablokov, Vassily B. Nesterenko and Alexey V. Nesterenko, "Chernobyl: The Consequences of the Catastrophe for People and the Environment", *Global Research*, http://www.globalresearch.ca.
64. Chris Busby, *The Health Outcome of the Fukushima Catastrophe: Initial Analysis from Risk Model of the European Committee on Radiation Risk*, March 30, 2011, http://llrc.org/fukushima/subtopic/fukushimarisk calc.pdf; "WSJ Interview: Japan Senior Political Figure Ichiro Ozawa", May 26, 2011, http://www.infiniteunknown.net.

IV

FDI IN RETAIL: DEVELOPMENT FOR WHOM?*

INTRODUCTION

On September 14, 2012, bowing to intense pressure from foreign corporations and foreign governments, especially the USA, the Union Cabinet of the Indian Government finally decided to go ahead and implement a decision it had taken 10 months earlier to allow foreign direct investment (FDI) in yet another important sector of the Indian economy, multi-brand retail, with a cap of 51 percent on foreign equity that ensures majority ownership. (A multi-brand retail store is one which sells several competing brands of the same product under the same roof. Shopping malls like Big Bazaar and Shoppers Stop are examples of multi-brand retail stores.)

Earlier, in January 2012, the government had notified the removal of the 51 percent cap on FDI in single brand retail (FDI in single-brand retail had been first permitted in 2006, subject to a cap of 51 percent foreign ownership), and fully opened up this sector to foreign investors, allowing them 100 percent ownership, with the condition that the single brand retailer should source 30 percent of its goods from India. FDI in cash and carry wholesale (a type of wholesale trade wherein customers pay for the wholesale goods in cash and not on credit, and have to arrange the transport for the goods themselves) had been permitted by the government in 1997. Then, it required

---

* *This essay was written in September 2012, soon after the UPA Government gave its approval to 51 percent foreign direct investment in FDI in multi-brand retail. The Introduction has been updated for this book.*

government approval. The approval requirement was relaxed and automatic permission granted in 2006.

The Foreign Hand

The Cabinet had first given its approval to the hitherto prohibited FDI in multi-brand retail on November 24, 2011 (to an extent of 51 percent). It also enhanced the cap on foreign equity investment in single-brand retail to 100 percent, thus offering sole ownership rights to foreign investors.

The decision led to a huge outpouring of protests all over the country, especially by traders' organisations. On December 1, 2011, crores of traders belonging to more than 10,000 traders' bodies across the country observed an all-India bandh and took out rallies protesting the government decision. Sensing an opportunity to score political points, the entire Opposition came out strongly in support of the protests. The widespread anger also caused a split in the ruling UPA coalition, and important allies of the Congress like the Trinamool Congress and the DMK also demanded a rollback of the Cabinet decision. Finally, on December 7, 2011, the government announced suspension of its decision to allow FDI in multi-brand retail. (The statement of the finance minister announcing this suspension did not say anything about single-brand retail, implying that the proposal to allow 100 percent FDI in single-brand retail still stood. With the Opposition indicating that it would not press for reversal of this decision, the government formally gave its approval to 100 percent FDI in single-brand retail through a press note on January 10, 2012.)[1]

Giant international retail corporations immediately expressed their deep disappointment with the government decision suspending FDI in multi-brand retail. They had spent millions of dollars on lobbying (a polite word for what is actually nothing but bribery) lawmakers in their home countries to help them set up shop in India. Such lobbying is legal in the USA, and companies are required to submit disclosure reports every quarter with the US Senate. According to reports filed by Walmart, a US corporation which is the world's largest retailer, it had spent around $25 million, or Rs 125 crore, since 2008, to lobby US lawmakers for help to gain access to foreign markets, including

India. Obviously, quite a bit of this money must have found its way into the pockets of Indian politicians and parties.[2]

The giant UK retailer Tesco commented: "The decision to defer FDI is a missed opportunity for Indian producers, farmers and consumers."[3] Senior officials of the German retail giant Metro too stated that the rollback was most unfortunate.[4] Even Microsoft, which is not directly affected by the decision, stated that it was "very disappointed" with FDI in multi-brand retail being put on hold, and stressed that "FDI in all forms is good" for India.[5]

Foreign corporations and their concubine governments mounted pressure on the Indian Government to push ahead with economic reforms and permit FDI in multi-brand retail. All the 'Big Three' international credit rating agencies expressed doubts about India's policy making and governance abilities. In April 2012, Standard and Poor's downgraded India's rating from 'stable' to 'negative', and then two months later, threatened to downgrade India's sovereign credit rating to junk grade, for failing to implement announced reforms;[6] soon after, Fitch downgraded India's credit rating outlook, citing inadequate economic reforms; and in August, Moody's too scaled down its forecast for India's economic growth. Large investment houses like Morgan Stanley and Goldman Sachs also raised questions regarding the country's growth prospects, saying that these were constrained due to acute lack of political will to implement reforms.[7]

In July 2012, the Asian edition of the US magazine *Time* carried a forlorn image of Prime Minister Manmohan Singh on its cover, under the headline "The Underachiever", and criticised him for being "unwilling to stick his neck out" on reforms.[8] Days later, the leading US daily *Washington Post* dubbed Manmohan Singh as a "tragic figure" who "is in danger of going down in history as a failure."[9]

In February 2012, the US Under Secretary of International Trade Francisco Sanchez called upon India to open multi-brand retail to foreign investment, saying that, "It is in India's interest to improve its business climate so it can attract investment and help continue grow its economy." The British Secretary of State for Business, Vince Cable, raised the issue when he visited India in January 2012; and in July 2012, George Osborne MP, Chancellor of the Exchequer, UK, called upon the Indian Government to be "more ambitious in retail liberalisation".[10]

In July 2012, US President Barack Obama too lent his voice to the chorus. Citing American business community's concern over the "deteriorating investment climate" in India, he called upon the Indian Government to implement another "wave" of economic reforms, and remove the limits and prohibitions on foreign investment.[11]

With the economy's foreign exchange crisis deepening (discussed later in this essay), the Indian Government finally decided to accede to the wishes of foreign corporations and their governments and open up the country's multi-brand retail sector to FDI, even at the risk of alienating itself from large sections of the Indian people, especially India's traders. On September 20, 2012, on the very day when traders' organisations and opposition political parties had called a *Bharat Bandh* to oppose this decision, it issued the final notification for allowing global retail giants like Walmart to open stores in India.

The BJP U-Turn

In September 2012, when the UPA Government granted approval to 51 percent foreign direct investment (FDI) in multi-brand retail, the BJP was in opposition and had vociferously opposed the UPA Government decision to permit FDI in retail. However, after coming to power, the BJP has silently reversed its position. At a press conference in Delhi in September 2014, a hundred days after the Modi Government assumed power, while the new Minister for Commerce and Industry Nirmala Sitharaman repeated the old BJP position that it would not allow FDI in retail, in the same breath, she also added that at the moment there was no move to reverse the UPA Government notification allowing 51 percent FDI in multi-brand retail.[12] In December 2014, replying to a question in the Lok Sabha, the Minister of State for Food and Consumer Affairs Raosaheb Patil Danve again stated that the new government had not yet taken a decision on the issue of multi-brand retail. So far as single-brand retail was concerned, he stated that the country had received $167.52 million FDI in this sector during April–September 2014, and six more proposals for investment in single-brand retail trading were under process for government approval.[13] On January 13, 2015, Jagdish Bhagwati, Professor at Columbia University and one of Modi Government's favourite economists, while delivering the Madhavrao Scindia memorial lecture in New Delhi, stated that Modi in his discussions with him had clearly indicated that he was not opposed to FDI in multi-brand retail. However, the BJP's traditional base was among shopkeepers. Within a year, once Modi consolidates himself, he would open up FDI in multi-brand retail.[14]

Now, finally, Finance Minister Arun Jaitley himself has set all speculation to rest. At a news conference at the BJP party headquarters on May 23, 2015, the finance minister stressed that governance involved "responsibility" and "continuity" and so the BJP was continuing with the UPA policy of allowing FDI in multi-brand retail.[15]

On each and every 'economic reform', whether it be privatisation of public sector insurance companies, or bringing back black money into the country, or expanding the Food Security Act, or permitting FDI in retail, the BJP has reversed/changed its stand. Not only is it continuing with the policies of the previous UPA Government, it is implementing them at an accelerated pace.

Propaganda

From the country's leading intellectuals and economists to corporate heads like Mukesh Ambani and Ratan Tata, all are claiming that allowing foreign retail giants into India's retail sector will be an important solution to the deepening economic crisis gripping the country. They are asserting that it will curb inflation and the common man will "get commodities of daily use at reduced prices". Not only that, it will benefit farmers as it will "bring modern technology to the country, improve rural infrastructure, reduce wastage of agricultural produce and enable our farmers to get better prices for their crop."[16] The commerce minister in the UPA Government, Anand Sharma, had in fact claimed that it would lead to the creation of ten million jobs in just three years![17]

What audacity! After implementing policies which have led to a quarter-of-a-million farmers committing suicides over the past decade, these people are now expressing concern about farmers! That the entry of foreign multinational corporations (MNCs) into the retail sector will enormously benefit the Indian economy is but a rehash of an old argument given by the Indian ruling classes two decades ago when they first welcomed MNCs to invest in the country (euphemistically known as the globalisation of the Indian economy). Indeed, it has enormously benefited the Indian elites: the number of high net worth individuals in India—those who have disposable assets of over $1 million (Rs 4.6 crore)—increased by 51 percent over the previous year to an estimated 1.27 lakh in 2009.[18] On the other hand, an overwhelming majority of the population—77 percent, or 836 million people—are living on Rs 20 or less a day; an appalling 87 percent of the rural population is unable to access the minimum recommended 2,400 calories per day![19] Finally, their argument about job creation is actually hilarious, coming from policymakers whose economic policies have given this country jobless growth for more than a decade now.[20]

But let's leave such broad criticisms aside. In this essay, we first analyse what will actually happen to India's retail sector when giant retailers from abroad enter the Indian economy; after that, we examine its so-called benefits for consumers and farmers.

1. India's Retail Sector: Statistics

While there are no authoritative figures available, the size of India's retail sector is estimated to be around $400–450 billion today (2011).[21] This sector is the second largest employer in the country after agriculture, and presently employs around 4 crore people, nearly 10 percent of the total employment in the country.[22]

From the point of view of job creation, this is probably the most important sector in the country today, as employment growth in agriculture and manufacturing sectors has virtually come to a standstill because of the economic reforms pursued over the past two decades.[23] It has become an 'employer of last resort', a kind of substitute for an absent social security programme. Thus, when a factory shuts down rendering workers jobless, or peasants find themselves idle during part of the year or get evicted from their land, or when young graduates fail to find jobs in the stagnant manufacturing sector, the retail sector absorbs them all. A skilled labourer turns into a street hawker, a farmer opens a paan–beedi shop, an educated unemployed youth hawks newspapers or takes up a door-to-door sales job, and a better off unemployed person starts a telephone booth and retails telecom cards as an 'add on' service.

According to the countrywide *Economic Census* carried out by the Central Statistical Organisation in 2005, the country had a total of 14.9 million retail outlets,[24] the highest in the world. India's retail sector is presently overwhelmingly dominated by small retailers, consisting of local kirana shops, owner-manned general stores, furniture stores, chemists, hardware–footware–garment–cutlery shops, stationery shops, bakeries, vegetable and fruit shops, paan and beedi shops, hand-cart hawkers, pavement vendors, etc. which together make up the so-called 'unorganised retail' or traditional retail sector. This sector accounts for around 93 percent of all retail sales. Organised retailing constitutes the remaining 7 percent. This includes the corporate-backed hypermarkets and retail chains, and also the privately owned large retail businesses.

Organised Retail: Already Booming

The organised retail sector has seen explosive growth over the past few years. According to a government sponsored study by the Indian Council for Research on International Economic Relations in May 2008, while the unorganised retail sector was expected to grow at about 10 percent per annum between 2006–07 and 2011–12, the organised retail sector was expected to grow at a much faster pace of between 45–50 percent per annum.[25] AT Kearney's (a global management consulting firm) 2011 edition of its *Global Retail Development Index* (this ranks the top 30 emerging countries for retail development on the basis of which global retailers can draw up their investment strategies) expects organised retail's share to increase from the present 7 percent to around 20 percent of India's retail market by 2020![26]

There were just three shopping malls in India in 1999, measuring less than one million square feet. Since then, the number of malls and total mall space in the country have increased at an accelerating pace. By the end of 2006, the country had 137 malls, and the total mall space had risen to 28 million square feet, with an average annual addition of 3.9 million square feet. Post-2006, the average annual addition of mall space doubled to 8 million square feet. By 2009, the country had 172 shopping malls with a total mall space of 52 million square feet; and by 2012, an additional 55 million square feet of mall space was expected to be ready, thus doubling the total mall space in the country within just three years.[27] Some of India's biggest corporate houses have entered the organised retail sector to set up retail chains, including Reliance (Reliance Fresh, Reliance Mart), the Aditya Birla Group (More), the Tata Group (Westside, Star India Bazaar, Landmark), the K. Raheja Group (Shoppers Stop, Crossword and Inorbit Mall) and the RP Goenka Group (Spencer's).

The furious pace of growth of the organised retail sector has adversely affected the small retailers. One survey found that 33–60 percent of the traditional fruit and vegetable retailers had suffered a 10–30 percent decline in sales and 20–30 percent decline in incomes across the cities of Bengaluru, Ahmedabad and Chandigarh.[28] With foreign giant MNC retailers like Walmart and Tesco now given permission to enter India, the unorganised retail sector in the country will be simply decimated.

In order to understand why this is bound to happen, it is necessary to first take a look at the size and economics of MNCs.

2. How Big Are MNCs?

The world economy today is increasingly dominated by a relatively few giant multinational corporations (MNCs). A MNC is a corporation, which, though it has its management headquarters in one country, operates in several countries. In the main, MNCs are headquartered in the rich nations—the United States, European Union and Japan, though in recent years, there has been a growth of MNCs in some third world countries too.

While mainstream economics discusses our era as one of intense and increased competition among businesses, the reality is quite the opposite. Each and every economic activity, in every conceivable sphere, be it manufacture of automobiles or semiconductors or medicines, or be it retail or transportation or information technology, or be it banking and finance, or be it the various sectors of agriculture, from seed manufacture to pesticide manufacture to wheat and rice production, is dominated at the global level by a handful of giant corporations. Note that here we are not talking of a few firms dominating a particular economic activity in a particular country, but their dominating that economic activity at a global level. The same MNC operates in twenty or fifty or more countries, and along with a handful of other such MNCs, dominates global production in that particular sector. To take an example, today five multinational firms produce nearly half the world's motor vehicles, and the ten largest firms produce 70 percent of the world's motor vehicles. The remaining large firms account for a sharply reduced proportion of the global market. In other words, there is a power law distribution thereafter: the twenty-fifth largest motor vehicle producer accounts for around one-half of one percent of the global market, and the fiftieth largest global producer accounts for less than one-tenth of one percent of global production.[29] This obviously means that these smaller firms are never going to be able to challenge the dominance of the big five, implying that in the coming years, they are either going to merge among themselves or be taken over by the bigger players. It also means that there is little to no chance that newcomers will arise to challenge the dominance of the handful of firms that rule global automobile production.

In 1999, in an aptly titled article "Let's Play Oligopoly!" the *Wall Street Journal* described the situation thus:

> In industry after industry the march toward consolidation has seemed inexorable.... The world automobile industry is coalescing into six or eight companies. Two US car makers, two Japanese and a few European firms are among the likely survivors.
>
> The world's top semiconductor makers number barely a dozen. Four companies essentially supply all of the world's recorded

> music. Ten companies dominate the world's pharmaceutical industry, and that number is expected to decline through mergers as even these giants fear they are too small to compete across the globe.
>
> In the global soft drink business, just three companies matter, and the smallest, Cadbury Schweppes PLC, in January sold part of its international business to Coca-Cola Co., the leader. Just two names run the world market for commercial aviation: Boeing Co. and Airbus Industrie.[30]

That was written more than a decade ago. Since then, corporate concentration has only increased. A more recent 2005 report by the international civil society organisation ETC Group examined the market share of the top 10 companies in many sectors, and made the astonishing finding that:[31]

- the world's top 10 seed companies control almost half of the $21,000 million global commercial seed market;
- in pesticides, the top 10 firms control 84 percent of the $29,566 million global pesticide market;
- in the animal pharmaceutical industry, the top 10 companies control 55 percent of the $20,255 million world veterinary pharmaceutical market; and
- the top 10 biotech companies account for almost three-quarters of the global biotech market.

Even these figures do not fully describe the monopoly power of the giant corporation. These figures do not capture the various strategic alliances and partnerships MNCs construct in order to extend their tentacles all over the globe. These include subcontracting agreements, management contracts, turnkey deals, franchising, licensing and product sharing. Thus, for instance, MNCs extensively subcontract their operations either in part or sometimes entirely to subcontractors in Third World countries to lower their labour costs; this volume is so huge that at least 40 percent of world trade is linked to outsourcing by multinationals. Thus, Nike does not manufacture even a single pair of shoes directly; it outsources all of its production to subcontractors in countries such as South Korea, China, Indonesia, Thailand and Vietnam.

To give another striking example, Microsoft, even though it is one of the most powerful companies in the world, has entered into multiple strategic alliances—with Ericsson, British Telecommunications, Telmex and others.

The world's major airlines have gone one step further and have coalesced into a handful of mega-alliances. Just one of these, the Star Alliance, includes: United Airlines, Continental Airlines and US Airways (United States); Air Canada (Canada); BMI (United Kingdom); Lufthansa (Germany); Brussels Airlines (Belgium); Swiss (Switzerland); Austrian (Austria); Spanair (Spain); Tap Portugal (Portugal); Lot Polish Airlines (Poland); Croatia Airlines (Croatia); Adria (Slovenia); SAS (Scandinavia); Blue1 (Finland); Aegean (Greece); Turkish Airlines (Turkey); Egyptair (Egypt); Thai (Thailand); Singapore Airlines (Singapore); Tam (Brazil); Air New Zealand (New Zealand); South African Airways (South Africa); ANA (Japan); Asiana Airlines (Korea); and Air China (China). These airlines are pooling their planes, catering services, training, maintenance and even their aircraft buying programmes to achieve greater economies of scale. The result is, in effect, a global fleet of aircraft operating under the leadership of a single dominant carrier, in this case United Airlines of the USA.[32]

In these and other ways, the rapid expansion of MNCs is creating a highly concentrated world economic system. The actual power wielded by these giant corporations over the global economy can be gauged by the revenues of the top 500 corporations in the world as compiled by *Fortune* magazine: their combined revenues are of the order of 35–40 percent of world GDP![33]

A recent study brings out even more starkly the crushing grip the world's largest MNCs have come to acquire over the global economy. There are more than 63,000 MNCs in the world (2003 figure). However, a study by the Swiss Federal Institute of Technology in Zurich that examined the relationships between 43,000 major MNCs discovered a vast web of interlocking ownerships that is controlled by a "core" of 1,318 giant corporations! These 1,318 corporations represented 20 percent of global operating revenues; however, through their shares, they collectively owned the majority of the world's large blue chip and manufacturing firms, and thus accounted for a further 60 percent of global revenues!![34] Without doubt, a handful of giant corporations are increasingly acquiring a controlling grip on the world economy, with enormous consequences for the future of Planet Earth.

MNCs and Competition

With a few gigantic firms dominating global production in every sector of the global economy, another important transformation that has taken place in the way the world economy operates is that these giant firms no longer compete with each other over prices!

Classical economic theory assumes the existence of a very large number of small firms engaged in 'cut-throat' competition with each other. None of these have any power over price, output and investment, which are all determined by the market.

The rise of the multinational corporation completely changes this situation. The giant corporation produces a significant share of the output of an industry. It is therefore able to control its price, the volume of its production, and the types and amounts of its investments. Therefore, even though in classrooms economics textbooks still teach classical economic theory, this theory is no longer valid in understanding the economics of MNCs.[35]

Since MNCs have enormous financial power, if they indulged in price competition with each other, it would be so destructive that the winner would also be considerably weakened. Therefore, instead of indulging in 'price warfare', they collude over prices. And if they have to collude over prices, why should they keep prices low? Therefore, they keep prices high, at a level which gives them maximum possible profits.[36] (When necessary, MNCs can also lower prices—as we see below, they sometimes do this to destroy small manufacturers, after which they raise prices once again.)

This does not mean that competition amongst MNCs does not take place anymore. It is as cut-throat as ever. Only that it now takes other forms. MNCs now compete with each other for reducing costs, over control of resources, and for market shares through product differentiation and advertising.

3. Impact of FDI in Retail on Small Retailers

Like in all other sectors, concentration is proceeding apace in the retail sector too. The global general merchandise retail market is controlled by a handful of powerful corporations like Walmart, Tesco, Carrefour and Metro, mainly headquartered in the US and Western Europe. These giant retailers are huge, much beyond our imagination. In 2009–10, the world's biggest general merchandise retailer Walmart had total global sales of $405 billion. Among the other biggies, Carrefour (of France) had annual sales of $163.8 billion, Metro (of Germany) $91.4 billion and Tesco (of UK) $90.1 billion.[37] These figures mean that Walmart alone sold more goods than all of India's 1.5 crore retailers combined! Obviously, once such giant mammoths start spreading their tentacles over the Indian retail sector, India's small retailers will just not be able to compete with them and will be destroyed, while India's corporate retailers will enter into collaborations with them, becoming their junior partners. Within a few years, India's vibrant retail sector will come to be dominated by a handful of giant MNC retailers.

The modus operandi of these giants is simple. Because of their size and financial muscle, big retailers like Walmart are able to source their supplies from the lowest cost producers at the global level, like China. In fact, Walmart procures billions of dollars worth of goods from China every year—according to one report in the *Washington Post*, more than 80 percent of the 6,000 factories in Walmart's worldwide database of suppliers are in China.[38] In the case of farm produce, MNC retailers will be able to source it from Indian farmers directly. (See Section 4 for more on this.) Therefore, they will be able to sell their products at cheaper rates than the small retailers. If necessary, Walmart and other big retail MNCs which have incredibly deep pockets are even willing to sell at a loss for several years, till the competition from small retailers is wiped out. Not just the kirana stores and street vendors will be forced out of business, the entire network of wholesalers and distributors will be destroyed.

Destruction of Small Retail in Developed Countries

The corporate choirs are crooning that this is an exaggeration, that small shops and supermarkets/hypermarkets can co-exist. They are lying, it has not happened anywhere in the world. Small retail has virtually been wiped out in the developed countries. In the US, during the fifteen year period 1992–2007, the share of the top four firms in total retail sales in five key retail areas has gone up sharply, as shown in Table 4.1.[39]

Table 4.1: Share of Top Four Firms in Retail Sales in US (%)

Retail Area	*1992*	*2007*
Food and Beverage Stores	15.4	27.7
Health and Personal Care Stores	24.7	54.4
General Merchandise Stores	47.3	73.2
Book Stores	41.3	71.0
Computer and Software Stores	26.2	73.1

Obviously, this domination by the big retail chains has been at the expense of small retailers. Robert Reich (former Secretary of Labour in the Clinton administration) has described their impact thus: Walmart turns "main streets into ghost towns by sucking business away from small retailers."[40] One study by Prof. Kenneth Stone of Iowa State University, USA found that small towns lose up to 47 percent of their retail trade after 10 years of Walmart stores nearby.[41]

In fact, the impact of big retailers, especially Walmart, on small businesses in the USA has been so destructive that people in several cities and communities like Cleveland, Chicago, Flagstaff, San Diego, Inglewood, Rosemead, Long Beach, Tucson, Spokane and New York City have organised and fought hard to prevent the entry of Walmart supercentres in their cities (with varying degrees of success). Walmart has used all kinds of tactics to try and browbeat its opponents into submission. These include setting up local front groups (over the period 2000–05, Walmart funnelled more than $4.3 million to front groups in ten California communities alone for running campaigns in its support), bribing opponents, funding vicious propaganda campaigns and adopting aggressive litigation tactics.[42]

In Europe, during the 1970s–80s when giant corporations were just coming into existence, many countries initially enacted laws, like *Loi Royer* in France and the *Loi de Cadenas* in Belgium, and also took other measures aimed at restricting the growth of large retailers. These included, for instance, imposing restrictions on big retailers to either completely shut down or open only for a limited number of hours on Sundays,[43] imposing limitations on size of new supermarkets and imposing restrictions on where new large shopping malls can be opened.[44] However, since the 1990s, monopolisation has accelerated in every sector of the economy in these countries, and so the political clout of monopoly corporations has also increased. Under pressure from the big retailers lobby, many European countries are therefore gradually lifting restrictions placed on the growth of large retail, accelerating the concentration of retail in the hands of a few giant retailers.

The consequences have been devastating for small retail. By 2005, the top five retailers accounted for around 65–75 percent of total grocery sales in several European countries, from Denmark to Sweden, Switzerland, Germany and the UK.[45] In the UK, there are several postal areas where Tesco, Britain's largest retailer, has almost total control of the food market![46]

Destruction of Small Retail in Third World Countries

After winning independence in the years following the Second World War, numerous Third World countries had initially attempted to carry out their industrial revolutions by adopting the model of autonomous capitalist development. Note that in this, they were only copying the strategy adopted by the developed countries from the USA to Germany in the 18th–19th centuries. One of the important policies implemented by most of them was to *limit the influx of foreign capital into their economies.*

However, this development model had inherent limitations. Due to changed historical circumstances, it was no longer possible for the underdeveloped countries to follow the Western model of capitalist development (discussing this is beyond the scope of this essay). And so, by the late 1970s, these models started failing, and these countries got entrapped in a foreign debt crisis. Their foreign creditors, the developed capitalist countries of the USA, Western Europe and Japan, acting in concert, now arm-twisted the Third World countries into removing restrictions and opening up their economies to inflows of foreign capital and goods.

One of the important policy changes made in all these indebted countries is that they have opened up their retail sector to large retailers from the West. This has had predictable consequences. From Turkey to Brazil to South Africa, in each and every Third World country that has permitted FDI in retail, within just a few years of the entry of giant retailers into their economies, they have driven millions of small retailers out of business to capture a large share of the retail market. Walmart entered Mexico in 1991; within a decade (2001), it had taken over nearly half (45.6 percent),[47] and by 2011, 55 percent of the retail market![48] The same story has been repeated in other Latin American countries: in Brazil, the share of street markets in fruit and vegetable sales declined by 27.8 percent between 1987 and 1996; in Argentina, the number of small stores dropped by 30 percent between 1984 and 1993, and employment in the retail sector declined by 26 percent over the same period; while in Chile, 'traditional' food and beverage retailers declined by approximately 20 percent in all segments over the period 1991–95.[49]

In East Asia, the supermarket share of retail food sales ballooned from less than 20 percent to around 50 percent over the decade ending around 2005.[50] The impact on small retail was so devastating that it led to riots, forcing several countries to impose controls on mega-retailers.[51]

With giant retailers now given permission to enter the Indian retail market, their impact is going to be no different; they will simply destroy India's small retail sector.

Job Creation Myth

For the very same reason, that these giant retailers will create jobs is also a myth. While they will employ a few thousand people, this is nothing compared to the millions of small retailers they will render jobless (apart from their adverse impact on small businesses and farmers, as discussed later in this essay). According to one estimate, if Walmart is allowed to enter India, one Walmart supermarket would displace over 1,300 small retail stores and render 3,900 people jobless; for every job created in a supermarket, around 17 jobs would be lost in the unorganised retail sector.[52] More than 4 crore people are employed in the retail trade in India, and if we think in terms of families, this means that more than 16 crore people are dependent on this sector for livelihood support. The entry of giant MNC retailers is going to have a devastating impact on the employment situation in the country.

Even the few jobs that will be created by these supermarket chains will be low-paid jobs. Walmart is known worldwide for paying wages far below industry standard. This is true for its home country too, the USA. Walmart is the largest private-sector employer in the United States, employing more than 1.4 million workers, one percent of the country's 140 million working population.[53] Walmart pays its workers, whom it calls 'associates', poverty or near poverty wages—the average wage at Walmart is $11.75 per hour or $20,774 per year, nearly six percent below the US federal poverty level. Not only that, because it is a big employer, whenever it opens a store in a town, its low wages force down wages in the local area, as other employers also have to lower wages in order to compete with it.[54] Worse, the company has a long record of worker abuse, including forced overtime (some off-the-clock), punishing workers for the slightest infraction, employing child labour, knowingly employing undocumented workers, discrimination against female employees, and relentless union-busting.[55] As a reward for such labour practices, Walmart's CEO Michael Duke got an annual salary of $35 million (in 2010), which constituted an hourly wage equal to the annual salary of the average Walmart employee![56]

Even before it gave the green signal to these lawless corporations to enter the country, the Indian Government over the past decade has been changing the country's labour laws to bring them in line with the labour practices of the giant retail chains and other foreign MNCs: easier hiring and firing, more short-term contracts, fewer benefits, and longer periods of overtime.

Retailing is probably the primary form of disguised unemployment/underemployment in the country. Given the lack of jobs in manufacturing and agriculture, retail activities such as door-to-door selling, plying a street cart or setting up a small store act as a last resort for the unemployed. Many in the retail trade are living below the poverty line. The opening up of the retail sector to FDI is going to push lakhs of these people already living below the poverty line into destitution.

4. Will Farmers Benefit?

If this was true, the MNC retailers should have benefited farmers in the US and Europe! On the contrary, corporate monopolies at every level, from giant agribusinesses to mammoth retail chains, have wrecked family farms, especially the smaller ones, in America. Presently less than one million Americans claim farming as their occupation. That figure was over 25 million in the 1950s.[57] Likewise, in Europe, every minute a farmer quits agriculture.

Across the developed countries, but for huge subsidies given by governments to farmers, agriculture would have collapsed by now. A 2010 report by the Organisation for Economic Cooperation and Development (an international economic organisation of 34 developed countries) explicitly states that farm subsidies rose by 22 percent in 2009, up from 21 percent in 2008. In just 2009, agricultural subsidies given by the industrialised countries totalled Rs 1,260 billion.[58]

MNCs Cartelise to Lower Purchase Prices

The reason for this deepening agricultural crisis in the developed countries is simple. Multinational corporations are gigantic, and so are able to monopolise the entire supply chain, from processing to trade to retail. Further, unlike what is taught in economics textbooks, they do not compete with each other, and instead cartelise amongst themselves, to lower the prices at which they buy goods from small producers and farmers. The farmers have no option but to sell their produce to these corporations at the prices offered by the latter. The giant retailers are thus in a position to drive down purchase prices at will, forcing farmers into ruin. This is the reason for the destruction of family farms in Europe and America.

A few examples. The impact of retail oligopoly on farmers can be judged by taking a look at how much of each dollar spent on food at the supermarket—called the retail food dollar—goes back to the farmer. In 1970, hog producers (those who raise pigs) in the US got 48 cents out of each retail dollar spent on pork; three decades later, their share had fallen to only 12 cents out of every retail dollar. This happened even though retail prices stayed stable, implying that the supermarkets had not shared any benefits with the consumers and had kept all the gains for themselves. In the UK, while it costs the consumer £1.45 to buy four pints (1 pint = 0.57 litres) of milk at a supermarket, the farmer receives just 58 pence (40 percent) of this. According to the Royal Association of British Dairy Farmers, dairy farmers are suffering a loss of 3 pence for every four pints. As a result, many small farmers have closed their dairy operations.[59]

The bigger a retailer is, the better able it is to extract lower prices from suppliers. The UK Competition Commission found that Tesco, the biggest supermarket in the UK, consistently paid suppliers 4 percent below the industry average, while smaller supermarkets paid above the average rate.[60]

The situation for the small farmers is becoming so bad that in February 2008, the European Parliament actually adopted a declaration that said:

> Throughout the EU, retailing is increasingly dominated by a small number of supermarket chains.... Evidence from across the EU suggests large supermarkets are abusing their buying power to force down prices paid to suppliers (based both within and outside the EU) to unsustainable levels and impose unfair conditions upon them.[61]

Strangling Growers in the Third World

Neither has big retail helped farmers in the Third World countries. A decade ago, Third World coffee producers earned $10 billion from a global market of over $30 billion. Now they receive less than $6 billion out of a global market of $60 billion. Likewise, cocoa farmers of Ghana now receive only 3.9 percent of the price of a typical milk chocolate bar, while the retail margin hovers at around 34.1 percent.[62] For every £1.00 that shoppers in the UK spend on bananas, plantation workers in Ecuador receive just 1.5 pence, while around 40 pence goes to the supermarkets; the remaining goes to line the pockets of the trading companies.[63] While the African producers as a whole get only 9 percent of the retail price of an exported apple, the retailers in the UK corner a 42 percent share.[64]

Imposing Unfair Conditionalities

The big retail corporations marginalise small farmers in other ways too, like by imposing stringent criteria for supply of their produce. Producers are typically expected to meet exacting product standards for their goods, adjust production volumes at short notice to meet short-term market trends, prevent deterioration of products through measures like provision of cold storage, and so on. Meeting these conditions requires high levels of investment in irrigation, transportation, storage facilities and packaging technology. The vast majority of smallholders do not have the financial or managerial resources to meet corporate buyers' demands, and so are being forced out and replaced by big farmers or the corporations themselves.[65]

For instance, in Brazil, Nestlé (a Swiss-based MNC) and Parmalat (an Italian MNC) first bought up the country's milk cooperatives in a series of aggressive takeovers, and then imposed standards that small farmers found difficult to meet. Thus, they demanded that farmers install milk refrigeration tanks on their farms. The smallest tanks needed at least 100 litres to be filled, but the average farm produced only 50 litres per day. Most small-scale farmers could not afford to install the coolers, which in any case were beyond their needs. Such conditions pushed over 50,000 dairy farmers out of their supply chains;

as a result, many went out of business altogether.[66] Likewise, in Argentina, corporate transformation of the supply chain saw the number of dairy farms falling from 40,000 in 1983 to 15,000 in 2001.[67] Walmart's overwhelming domination of Mexico's retail trade is one of the important reasons that has forced over 1.25 million small Mexican farmers—25 percent of the country's farmers—to quit farming over the last two decades.[68]

An investigation by the UK Competition Commission in 1999 also made similar findings. It found that suppliers to grocery supermarkets were forced to accept numerous conditions by the giant retailers, including: discounts (sometimes retrospectively); imposing charges and making changes to contractual arrangements without adequate notice; and unreasonably transferring risks from the buyer (supermarket) to the supplier. Such practices exerted downward pressure on the incomes of farmers and workers involved in the supply of goods to such retail chains.[69]

MNCs take advantage of their monopoly power to even indulge in *unfair trading practices* with small farmers. These can include: delaying payment for produce; lowering prices at the last minute; buying less than the amount agreed to; non-transparent weighing and grading of produce; charging high interest rates for credit; and changing quality standards without adequate notice.[70]

Impact on Small Farmers in India

Given all this evidence, it is obvious that the entry of giant corporate retailers into India's food market will have a devastating impact on India's 650 million farmers.

Presently, because of the APMC* Acts, the farmer has the option to sell his agricultural goods in any mandi (wholesale market) either himself or through any agent who gives him the best rate. Because there is no single buyer, farmers get a better price. Now, the Central government is pressurising the states to amend their APMC Acts, so

* *APMC or Agricultural Produce Market Committee: A marketing board established by state governments in India, in order to facilitate farmers to sell their produce to traders/agents and get reasonable prices.*

as to allow agribusiness corporations to enter into direct contracts with farmers.[71] One eventual consequence of this is going to be that the system of mandis is gradually going to get dismantled. This is because MNCs have huge financial strength and will initially pay better prices to the farmers than the mandis (they are already doing this in many states that have modified their APMC Acts). Therefore, in the coming years, the MNCs will gradually acquire monopoly over the buying of agricultural produce from farmers.

As mentioned earlier, MNCs do not compete with each other over prices; either they will operate in different domains, or they will cartelise. Once the mandis close down and the MNCs acquire monopoly over purchase, they will then start lowering procurement prices, as they have done all over the world. The farmers will have no option but to sell to them. Additionally, the giant corporations/retailers will now be in a position to impose conditions like strict adherence to quality and schedule on the farmers, which will be very difficult for our small tomato and potato farmers to meet.

Finally, a brief look at the claim by Prime Minister Manmohan Singh and other 'friends of Indian farmers' that FDI in retail would benefit farmers by creating modern storage facilities which will help reduce the huge post-harvest losses of fruits and vegetables in the country. It is a ridiculous argument. It is the duty of the government to set up these facilities in the public sector; or else, the government can provide incentives and get farmers' cooperatives to set up these facilities. On the other hand, if foreign multinational retailers create these facilities, they will do so for their own benefit, and not for benefit of farmers. MNCs are not social workers!

Then why is the government not investing in creating these facilities, why is it pushing for agribusiness corporations and giant retailers to set them up? It is a part of the sordid globalisation agenda being implemented by India's servile rulers at the behest of the World Bank and India's foreign creditors. The global agribusiness corporations are seeking to acquire control over India's agricultural sector, and so they are pressurising the Indian Government to reduce its capital investment in agriculture, and the Indian Government is dutifully implementing their wishes.[72]

Over the last two decades, ever since the Government of India began opening up the country's economy to FDI inflows in the name of 'helping the Indian farmer', the agricultural sector has sunk deeper and deeper into crisis. It has led to a massive increase in the indebtedness of the peasantry. Not only have seven-and-a-half million farmers abandoned agriculture over the past decade, it has spurred the worst-ever recorded wave of suicides in the country's history.[73] The latest of these policies, FDI in retail, will have even more catastrophic consequences.

5. Big Retail Destroys Small Businesses Too

As discussed earlier, big retailers like Walmart have the financial strength to source their supplies from the lowest cost producers at the global level. For instance, in 1995, 6 percent of Walmart's total merchandise sold in the United States was imported. By 2005, 60 percent of its total merchandise was imported, from more than 6,000 suppliers in 63 countries.[74]

With the government permitting corporations like Walmart to set up shop in India, Indian businesses will soon have to compete with lowest cost products from around the world. Even if Indian businesses are able to somehow withstand this competition, Walmart can still destroy them by deliberately lowering prices, as it has the financial capacity to withstand losses. When Parmalat, a world leader in dairy products, entered South Africa's dairy market during the 1990s, it gained market share by offering dairy products to retailers at reduced rates, thereby undercutting local processors and distributors, many of whom shut down as a result.[75] Walmart's entry into India will similarly destroy small businesses here too.

Marginalising Workers

Walmart is so big and buys so much from its suppliers that it is able to dictate terms to them. It forces them to sell their products at rock bottom prices, thereby further worsening the conditions of the workers in the supplier countries.

Business has no ethics. Walmart has no problems in sourcing its products from countries where child labour, slave labour and suppression of human rights are commonplace. Workers in Honduras working for Walmart work for 88 hours a week in 14 hour shifts, making 43 cents an hour, which meets only 54 percent of the cost of survival. Clothing sold by Walmart is often made by young women in Bangladesh, who are forced to work from 7 am to 8 pm, seven days a week, paid 9 cents to 20 cents an hour, denied health care and maternity leave, allowed only monitored bathrooms visits, and are fired if they dare ask for their rights.[76] Despite such terrible working conditions, the share of Bangladeshi workers' wages in the final retail price of a shirt in North American markets was only 1.7 percent; the profit of the Bangladeshi employer was another 1 percent; while 'gross commercial profit, rent and other income of distributors' accounted for 71.8 percent.[77]

Walmart sources heavily from China because of the Chinese Government's ban on trade unions, its willingness to harshly punish anyone trying to organise a workers' movement, and because courts and regulatory bodies are willing to overlook labour violations. And so Walmart is able to pit suppliers against each other and squeeze them for the lowest price. The result is that low wages, long hours and poor conditions are common in factories in China supplying goods to Walmart. These factories go to the extent of employing children below the age of 16 (China's legal working age), force workers to work 15 hours a day, seven days a week, pay them very low wages, and expose them to dangerous machinery and harmful chemicals like lead, cadmium and mercury.[78]

Once Walmart and other giant retailers set up their retail chains in India, the workers in Indian factories will have to compete with such low paid workers to survive. It will be a race to the bottom of the wage and benefit scale.

6. Will Consumers Benefit?

The propaganda is that supermarkets will eliminate middlemen, leading to lower consumer prices. This is another myth. In reality, corporate retail establishes complete monopoly over the whole supply chain to become producer, wholesaler, distributor and retailer, all together. Thus, corporate retailers become giant middlemen themselves. Once they succeed in this, why will they transfer some of their huge margins to consumers and lower consumer prices?

On the contrary, MNCs take advantage of their monopoly position to raise consumer prices and earn superprofits! As discussed earlier, MNCs do not engage in price competition with each other; they collaborate to keep prices high. Initially, while the retail giants are taking on the existing small retailers, consumers may benefit from lower prices for a short while. But once the MNC retailers acquire a monopoly over the market, they hike prices. Even when supplier prices fall due to cost economies, they do not lower consumer prices. This has been the experience the world over, from Nicaragua and Argentina to Kenya and Thailand and Vietnam: prices in the supermarkets in all these countries are an estimated 10–14 percent higher than in traditional markets.[79]

An official report prepared in June 2011 by the French Government's food price watchdog charged supermarkets with squeezing producers by paying lower prices, but not passing on the gains to customers. With the result that the supermarkets were earning fabulous profits: margins on apples and bananas stood at around 140 percent and for carrots and lettuce at 110 percent; while the margin on pork loin had risen to 55 percent from 39 percent a decade ago.[80] Similarly, the UK National Farmers' Union also found that declining farmgate prices (price received by the farm for its produce) in the UK are not being passed on to consumers. Sharp falls in producer prices for milk and lamb during the 1990s, for example, did not translate into lower retail prices for these goods.[81] In the US, supermarkets raised tomato prices by 46 percent between 1994 and 2004 while prices paid to producers fell by 25 percent.[82]

The same story is being played out in the tea gardens of India. A study by the NGO ActionAid International some years ago found that large buying companies, operating on behalf of corporate entities, had formed cartels to drive down auction prices: auction prices for tea had fallen by around 33 percent in southern India, from 69 rupees per kg in 1998 to 46 rupees in 2004, and by nearly 12 percent in northern India within the same timeframe. The prices had in fact fallen to below the cost of production, estimated to be approximately 75 rupees per kg in 2004. This had ruinous effects on small-scale tea farmers and plantation workers. However, the falling auction prices did not result in a lowering of the price paid by consumers—the retail market prices continued to be high, at around 160 rupees a kg. With the result that the large tea companies reaped large profits: shareholder dividends issued by Hindustan Lever, which is estimated to have a 34 percent share of the Indian packaged tea market, have more than quadrupled since 1996.[83]

7. FDI in Retail: For Whose Benefit?

Clearly, the government decision to allow 'FDI in Retail' is going to have calamitous consequences for India's dynamic retail sector. Lakhs of small shopkeepers and street vendors will be forced out of business, rendering millions of people unemployed. Not only that, it will have devastating consequences for small businesses and small farmers too, who are already in crisis due to the gradual opening up of the economy to foreign capital over the last two decades. Neither will consumers benefit; 'FDI in Retail' is not going to lead to lower consumer prices and help control inflation in any way.

If it is going to have such ruinous consequences, why is the Government of India allowing giant foreign retailers to set up supermarkets–hypermarkets in India? Why are our country's rulers mortgaging the interests of the people of the country to benefit big foreign corporations?

Globalisation: India on 'Sale'

It is happening not just in the retail sector, it is happening with every sector of the country's economy. For the last more than two decades, successive governments at the Centre have been running the economy solely for the profiteering of giant foreign corporations of the developed capitalist countries and their Indian collaborators, the big Indian corporate houses.

It all began in 1991. The country was entrapped in a foreign exchange crisis. India's creditors, the developed countries (the triad of the United States, the West European countries and Japan) forced the Government of India to take a 'Structural Adjustment Loan' from World Bank–IMF to tide over the crisis. The loan package was a strict quid-pro-quo. In return for the loan, the Indian Government agreed to implement a series of market reforms. The World Bank and IMF are institutions directly controlled by the triad, and therefore the loan conditionalities were designed to benefit the corporations (that is, the MNCs) of the developed countries. These reforms included opening up the economy for imports and investments by giant multinational corporations of the developed countries, handing over control of public sector enterprises to them and removal of all controls on their profiteering in the name of 'freeing the market'.

As we have explained elsewhere,[84] it is an inherent logic of these reforms that their implementation can only lead to a worsening of the country's foreign exchange crisis, and that is precisely what has happened.

Two decades of globalisation have led to:

i) a sharp rise in our trade deficit, from $2.8 billion in 1991–92 to a whopping $189.7 billion in 2011–12;
ii) a sharp rise in our current account deficit—to $78.2 billion for the financial year 2011–12, the highest level since 1991;
iii) a sharp rise in our external debt—it stood at an astronomical $346 billion in end-March 2012, a rise by more than 4 times over 1991–92![85]

This spiralling whirlpool of foreign debt has made the country more and more dependent on foreign exchange inflows (or FDI) to prevent the economy from once again plunging into foreign exchange bankruptcy. And so the foreign corporate armies and their concubine governments are able to impudently trample upon our honour and dignity, yankee-kick us into implementing more and more economic reforms, force us to open up more and more sectors of the economy for gigantic multinationals to invest and plunder . . .

The approval given to foreign corporations to invest in the retail sector is but a continuation of these globalisation policies being implemented in the country over the last two decades. Large multinational retailers like Walmart, Tesco, Carrefour and Metro are facing saturated home country markets, and are looking for better pastures. Additionally, they are also facing increasing opposition in their home countries due to their impact on local communities. So, they have been keen to expand into India, and mounted pressure on the Indian Government to open up this sector for foreign investment.

India's elites have been euphoric over globalisation. The capitalist classes are no longer interested in the long-term growth prospects of the economy; they are keen to become the junior partners of foreign MNCs and increase their profits. The swanky upper classes are in raptures over the entry of foreign MNCs, as the world's most trendy consumer goods are now available in the country. And so, for their narrow selfish interests, the Indian elites too demanded that the Indian Government open up the retail sector for FDI. Their faithful servants, India's traitorous intellectuals, launched a huge propaganda offensive to convince the Indian people that 'FDI in Retail' will benefit the economy and the people, lower prices, improve farm incomes, blah blah blah.

The mainstream political parties essentially represent the interests of the Indian elites. With large sections of the local elites in favour of opening up the retail sector to FDI, the worsening foreign exchange crisis and mounting foreign pressure finally pushed the Indian Government to ignore the countrywide protests and grant permission to foreign retail giants to invest in India.

We Must Advance Our Struggle!

Friends, our nationwide struggle to prevent the entry of foreign multinational corporations into the retail sector has not prevented the Indian ruling classes from going ahead with their sordid agenda.

Clearly, a lot more needs to be done. We need to intensify our struggle. There are many amongst us who are gripped by a sense of despondency. A common refrain is that if the opposition parties couldn't prevent the policy from being implemented, what can we, the ordinary people, do. We need to be clear that the opposition of the mainstream political parties to this policy was only out of opportunism, to take advantage of the tremendous public anger against this policy. Which is why they made no attempt to mobilise people for a determined struggle against this policy, and all they did was to give a call for a ritualistic one-day *Bharat Bandh*. This is just as has happened in the past. Over the last two decades, different combinations of parties have been in power at the Centre; whenever the ruling coalition has implemented economic reforms, each time, the then Opposition has protested; but when in subsequent elections, the latter has come to power, it has only implemented yet more reforms. In reality, globalisation is the consensus policy of India's entire ruling elite and its political parties.

There is no need to be despondent about the fact that there are no tall leaders to follow. Leaders are not born in vacuum; they are born out of social movements. The biggest and tallest trees all ultimately sprout from the Earth.

We need to deepen our struggle, involve more people in it. There are a very large number of common people who have been hoodwinked by the intense government and media propaganda and believe that this policy will indeed benefit Indian farmers and consumers. Therefore, it is important to continue with our campaign to educate the common people about the disastrous effects of this policy

Of course, just increasing consciousness is not enough. We will need to organise various forms of creative protests and motivate people to join them in increasing numbers.

Ultimately, our struggle against FDI in retail is a part of the growing nationwide movement against globalisation, against the sell-out of our country to foreign and Indian big business houses by India's ruling classes. As more and more people join this struggle, it will strengthen and become a powerful force to transform society, and build a new India, where development does not mean profit maximisation of a few big corporations, but fulfilment of the basic needs of all people—healthy food, invigorating education, good quality healthcare, decent shelter, clean pollution-free environment—that will create the conditions for the full development of the enormous inherent potential of all human beings. Bringing into existence such a system is possible today—it is no longer a utopia that it was earlier—because of the enormous advancement in human knowledge and human capabilities and the giant leaps in science and technology achieved since independence.

The ruling classes of course want us to believe that it is not possible to change the present corporate centric, profit oriented system. But like all social systems that existed in the past, the present system too is a historical entity. As Buddha said a very long time ago:

> Anything that comes into being is also destined to pass away.

References

1. "100% FDI Nod for Single Brands", *Hindustan Times*, December 7, 2011, http://www.hindustantimes.com; "India: FDI in Single Brand Retail Increased to 100%", November 12, 2012, http://www.mondaq.com.
2. Rajinder Puri, "Did Walmart Bribe Indian Politicians?" *The Statesman*, December 12, 2012, http://www.asianewsnet.net; Venky Vembu, "From Enron to Wal-Mart: The Dirty Business of 'Lobbying'", December 11, 2012, http://www.firstpost.com.
3. Deepal Jayasekera, "Indian Government Puts Retail Sector Restructure on Hold", December 8, 2011, http://www.wsws.org.
4. "Retail FDI on Hold, India Inc Unhappy", December 6, 2011, http://info.shine.com.
5. "Microsoft 'Disappointed' with Hold Back on Retail FDI", December 9, 2011, http://businesstoday.intoday.in.
6. Mayur Shetty, "Standard & Poor's Warns India of a Downgrade to Junk Category", *TNN*, June 11, 2012, http://timesofindia.indiatimes.com; Amol Sharma, Sudeep Jain, "India Gets Downgrade Warning", April 25, 2012, http://online.wsj.com.
7. "Fitch Downgrades India's Credit Rating from Stable to Negative", June 19, 2012, http://indiatoday.intoday.in; "PM Concerned Over Moody's Forecast on Economy", *PTI*, August 11, 2012, http://www.hindustantimes.com.
8. "Time Magazine Dubs Manmohan Singh as 'Underachiever'", *PTI*, July 8, 2012, http://articles.timesofindia.indiatimes.com.
9. "After Time, Washington Post Calls PM Manmohan Singh a "Tragic Figure"", September 5, 2012, http://indiatoday.intoday.in.

10. "In India's Interest to Improve Business Climate to Attract More FDI: US Official", *PTI*, February 20, 2012, http://articles.economic times.indiatimes.com; "UK Wants India to Open Retail, Raise FDI Limit in Defence", *PTI*, January 14, 2011, http://articles.economic times.indiatimes.com; "India to Go Ahead with FDI in Multi-Brand Retail: Minister", July 27, 2012, http://www.fibre2fashion.com.
11. "Investment Climate in India Deteriorating, Time to Make Difficult Reforms: Barack Obama", *PTI*, July 15, 2012, http://www.ndtv.com.
12. "India to Disallow FDI in Multi-Brand Retail: Nirmala", September 8, 2014, http://www.thehindu.com.
13. "Government Considering 6 FDI Proposals in Single-Brand Retail", *PTI*, December 16, 2014, http://economictimes.indiatimes.com; "India Attracts $259 Mn FDI in Single Brand-Retail Since April 2010", *PTI*, December 23, 2014, http://economictimes.indiatimes.com.
14. "Confident That NDA Will Open Up Retail to FDI: Bhagwati", January 14, 2015, http://www.livemint.com.
15. "Jaitley on FDI in Retail: Governance Involves Responsibility and Continuity", May 23, 2015, http://www.business-standard.com; "Nuclear Bunker for Retail 'Continuity'", May 23, 2015, http://www.telegraphindia.com.
16. "Youth Congress Meet: PM and Sonia Vow to Bring Lokpal, Defend FDI", *India Today*, November 29, 2011, http://indiatoday.intoday.in.
17. "FDI in Multi-Brand Retail Will Create 10 Million Jobs: Anand Sharma", *Times of India*, November 26, 2011, http://timesofindia.indiatimes.com.
18. "High Net Worth Individuals in India Up 51% in 2009", *Financial Express*, June 24, 2010, http://www.financialexpress.com.
19. Amit Sengupta, "So, Where Have All the Poor Gone?", *Hardnews*, January 2010, http://www.hardnewsmedia.com; Utsa Patnaik, "Trends in Urban Poverty Under Economic Reforms: 1993–94 to 2004–05", http://www.indiaenvironmentportal.org.in.
20. *India Becoming a Colony Again*, Lokayat Publication, Pune, 2010, pp. 54–57; available online at www.lokayat.org.in.
21. The figure of $400 billion is cited in numerous newsreports. See for example: "FDI in India: Just 4 Percent of India's Retail is Organised," *Times of India*, November 30, 2011, http://timesofindia.india times.com; "FDI in Retail: Only 4 Percent is Organised, Says CII", *Business Today*, November 30, 2011, http://businesstoday.intoday.in. This is probably based on the Business Monitor International (a renowned multinational credit risk and political risk rating agency)

India Retail Report for the second quarter of 2011, which says that total retail sale in India was $395.96 billion in 2011. The 2011 edition of *Global Retail Development Index (GRDI)* published by AT Kearney, the well-known international management consultancy firm, puts the size of India's retail market at $435 billion, while the international financial conglomerate Citigroup in its *India Microscope* report estimates its size at $470 billion.

22. Most newsreports and articles cite this figure. This probably comes from the National Sample Survey Organisation's survey of employment and unemployment in 2009–10, according to which the service sector category that includes the wholesale and retail trade (besides the much smaller segment of repair works for automobiles and personal and household goods) provided jobs for 44 million people out of a total workforce of 459 million. (C.P. Chandrasekhar, "Retreat on Retail", *Frontline*, December 17–30, 2011, http://www.frontlineonnet.com.)
23. *India Becoming a Colony Again*, op. cit., pp. 54–57.
24. *India in Business: Industry and Services*, Ministry of External Affairs, Government of India, http://www.indiainbusiness.nic.in.
25. Mathew Joseph et al., *Impact of Organized Retailing on the Unorganized Sector*, Indian Council for Research on International Economic Relations, May 2008, p. vi, http://dipp.nic.in.
26. *GRDI 2011*, AT Kearney, http://www.slideshare.net.
27. Mathew Joseph et al., *Impact of Organized Retailing on the Unorganized Sector*, op. cit., p. vi; "120 Million Square Feet Mall Space by Q1, 2011: Malls of India Report", September 16, 2009, http://www.indiaretailing.com; *India Organised Retail Market 2010*, Knight Frank India, http://online.wsj.com.
28. "Multinational Corporations: A Key to Global Poverty Reduction", January 9, 2006, http://www.globalenvision.org.
29. John Bellamy Foster et al., "Monopoly and Competition in Twenty-First Century Capitalism", *Monthly Review*, April 2011, http://monthlyreview.org.
30. John Bellamy Foster et al., "The Internationalization of Monopoly Capital", *Monthly Review*, June 2011, http://monthlyreview.org.
31. *New Report on Corporate Power – Oligopoly, Inc. 2005*, Communiqué, ETC Group, November–December 2005, http://www.etcgroup.org.
32. John Bellamy Foster et al., "The Internationalization of Monopoly Capital", op. cit.
33. John Bellamy Foster et al., "Monopoly and Competition in Twenty-First Century Capitalism", op. cit.

34. Andy Coghlan and Debora MacKenzie, "Revealed – The Capitalist Network That Runs the World", *New Scientist*, October 24, 2011, http://www.newscientist.com.
35. For more on this theory, see endnotes 29 and 30.
36. For more on this theory, see: Paul Baran and Paul Sweezy, *Monopoly Capital*, K.P. Bagchi and Company, Calcutta, 1994.
37. "Global Retailing – International Retail Factsheet", IGD, June 3, 2010, http://www.igd.com.
38. Peter S. Goodman and Philip P. Pan, "Chinese Workers Pay for Walmart's Low Prices", *Washington Post Foreign Service*, February 8, 2004, http://www.washingtonpost.com.
39. John Bellamy Foster et al., "Monopoly and Competition in Twenty-First Century Capitalism", op. cit.
40. Vijay Prashad, "Shop and Awe", *Frontline*, December 17–30, 2011, http://www.frontlineonnet.com.
41. Kenneth E. Stone, "Impact of the Walmart Phenomenon on Rural Communities", published in *Proceedings: Increasing Understanding of Public Problems and Policies—1997*, Farm Foundation, Chicago, USA, http://www2.econ.iastate.edu.
42. There are several articles and reports on this on the internet. See for example: "Shameless: How Walmart Bullies Its Way into Communities Across America", *Walmart Watch Report*, 2005, http://www.maine.com; "Walmart's Expansion Fight Now Rests with Gov. Brown", *Los Angeles Times*, September 3, 2011, http://articles.latimes.com; "Walmart Fight Heats Up in California", *Christian Science Monitor*, June 19, 2007, http://www.csmonitor.com; Robert Smith, "New York City Officials to Walmart: Keep out", *NPR*, February 4, 2011, http://www.npr.org.
43. "Supermarkets Fed Up with Sunday Shopping Rules", *Dutch News*, July 5, 2011, http://www.dutchnews.nl; Mark Faithfull, "Europe Still Divided by Sunday Shopping Conundrum", April 2006, http://www.icsc.org.
44. Horst Raff and Nicolas Schmitt, "Imports and the Structure of Retail Markets", June 2011, p. 2, http://econstor.eu; "Liberalisation Set to Revolutionise French Retailing", *Data Monitor*, April 9, 2008, http://about.datamonitor.com; Ken Baar, "Legislative Tools for Preserving Town Centres and Halting the Spread of Hypermarkets and Malls Outside of Cities", Institute for Transport and Development Policy, New York, USA, www.itdp.org.
45. "Grocery Market: Proposed Decision to Make a Market Investigation Reference", Office of Fair Trading, March 2006, http://www.ppa.co.uk;

Shekhar Swamy, "How the World Burnt Its Fingers", *The Hindu Business Line*, August 25, 2011, http://www.thehindubusinessline.com.

46. "Tesco Plc: Overview", September 2004, http://www.corporatewatch.org.
47. Leonardo Iacovone et al., "Walmart in Mexico: The Impact of FDI on Innovation and Industry Productivity", January 2009, http://spot.colorado.edu.
48. "A Case Analysis of the Wal-Mart De Mexico", http://www.otherpapers.com; Di Gregorio et al., "Competition between Emerging Market and Multinational Firms: Wal-Mart and Mexican Retailers", http://www.allbusiness.com.
49. Nivedita Menon, "Indian Government's Claims About Corporate Retail and the Reality: Shankar Gopalakrishnan", *Kafila*, November 30, 2011, http://kafila.org/2011.
50. C.P. Chandrasekhar, "Experience so Far", *Frontline*, December 17–30, 2011, http://www.frontlineonnet.com.
51. "Indonesia Will Have Zoning to Restrict Big Retail Chains", *India Retailing*, December 28, 2007, http://www.indiaretailing.com; Mohan Guruswamy, Kamal Sharma, *FDI in Retail—II: Inviting More Trouble?* Centre for Policy Alternatives, New Delhi, February 2006, http://cpasindia.org; Anuradha Kalhan, Martin Franz, "Regulation of Retail: Comparative Experience", *Economic and Political Weekly*, August 9, 2009, http://environmentportal.in.
52. T.K. Rajalakshmi, "Sustained Resistance", *Frontline*, December 17–30, 2011, http://www.frontlineonnet.com.
53. Henry Blodget, "Walmart Employs 1% of America. Should It Be Forced to Pay Its Employees More?" *Business Insider*, September 20, 2010, http://articles.businessinsider.com.
54. Dave Jamieson, "Walmart Minimum Wage of $12 Wouldn't Drive Up Prices, Says Study", *Huff Post*, April 19, 2011, http://www.huffingtonpost.com; Rachel Johnson, "California Walmart Workers Win Settlement Over Wage Violations", May 13, 2010, http://www.californiaprogressreport.com.
55. Stephen Lendman, "Global Sweatshop Wage Slavery", February 25, 2010, http://www.thepeoplesvoice.org.
56. Jonathan Turley, "Walmart CEO Makes Average Workers Annual Salary Every Hour", July 3, 2010, http://jonathanturley.org.
57. P. Sainath, "FDI in Retail—UPA 'Retired Hurt'", *The Hindu*, December 12, 2011, http://www.thehindu.com.
58. Devinder Sharma, "FDI in Retail: Whom Are You Kidding, Mr PM?"

November 30, 2011, http://www.rediff.com.

59. Shekhar Swamy, "How FDI in Retail Will Hurt Farmers", *The Hindu Business Line*, December 25, 2011, http://www.thehindubusiness line.com.
60. *Power Hungry: Six Reasons to Regulate Global Food Corporations*, Actionaid International, January 2005, www.actionaid.org.uk.
61. Jayati Ghosh, "Multinational Retail Firms in India", *Macroscan*, December 12, 2011, http://www.macroscan.org.
62. Mohan Guruswamy, Kamal Sharma, *FDI in Retail—II: Inviting More Trouble?* op. cit.
63. *Power Hungry: Six Reasons to Regulate Global Food Corporations*, op. cit.
64. Dipankar Dey, "FDI in India's Retail Trade: Some Additional Issues", *Aspects of India's Economy*, No. 43, Research Unit for Political Economy, July 2007, http://rupe-india.org.
65. *Power Hungry: Six Reasons to Regulate Global Food Corporations*, op. cit.
66. Ibid.
67. Nivedita Menon, "Indian Government's Claims About Corporate Retail and the Reality: Shankar Gopalakrishnan", op. cit.
68. Shekhar Swamy, "How FDI in Retail Will Hurt Farmers", op. cit.
69. Dipankar Dey, "FDI in India's Retail Trade: Some Additional Issues", op. cit.
70. *Power Hungry: Six Reasons to Regulate Global Food Corporations*, op. cit.
71. "States to Adopt News Laws for Contract Farming", *Economic Times*, August 31, 2005, taken from IBEF, http://www.ibef.org. On how the Centre and the World Bank are arm-twisting unwilling state governments, see: Gautam Dheer, "Deadline Draws Near, Punjab Still to Amend APMC Act", *Express India*, March 3, 2008, http://www.expressindia.com.
72. For more discussion on this, see: *India Becoming a Colony Again*, op. cit., pp. 33–38; Neeraj Jain, *Globalisation or Recolonisation?* Lokayat publication, Pune, 2006, available on internet at www.lokayat.org.in.
73. P. Sainath, "FDI in Retail—UPA 'Retired Hurt'", op. cit.
74. "Wal-Mart's Impact on India's Suppliers—No FDI in India", http://www.indiafdiwatch.org; "Criticism of Walmart", *Wikipedia*, sourced on January 28, 2012, http://en.wikipedia.org.
75. *Power Hungry: Six Reasons to Regulate Global Food Corporations*, op. cit.
76. "Boycott Walmart", http://www.1worldcommunication.org.
77. Dipankar Dey, "FDI in India's Retail Trade: Some Additional Issues", op. cit.
78. There are numerous articles on working conditions in Walmart's China

suppliers available on the internet. See for example: David Barboza, "In Chinese Factories, Lost Fingers and Low Pay", *The New York Times*, January 5, 2008, http://www.nytimes.com; Peter S. Goodman and Philip P. Pan, "Chinese Workers Pay for Wal-Mart's Low Prices", op. cit.

79. Nivedita Menon, "Indian Government's Claims About Corporate Retail and the Reality: Shankar Gopalakrishnan", op. cit.
80. C.P. Chandrasekhar, "Experience so Far", op. cit.
81. *Power Hungry: Six Reasons to Regulate Global Food Corporations*, op. cit.
82. Nivedita Menon, "Indian Government's Claims About Corporate Retail and the Reality: Shankar Gopalakrishnan", op. cit.
83. *Power Hungry: Six Reasons to Regulate Global Food Corporations*, op. cit.
84. See Neeraj Jain, *Globalisation or Recolonisation?* op. cit.; also see Essay III of this book.
85. "Balance of Payments: Current Account Deficit Surges to 4.2% of GDP in FY2012", June 30, 2012, http://www.derivatives.capitaline.com; "India's Current Account Deficit Widens", *PTI*, June 29, 2012, http://timesofindia.indiatimes.com; "Mecklai Graph: India's External Debt at USD 345 Bn, Up 13%", September 11, 2012, http://www.moneycontrol.com.

V

COKE–PEPSI: DESTROYING HEALTH, ENVIRONMENT AND LIVELIHOODS

PROLOGUE*

Multinational corporations (MNCs) are entering India in a big way. Ever since 1991, when India's rulers began the globalisation of the Indian economy, successive governments have rolled out the red carpet for them. Laws are being rewritten, controls are being relaxed, regulations are being modified, to remove all obstacles to their operations in India, enable them to make super-profits, and repatriate them back to their home countries.

MNCs are huge. They are so big that they can gobble up entire countries. Walmart—the retailing giant (2011 revenue $446.95 billion)—has a revenue that exceeds the respective GDPs of 174 countries.[1] *Shell is bigger than Pakistan and Bangladesh combined. Ford is bigger than New Zealand. In 2009, of the 100 largest economic entities in the world, 44 were corporations. Their combined revenues were $6.4 trillion, an amount that was larger than the combined economies of 155 countries.*[2]

MNCs are non-transparent, autocratic entities, dedicated to a single purpose—accumulating more and more profits. Since the 1980s, with more and more countries accepting globalisation and allowing MNCs to enter and gradually dominate their economies, they have been able to spread their tentacles throughout the world. They now dominate the global economy. Each and every economic activity, in every conceivable sphere, be it manufacture of automobiles or semiconductors or medicines, or be it retail or transport or IT, or be it banking and finance, or be it pesticide

* *This essay was originally written in 2012. It has been slightly updated for this book.*

manufacture or wheat or rice production, is dominated at the global level by a handful of giant corporations. The same MNC operates in several countries, and along with a handful of other MNCs, dominates global production in that particular sector. To give a few examples: today five MNCs produce nearly half the world's motor vehicles; four companies essentially supply all of the world's recorded music; ten companies dominate the world's pharmaceutical industry; the top ten pesticide firms control 84 percent of the global pesticide market; and so on.[3]

The actual control exerted by MNCs over the world economy is much more than that suggested by the above figures. Three complex systems theorists at the Swiss Federal Institute of Technology in Zurich undertook a study of the linkages between 43,000 multinational corporations in the world. They constructed a model of which corporations controlled the others through shareholding networks, and came up with astounding findings. Their analysis revealed a "core" of 1,318 corporations, each of which had ties with 20 companies on the average. What's more, although these 1,318 represented 20 percent of global operating revenues, through their shares these 1,318 collectively owned the majority of the world's large blue chip and manufacturing firms—the "real" economy—representing a further 60 percent of global revenues. And when the team further untangled the web of ownership, they found that much of the ownership of these 1,318 companies was held by a "super-entity" of just 147 companies![4]

The takeover of the world economy by giant corporations has had calamitous consequences for the mass of humankind. On the one hand, a tiny number of people now control a huge amount of wealth. A recent study by the NGO Oxfam showed that the richest 1 percent in the world had increased their share of global wealth from 44 percent in 2009 to 48 percent in 2014 and at this rate will own more than 50 percent in 2016. Implying that by 2016, 1 percent of the world's population will own more wealth than the other 99 percent! Of the remaining 52 percent of global wealth, 46 percent is owned by the next 19 percent of the world's population. The bottom 80 percent share just 5.5 percent of the global wealth.[5]

Another listing, by the American business magazine Forbes, tracked the wealth of the world's billionaires. In 2014, a total of 1,645 people *made it to the list, and represented a combined wealth of $6.4 trillion, or roughly 8 percent of the global GDP of 2014. Their average worth was $4.7 billion, up from $4.2 billion in 2013.[6] And, on the other hand, the bottom half of the world's population, 3 billion people, are living on less than two dollars (Rs 100) a day, with most of them either chronically malnourished or continually concerned with where their next meal will come from. Over a billion have no access to clean water, 1.5 billion have no electricity and 2.5 billion have no sanitation facilities.[7]*

The MNCs' ruthless quest for profit accumulation is now beginning to threaten the very existence of life on planet Earth. The problem of global warming is rapidly becoming worse, leading to accelerated melting of ice sheets and glaciers, rise in sea levels, and more frequent extreme weather events—like record high temperatures, prolonged and severe droughts, heavy rainfalls and floods and devastating hurricanes. Scientists fear that the crisis may soon become irreversible. Yet, the developed countries led by the USA are simply unwilling to sign any global treaty to control global warming, because it would affect MNC profits.

Such is the nature of these monstrous corporations who are now being allowed an unfettered entry into India. They are moving quickly to take control of each and every sector of the Indian economy—from agriculture to industry to finance to services, and now retail too. Along with their collaborators—India's big business houses, they are seizing control of the country's natural resources—forests, rivers, seas, mineral wealth. The entire economy is being pulverised and remoulded, to squeeze out the maximum possible profits. Even essential services—health, education, transport, electricity—are being taken over by private capital, to be transformed into mere means for profit accumulation. India's rulers have become so myopic in their greed that they are allowing MNCs to exploit even the most fundamental resource of all, necessary for sustaining life: groundwater reserves!

Amongst the most monstrous of the MNCs entering India are the carbonated soft drink giants, Coca-Cola and PepsiCo. They are notorious—for what they make, how they make it, and how they sell it. (It's actually the same with all multinationals.) This essay focuses on the activities of these two corporations, to illustrate the impact the entry of MNCs into India is going to have on our lives.

Introduction

Thanda matlab Coca-Cola... Yeh pyaas hai badi... Through such advertisements featuring the country's most popular film stars and cricketers, Coke and Pepsi have so mesmerised the Indian youth that today thirst has become synonymous with these cold drinks. Even though it's only two decades since these two corporations began operations in India (Coca-Cola was in India earlier too, but had been kicked out in 1977), they already control over 95 percent of the country's soft drink* market. However, their success has nothing to do with the quality of their products; as we see below, their products are nothing but a toxic brew. Their success is, firstly, because of their giant size: they are so big that competition with them is simply not possible; and secondly, because of their huge advertising budgets: they spend hundreds of crores of rupees to influence and control our minds.

Before we take a look at the operations of these corporations in India, let us take a brief look at the cola story globally.

1. The Coke–Pepsi Story

Coca-Cola was invented in 1886 by John Pemberton, a pharmacist. Soda water was very popular in the US in those days. Shopkeepers would add various extracts to the mineral water they sold at their soda fountains so as to please their patrons. Pemberton came up with the idea of mixing the extract of coca leaf—known to be an ideal nerve tonic and stimulant, with the extract of cola nut—another powerful stimulant said to be invigorating and able to cure hangovers, and gave his product the name Coca-Cola. The combination of two powerful stimulants, accompanied by a massive advertising campaign, sent sales zooming. By 1929, Coca-Cola Company dominated the US soft drink market and was among the 125 largest US companies in terms of sales.[8]

* *Non-alcoholic drinks can be classified into fruit drinks and soft drinks. Soft drinks can further be classified into carbonated and non-carbonated drinks.*

Pepsi was invented by Caleb D. Bradham, also a pharmacist and a soda fountain owner. Sometime in the 1890s, he came up with a mixture that he labelled Pepsi-Cola as he felt that the drink could relieve dyspepsia (upset stomach) and the pain of peptic ulcers. The drink initially became quite popular and sales boomed; but then, in the 1920s, disaster struck the Pepsi-Coia Company as a result of fluctuations in the price of sugar following World War I, and it twice went bankrupt. In 1931, the company was finally acquired by Charles Guth. He adopted a new marketing strategy to challenge Coca-Cola. First he changed its composition to make it taste similar to Coke, and then he priced it in such a way that the customer would get the same quantity at half its price. Those were the years of the Great Depression. With Coca-Cola unwilling to lower its high prices because of its monopoly position, Pepsi's pricing strategy clicked with customers and its sales took off. By the end of World War II, Pepsi had gained a toe-hold in the US market. In 1950, it had a 10 percent share in the US carbonated soft drinks market, as compared to 47 percent for Coke. Having become big, it now abandoned its *Twice as much for a nickel* campaign; since then both these giants have not indulged in price wars and have only indulged in advertising wars.[9]

Coca-Cola of course was much bigger. While the people of its home country were busy slugging it out with the Germans in the battlefields of World War II, Coca-Cola was planning ahead...

Coca-Cola During World War II[10]

In 1929, Coca-Cola entered Germany with the subsidiary Coca-Cola GmbH. Germany was soon to become the company's second biggest market. Coca-Cola's success in Germany rested, in part, on its ability to establish itself as a German brand in the minds of consumers. The company sponsored many Nazi events, including the 1936 Olympics, and would situate billboards and advertisements in close proximity to Nazi leaders at rallies and in magazines. The strategy of direct association with Nazi leaders sent a strong message to the German people that Coke was on Germany's side and helped the company towards financial success. By 1939 when the Second World War broke out, Coca-Cola had established itself to such a degree that

Max Keith, the chief of its German operations, was appointed to the 'Office of Enemy Property'. Coca-Cola had clearly become a part of the Nazi state.

This close association with the fascist regime paid off handsomely —sales zoomed from zero cases (crates) in 1929 to four million in 1939. So successful was Coca-Cola in Germany that even when the country was being destroyed in 1944, the company sold two million cases.

While Coke was rubbing shoulders with the Nazis and pretending to be a German company, it also used the opportunity offered by World War II to establish itself as a patriotic morale booster for American soldiers. The president of the company, Robert Woodruff, announced Coca-Cola's wartime policy in 1941 after the bombing of Pearl Harbour: "We will see that every man in uniform gets a bottle of Coca-Cola for five cents wherever he is and whatever it costs." Coca-Cola Company managed to convince the War Department that Coke would boost morale, and the US Government agreed to fund the installation of 64 bottling plants just behind the warfront. The bottling plants were shipped to the front lines and moved as the battlefront moved. Coke literally went to war with the rest of America.

Not one to miss an advertising opportunity, Coca-Cola's wartime advertising in the United States now highlighted its 'contributions' to the war effort. Coke became the patriotic drink! It was an advertising coup. After the war, millions of soldiers came home with a strong attachment to Coke, thus bolstering the company's sales. Its ingenious wartime advertising strategy helped establish Coke as the leading soft drink brand in the US, and helped it become the American icon that it is today.

Unbeknownst to the population in the United States and the American soldiers fighting in Europe, their enemy was enjoying the same beverage in Germany with a similar patriotic zeal. Coke had placed one foot in both the camps; irrespective of who lost the war, Coke was going to win.

Coke–Pepsi Become MNCs

At the end of World War II, the US emerged as the most powerful economic and military power on Earth. A wave of independence struggles was sweeping across the countries of Asia and Africa. To consolidate their independence and allow local industry to develop, the newly independent countries were imposing restrictions on foreign investments by the developed countries (that is, the USA, Western Europe and Japan). Taking advantage of its financial strength, the US doled out grants and loans to these countries to create an opening in their markets for export of goods and capital by its corporations; it even militarily intervened where possible to force their rulers to bend to its wishes. As US President Eisenhower put it: "A serious and explicit purpose of our foreign policy is the encouragement of a hospitable climate for investment in foreign nations."[11] US corporations, including of course Coca-Cola and Pepsi, now began to spread their tentacles worldwide, backed by a string of US military bases spread across the globe.

By the late 1970s, the independent capitalist development models of the Third World countries (that is, the countries of Asia, Africa and Latin America) had started failing, and their rulers started borrowing heavily from the developed countries. The debt rapidly accumulated and soon became unpayable. The US seized the opportunity to pressurise these countries to fully open up their economies to foreign investment—the so-called *globalisation* of the world economy began. This enabled the corporations of the developed countries to expand their international operations and dominate the global market to such an extent that they now started being called multinational corporations (MNCs).[12] Coca-Cola and PepsiCo too became behemoths straddling the entire globe, selling in more than 200 countries.

Like other MNCs, the history of expansion of Coca-Cola Company and PepsiCo worldwide is a history of manipulation, trickery, thuggery and even genocide; profit is all that counts. A few examples:

- Since their basic product is soft drinks, which requires a lot of water, they have been seizing control of and over-exploiting aquifers of local communities, creating water scarcities for the people. Thus, in Mexico, Vicente Fox, during his presidency (2000–06), privatised water resources and handed them over to corporations, depriving people of access to them. Fox—a former president of Coca-Cola Mexico—gave as many as 27 concessions to Coca-Cola! Nineteen of these concessions were for extraction of water from aquifers and from 15 different rivers; and 8 were for the right to dump its industrial waste into public waters![13]

- Coca-Cola has been involved in exploiting and repressing workers all over the world. In Colombia, Coca-Cola has attempted to destroy the workers' union, Sinaltrainal, by hiring armed thugs. These groups work in close collaboration with the US-backed Colombian military and the dictatorial Colombian Government. Several workers have been murdered by these death squads, including the president of the union, Luciano Romero.
- In Turkey, Coca-Cola got the local police to intimidate and torture workers protesting outside its bottling plant against being illegally dismissed.
- In Peru, Coca-Cola refused to implement court orders for reinstatement of 60 workers whom it had illegally dismissed.
- In Chile, workers at its plants work 16 hours a day, and are not even paid the minimum wage.[14]

Today, these two corporations, which basically sell almost the same product despite whatever their advertisements might say, control over 70 percent of the world's carbonated soft drink (CSD) market.[15] (While Coke and Pepsi remain their most valued brands, both companies have diversified their portfolios. The Coca-Cola Company has a portfolio of more than 3,500 beverages, including fruit juices, energy and sports drinks, teas and coffees, and milk- and soy-based beverages. PepsiCo also has a portfolio of hundreds of brands; apart from that, it has expanded into snack and nutrition foods too. Despite this diversification, CSDs still account for a leading 40 percent volume share of the global soft drinks industry.[16]) The total annual revenues of these two corporations exceeded $100 billion last year (2011). Coca-

Cola reported sales of $46.77 billion for the year ending December 2011 while PepsiCo had 2011 sales of $66.50 billion of which 34 percent was from beverages.[17]

Since their profits depend upon making people drink more and more soft drinks, Coca-Cola and Pepsi use every trick in the book to make people drink more, including lacing their drinks with addictives, huge advertising and marketing campaigns, and bribing policy makers. And so the global consumption of CSDs has been rising every year: it has increased at a compound annual growth rate of 2.1 percent over the past five years to top 198 billion litres in 2011; and is forecast to reach 224 billion litres in 2016![18]

The rise has been the steepest in the United States, the home country of Coke and Pepsi, where people have been bombarded by one of the most intense advertising campaigns in the world. Consumption of CSDs in the United States has gone up ten-fold since the 1940s: from only about 21.3 litres per person per year in 1942 to a whopping 212 litres in 1998—which means that every American man, woman and child drank an average of two 300 ml bottles of CSDs made by Coca-Cola and Pepsi every day![19] (Since then, due to rising consciousness about their adverse health impacts, US consumption has steadily declined, but is still the highest in the world.)

Let us first examine the contents of these soft drinks, which have been so successfully marketed by Coca-Cola and Pepsi all over the world that on an average, every person in the world drinks one 300 ml bottle every four days! In the subsequent chapter, we take a look at their marketing techniques, which have made them so successful.

2. CSDs: A Toxic Brew

Coca-Cola and Pepsi have consistently portrayed their products as being positively healthful and life enhancing. According to the chairman and CEO of Coca-Cola:

> Actually, our product is quite healthy. Fluid replenishment is a key to health. . . . Coca-Cola does a great service because it encourages people to take in more and more liquids.[20]

Not only that, these companies also claim that soft drinks contribute positively to a well-balanced diet. A poster that the National Soft Drink Association of the USA provided to teachers stated:

> As refreshing sources of needed liquids and energy, soft drinks represent a positive addition to a well-balanced diet. . . . These same three sugars also occur naturally, for example, in fruits. . . . In your body it makes no difference whether the sugar is from a soft drink or a peach.[21]

The reality is quite the opposite. Consider just the known facts about the contents of Coke–Pepsi drinks* and their effects on us. (*The examples given below are all from the US,* as that is where the effects are most visible, because that is where people have been drinking Coke–Pepsi for decades.)

i) Acids

Acids are added to give 'bite'. Soft drinks contain numerous acids, such as acetic, fumaric, gluconic and phosphoric acids. The combination and strength of these acids is so strong that a plumber can use a soft drink to unclog a severely clogged drain, or if a car battery is corroding one can use a soft drink to dissolve the corrosion.

The stomach maintains a very delicate acid–alkaline balance. Excessive consumption of soft drinks disturbs this balance, thereby creating a constant acid state. This can then cause inflammation of the stomach and erosion of the gastric lining, a condition known as gastronomic distress, which is very painful and disrupts digestion.[22]

The phosphoric acid present in Coke and Pepsi causes the body to waste its much-needed alkaline minerals (sodium, potassium, magnesium and calcium) to neutralise the acid, thus causing problems like weakening of bones, colitis, heart disease, indigestion and anaemia.[23] According to doctors, phosphoric acid, in combination with fructose present in soft drinks, may also block iron absorption into the body.[24]

---

* *Note that when we are talking of Coke–Pepsi drinks, we are referring to all the products made by Coca-Cola and PepsiCo, like Coca-Cola, Mirinda, Fanta, Pepsi, Sprite and 7UP.*

ii) Caffeine

Most soft drinks contain caffeine. A 300 ml bottle of Coke–Pepsi normally has 30–40 mg of caffeine.[25] This is added deliberately, for its physiological effects: caffeine is an addictive drug whose potency increases when it is consumed cold, causing customers to drink more soft drinks.[26]

The amount of caffeine in soft drinks can have distinct physical and behavioural effects: it can cause nervousness, irritability, sleeplessness and rapid heartbeat. Studies show that drinking the caffeine equivalent of two to three bottles of soft drinks per day (100 mg/day) produced physical dependence (addictiveness) in people, causing them to suffer withdrawal symptoms like tiredness and headache when they stopped consumption.[27]

Caffeine's addictiveness is probably one reason why six of the seven most popular soft drinks in the US contain caffeine. An official of the British soft drinks manufacturer Hero Drinks Group has in fact forthrightly admitted that caffeine "is added mainly for its stimulatory effects."

Companies can, but prefer not to, make caffeine-free colas; they account for only about five percent of the volume of colas made by Coca-Cola.[28] In today's world of saturated markets, every means to increase sales goes . . .

Like phosphoric acid, caffeine too causes decalcification of bones. Caffeine increases the excretion of calcium in urine. Drinking one 300 ml bottle of caffeine-containing soft drink causes the loss of about 20 mg of calcium, or two percent of the recommended daily consumption.[29]

Caffeine can also cause maternal fertility problems. The US Food and Drug Administration (FDA) gave a warning way back in 1981 that "pregnant women should avoid caffeine containing foods and drugs, if possible, or consume them only sparingly."[30]

iii) Excessive Sugar

Soft drinks contain an enormous amount of refined sugar, and that too of a particularly harmful variety, high fructose corn syrup.

Each 300 ml bottle of soft drink contains the equivalent of 8–9 teaspoons of sugar[31]—to counter the bitter taste of all the various additives in this brew.

The excessive sugar found in soft drinks also functions like an addictive. To digest it, the small intestine needs a large amount of water, which it draws from other parts of the body. As a result, soon after drinking a soft drink to quench one's thirst, one feels thirsty yet again, and reaches out again for another bottle of soft drink. This, in combination with caffeine, and backed by an intense marketing campaign (discussed later), is what is responsible for the soaring consumption of CSDs worldwide.

Because of the large amount of sugar in soft drinks, the massive consumption of soft drinks worldwide is leading to a myriad of pathologies, most importantly, obesity and obesity-related diseases, especially diabetes and heart disease.

The Obesity 'Epidemic'

The US is in the grip of an "epidemic" of obesity, according to the US Surgeon General.[32] Today, two out of three adults (69 percent) in the US are overweight, and one in three (36 percent) is obese.* Obesity has become the number-one health problem in the United States, according to Dr. Julie Gerberding, director of the Centers for Disease Control and Prevention (CDC), a component of the Department of Health of the United States Government.[33] It has become an even bigger threat to people's health than tobacco! Over the period 1993–2008, while the proportion of smokers among American adults fell by one-fifth, obesity rates nearly doubled. With the incidence of smoking declining and that of obesity rising, a recent study conducted by researchers from Columbia University and the City College of New York (USA) found that obesity is causing as much, if not more, disease than smoking.[34]

---

* *Overweight and obesity are defined in terms of Body Mass Index (BMI), defined as a person's weight in kilograms divided by the square of his height in metres (kg/m^2). According to the WHO, a person with BMI greater than or equal to 25 is overweight, and with BMI greater than or equal to 30 is obese.*

This obesity epidemic is directly related to the rising consumption of soft drinks (and also consumption of fast food, like hamburgers and doughnuts) in the United States. A can (355 ml) of soft drinks provides about 150 calories, and the average American drinks nearly 2 cans of soft drinks a day. A study by doctors at Brigham and Women's Hospital in Boston (USA), an affiliate of Harvard Medical School, found that women who had increased their soft drink consumption over a four-year period from one or fewer drinks per week to one or more per day gained an average of about 4.5 kilograms. The *Nurses' Health Study*, which tracked the health of nearly 90,000 women over a eight-year period, was published on August 25, 2004 in the *Journal of the American Medical Association*.[35] Another 20-year study on 120,000 men and women found that people who increased their sugary drink consumption by one 12-ounce (355 ml) serving per day gained more weight over time—on average, an extra pound (0.45 kg) every four years—than people who did not change their intake.[36]

And So, the Diabetic 'Epidemic'

It's common medical sense that obesity is a primary risk factor for diabetes. And so, predictably, the *Nurses' Health Study* also found that women who consumed one or more servings of soft drinks daily (a figure which is less than the US national average), had nearly twice the risk of developing type 2 diabetes as compared to women who drank less than one serving per month.[37] Numerous other studies, including one presented recently at a meeting of the American Heart Association in March 2010, have also confirmed these findings.[38]

And so the obesity 'epidemic' has spawned a diabetes 'epidemic'. In 2010, 25.8 million Americans had diabetes—8.3 percent of the US population; another 79 million American adults had pre-diabetes, a condition in which a person's blood glucose levels are higher than normal, but not high enough for diagnosis as diabetes. Together, this means that more than one-third of the American population has either diabetes or pre-diabetes![39] The CDC predicts that 45 to 50 million Americans could have diabetes by 2050. It has warned that if current trends continue, one in three Americans born in 2000 will develop diabetes during their lifetime.[40]

With soft drink consumption booming world wide, the obesity–diabetic epidemic is not confined to the United States; it has crossed over to Europe, and has penetrated even the poorest countries, especially in urban areas. The World Health Organisation (WHO) says that an escalating global epidemic of overweight and obesity—"globesity"—is taking over many parts of the world. In 2008, nearly 35 percent of the world adult population was overweight or obese. The number of obese people in the world had doubled over the period 1980–2008; and by 2008, nearly half a billion adults were obese worldwide.[41]

The globesity epidemic is leading to a global type 2 diabetes epidemic: according to a study by an international team of researchers published in the *Lancet*, the number of adults with diabetes worldwide has more than doubled between 1980 and 2008, to 347 million—meaning that nearly 10 percent of all adult men and women worldwide were diabetic in 2008![42]

Stroke, Vascular and Other Diseases

Apart from diabetes, consumption of soft drinks also increases the risk of heart disease, stroke, cancer and other diseases, and causes severe social and psychological problems.

Middle-aged adults who drink more than one soft drink daily, either diet or regular, have a nearly 50 percent greater rate of developing metabolic syndrome, according to data released by the *Framingham Heart Study*, a project of the National Heart, Lung and Blood Institute, USA. Metabolic syndrome is a constellation of conditions—high blood pressure, high insulin levels, excess weight (especially around the abdomen), high levels of triglycerides and low levels of HDL (good) cholesterol—that increase the risk of heart disease.[43]

Another study carried out by researchers at the Cleveland Clinic's Wellness Institute and published in the *American Journal of Clinical Nutrition* examined the effects of CSDs on brain stroke risk. The study concluded that the excessive sugar in sodas caused blood glucose and insulin levels to spike, which over time may lead to glucose intolerance, insulin resistance and inflammation. These physiological changes influence atherosclerosis, plaque stability and thrombosis—

all of which are risk factors for ischemic stroke (brain stroke which occurs when artery to the brain is blocked).[44]

There is also convincing evidence that regular consumption of soft drinks induces the production of uric acid and leads to high levels of blood uric acid, causing gout. (Gout is a form of inflammatory arthritis.) People consuming a can of sugar-sweetened beverages a day had 50 percent, and even as much as 75 percent, higher risk of gout as compared to people who rarely had such drinks.[45]

The Sugar in Colas: More Toxic

The high fructose corn syrup present in colas is made from corn through a complicated chemical and enzymatic process, and contains 55 percent fructose and 45 percent glucose. It is used extensively as a sweetener in making soft drinks and processed foods, as it is cheaper than sugar, has a longer shelf life, and mixes very easily with other ingredients. However, this form of sugar is more dangerous for the body than ordinary sugar. While every cell in the body can metabolise glucose, the fructose in high fructose corn syrup can only be metabolised in the liver. Excessive consumption of high fructose corn syrup containing soft drinks therefore overworks the liver, damaging it. It causes a condition known as scarring of the liver, which can ultimately lead to cirrhosis and liver failure.[46]

Children: Worst Victims of Obesity–Diabetic Epidemic

Habits about eating and drinking formed during childhood often continue into adulthood. So Coke–Pepsi especially target children in their advertising and marketing campaigns. Their efforts have borne fruit. Almost half of all children in the United States between the ages of 6 and 11 drink CSDs, with the average drinker consuming one and a half bottles per day. Teenagers are the most avid consumers of all, with teenage consumption in the USA tripling over the period 1977–78 and 1999–2002. By 1999–2002, the average 13- to 18-year-old teenager was consuming the equivalent of two bottles (of 300 ml) of CSDs a day! And since not every teenager consumes CSDs, if we exclude the non-consumers, the daily beverage consumption for all 13- to 18-year olds in the US was an astounding 2.7 bottles (830 ml to be more precise) a day!

What is even more unbelievable: one-fifth of one- and two-year-old children consumed soft drinks. These toddlers were drinking an average of 200 ml—one cup—per day (in the mid-1990s)![47]

Nutrition experts recommend that most of the body's daily calorie needs should be met by eating carbohydrate containing foods like vegetables, fruits and whole grains, which also provide useful nutrients to the body, and that foods containing added sugars should be avoided. Added sugar is the sugar added to processed food and drinks while they are being made, as well as sugar added while cooking food at home. (It does not include naturally occurring sugars, such as those in milk and fruits.) This added sugar provides only 'empty' calories to the body; it contains no essential nutrients like proteins, vitamins and minerals, and is added solely for its taste.

According to the American Heart Association and other bodies, children aged 13 and below and adolescent girls (who are not active) should not consume more than 80 calories and 20 grams of added sugar per day; for adolescent boys, the recommended limit is 133 calories and 33 grams of sugar.[48] One 300 ml serving of CSD contains around 135 calories and 35 grams of added sugar, much more than the recommended amount of sugar that most children should consume in an entire day. But almost half of all US children consume one and a half bottles of soft drinks every day! US teenagers consume even more, nearly three bottles of CSDs every day.[49] On top of it, children do not only consume soft drinks. They also consume fruit drinks, chocolates, cookies, cakes, ice creams and other such foods, all containing added sugar, every day!

And so it is no surprise that children are the worst victims of the obesity–diabetic epidemic. Childhood obesity has tripled in the USA over the past three decades. In 2008, nearly one of every three (32%) children between the age of 6–19 was overweight, while one in six (17%) was obese.[50]

For children, obesity is a bigger tragedy for many reasons. Obese children and teenagers often suffer from psycho-social problems due to prejudice, discrimination and taunts from other children. This leads to low self esteem, preventing them from living up to their full potential. More than two-thirds of obese children and teenagers have at least one cardiovascular risk factor (e.g., hypertension, high cholesterol, etc.), and 39 percent have two or more risk factors.[51]

A recent study by the University of Sydney came to more alarming conclusions. It found that children who drank one or more soft drinks every day had narrower arteries in the back portion of their eye—a factor linked to higher risk of heart disease and high blood pressure.[52]

Even more worrying is that obese children are increasingly being diagnosed with type 2 diabetes. Earlier, type 2 diabetes was practically unheard of in young people under 30, hence its other name—adult-onset diabetes (almost all children with diabetes used to suffer from type 1 diabetes). But type 2 diabetes isn't just for adults anymore! The number of children with this condition has skyrocketed within the last 20 years. When these children grow up, they'll face complications such as amputations, blindness, heart attacks and kidney failure.[53]

Other conditions linked to childhood obesity include asthma, fatty liver disease and sleep apnea.[54]

Decalcification in Children

Bone development mainly depends upon how much bone mass is built up in early life, especially up to the age of 18. Calcium (together with Vitamin D) plays an important role in building up bone density during childhood. Today, numerous studies have established that drinking carbonated soft drinks leads to bone weakening, as the acids and caffeine in soft drinks leach out calcium from the bones, which then passes out of the body through urine. And children are the most avid drinkers of these calcium-leaching soft drinks! On top of it, children who drink too many soft drinks tend to drink less milk and so have a lower calcium intake.

The loss of calcium, combined with children drinking soft drinks instead of milk, is leading to weaker bones. Studies show that children who drink soft drinks are 3–5 times more likely to break a bone as compared to those who avoided CSDs. This also makes children more susceptible to osteoporosis (a disease in which bones become porous and hence more prone to fractures) in later life. For girls, this is even more damaging as they are more prone to osteoporosis in later life.

In 2002, the US National Osteoporosis Foundation estimated that 10 million Americans had osteoporosis. Another 34 million had low bone mass and were at increased risk for the disease. That's a total of nearly 15 percent of the population at risk for osteoporosis! Obviously, this huge number is directly related to booming CSD consumption.[55]

Economic Costs of Obesity–Diabetic Epidemic

According to the US Surgeon General, obesity-related diseases account for more than 300,000 deaths every year; one out of every eight deaths in America is caused by an illness directly related to overweight and obesity.[56] By one estimate, the US spent $190 billion on obesity-related health care expenses in 2005.[57]

Impact on Teeth

Soft drinks have emerged as one of the most significant dietary sources of tooth decay, affecting people of all ages, more specifically children.

The white visible section of the teeth is called the tooth enamel. It's made up of minerals, especially calcium and phosphate. There are naturally occurring bacteria in everyone's mouths. When these bacteria come in contact with sugar, acid is produced. This acid, in combination with the extra acid in the soft drinks, dissolves some of the tooth's strengthening minerals (calcium and phosphate) from the tooth surface. Each time one sips a cold drink, the acid attack lasts for around 20 minutes.

Saliva is the body's natural defence against tooth demineralisation. It helps wash sugars from the mouth and contains bicarbonate that helps neutralise the acid production. Saliva additionally contains calcium and phosphate, and so it also remineralises the surface of the damaged teeth. But if 'acid attacks' occur too often, as when soft drinks are sipped throughout the day (as is often the case with teenagers), the saliva won't have enough time to repair the damage done, and a cavity will eventually develop in the tooth.[58]

iv) Other Additives

A commonly used preservative in soft drinks is sodium benzoate. In acidic solutions (like colas), sodium benzoate can break down into benzene, a known carcinogen. Levels in soft drinks can be up to 40 times higher than recognised 'safe' doses.[59]

The characteristic dark brown colour of brown carbonated drinks like Coke and Pepsi comes from caramel colouring. There are four types of caramel colourings. The caramel colouring used in colas is sulphite ammonia caramel (E150d). The making of this caramel colour involves a chemical process that adds a chemical, 4-methylimidazole or 4-MEI, to the caramel. Studies show this chemical to cause cancer in laboratory animals; and the US State of California recently added 4-MEI to its list of chemicals known to cause cancer. Tests show that colas contain 4-MEI in quantities several times higher than the safe limit set by California State. In 2011, the Center for Science in the Public Interest* petitioned the US FDA to ban this kind of caramel colouring.[60]

v) And in India, Pesticides too!

As if all this was not terrible enough, tests carried out by the Centre for Science and Environment (CSE), a public interest advocacy group based in New Delhi, of 12 leading soft drinks produced and marketed in India by Coca-Cola Company and PepsiCo, showed that all samples contained high levels of pesticides and insecticides. The levels were high enough to cause cancer, damage to the nervous and reproductive systems, birth defects and severe disruption of the immune system. CSE also tested two soft drink brands sold in the US, to see if they contained pesticides. They didn't![61]

vi) Diet Sodas: More Poisonous

Diet sodas are advertised by Coca-Cola and PepsiCo as the healthy, sugar-free alternative to Coke and Pepsi, and their sales have zoomed worldwide. Diet Coke is now the second most consumed carbonated beverage in the world, with annual sales topping $1 billion.

---

* *An independent, non-profit, US-based health advocacy organisation.*

The most important health benefit claimed for diet sodas is that they are low-calorie and so do not damage the heart. However, numerous studies have shown that this is just another lie propagated by these corporations. The reality is that diet sodas too lead to weight gain and therefore heart disease risk. One such study presented at a meeting of the American Diabetes Association in June 2011 showed that diet soda drinkers had waist circumference increases of 70 percent greater than non-diet soda drinkers. And those that consumed two or more diet sodas a day experienced waist size increases that were a shocking six times greater than those who did not drink diet soda. This is probably because the sweetness of artificial sweeteners in diet sodas confuses our body, provoking it to release insulin and other hormones that control blood glucose, disturbing the hormone balance and leading to weight gain.[62]

The internationally renowned *Framingham Heart Study* mentioned earlier also came to the same conclusion. It found that people who drank more than one can of diet soda daily had a 48 percent greater rate of either having or developing metabolic syndrome, which increases heart disease risk; the risk was the same as for those who consumed regular soda![63] Two other studies, one led by Adam Bernstein, research director at the Cleveland Clinic's Wellness Institute and published in the *American Journal of Clinical Nutrition*, and another led by Hannah Gardener of the Columbia University Medical Center, USA and published in the *Journal of General Internal Medicine*, that examined the relationship between regular consumption of diet soda and the risk of stroke also found that diet soda increases the risk of heart attack. Both found that adults who drank diet soda daily had a 43 percent increased risk of heart attack or stroke compared to those who never drank diet soda.[64]

That is not the end of bad news for Diet Coke–Pepsi drinkers. Not only do diet sodas contain tooth and bone destroying acids, psycho-addictive caffeine and cancer causing sodium benzoate like in regular sodas, additionally, they also contain the extremely toxic artificial sweetener, aspartame.[65]

Aspartame is probably one of the most controversial food additives in history. Both the US FDA and the CDC have admitted to a long list of adverse effects associated with ingestion of aspartame. The list includes numerous symptoms connected to impaired neurological function, including: headache, aggressive behaviour, disorientation, hyperactivity, extreme numbness, excitability, memory loss, loss of depth perception, liver impairment, cardiac arrest, seizures, suicidal tendencies, severe mood swings, muscle weakness, abdominal pains and cramps, vision deterioration, skin rashes and joint and musculoskeletal pain. Furthermore, according to researchers and physicians studying the adverse effects of aspartame, the following chronic illnesses can be triggered or worsened by ingestion of aspartame: brain tumours, multiple sclerosis, epilepsy, chronic fatigue syndrome, Parkinson's disease, Alzheimer's disease, mental retardation, lymphoma, fibromyalgia and diabetes. The most recent evidence shows that aspartame ingested at half the levels that are currently found in soft drinks raises the risk of otherwise rare brain tumours known as lymphomas.[66]

Compelling evidence presented by numerous eminent scientists and consumer groups with regard to aspartame's toxicity forced the US FDA to initially deny approval to aspartame. The ban continued for eight years. Eventually, however, corporate muscle and political skulduggery won out over scientific rigour, and aspartame was approved for use in 1981. The FDA's about-turn opened the floodgates for aspartame's swift approval by more than 70 regulatory authorities around the world. (See the appendix for this story.)

3. Deception Unlimited

Even though soft drinks have been around for over a hundred years, it is only in the last two decades or so that researchers have started studying their effects on human health. Their startling findings summarised in this essay, that the soft drinks made by Coca-Cola and PepsiCo are toxic brews, will appear to most readers to be far-fetched: because people have got used to seeing soft drink advertisements umpteen times daily; because Coke and Pepsi have become ubiquitous—they are available everywhere, from the corner paan-shop to shopping malls to cinema halls and even hospital canteens (and many of them keep no other drink); because people see everyone around them consuming Coke–Pepsi drinks many times a day to quench thirst . . .

Most readers would also be thinking: 'Coke–Pepsi are MNCs. Their drinks are consumed by millions of people the world over. Surely, if they are so toxic, there would have been an uproar against them.'

To draw a parallel, it has been the same with tobacco. It was 60 years ago (1962) that the harmful effects of tobacco were authoritatively established in a report by the Royal College of Physicians (UK); it was way back in 1964 that the US Surgeon General announced that smoking causes lung cancer; but it has taken decades of struggle by anti-tobacco activists to force governments to act to discourage smoking, and even today tobacco advertising is only partially banned in most countries. Despite all the evidence, many smokers still refuse to believe that smoking is harmful to health. Presently there are about 1.1 billion smokers in the world, despite the fact that lung cancer is the most common form of cancer worldwide and 5 million smokers die due to tobacco-related illnesses every year. Till the late 1990s, the cigarette industry continued to deny that smoking was injurious to health, and to this day continues to deny that nicotine is addictive.

Most of us are ignorant of the reality of the world we live in. Most of us are unaware of the power wielded by giant multinational corporations (MNCs) over our daily lives. In today's globalised world, MNCs dominate the global economy and are able to influence policymakers to such an extent that no government dares to take action against them for their environmental–social–economic–health crimes. Neither are these crimes reported in the media, because this too is dominated by MNCs. On the contrary, MNCs have transformed all the means of education, information and entertainment—the global television, newspaper, music, film and publishing industry—into means for their propaganda, and through that, they are able to influence and even determine what we read, think and see; they also control our dreams, desires and tastes, and even what we eat and drink.

An important objective of the MNC-controlled global propaganda machinery is to transform human beings from thinking beings into consuming pigs. The principal means by which MNCs do this is through advertising and marketing—MNCs earn such huge super-profits that they are able to spend billions of dollars on this. They hire the brightest minds and pay them fat salaries, and the sole job of these 'intellectual merenaries' is to use their intellect, skills and creativity to manipulate our minds and convince us to consume more and more and more . . .

Hyper-Consumerism

In 1877, Chief Sitting Bull of the Lakota nation* said of the European invaders who were destroying his people and their way of life,

> The love of possession is a disease with them.[67]

Disease is an apt term, because the desire to possess more and more is not inherent to the nature of human beings; it is acquired. The Native American chief was able to perfectly identify the disease, because he came from a different culture. Prominent US historians have written of Native Americans:

> They are all equal. . . . Neither is richer or poorer than his companion and all unanimously limit their desires to that which is useful and precisely necessary, and are contemptuous of all other things, superfluous things, as not being worthy to be possessed . . .[68]

Despite what neoclassical economists may tell us, people do not have an inherent, insatiable desire to acquire more and more goods, to consume without end. Anthropologists studying 'primitive' societies have found very different human relations and human nature than the highly competitive, dog-eat-dog, selfish characteristics that have dominated during the modern, capitalist period. People lived in cooperation with each other in egalitarian societies. There were no bosses or rulers. There was no obsession with private property. Behaviour was characterised by generosity rather than selfishness.[69]

---

* *The Lakota people are an indigenous people of the Great Plains of North America.*

The desire to possess and consume limitlessly has been artificially created, it is a product of capitalism. Ever since capitalism came into being 500 years ago, cooperation and sharing inherent among human beings has been downplayed, while aggressive competitiveness, greed and individualism have been promoted so as to create the conditions for the growth of a system whose central feature is accumulation, accumulation and even more accumulation of profits. And along with this, a culture of consumerism has also been promoted: because only when goods are sold can profits be made.

In today's world of monopoly capitalism, this has taken on a newer form, hyper-consumerism—to purchase–possess–consume more and more, without any relation to basic human needs or happiness. Buy, buy and buy, so that MNCs can make more, more and more profits . . . This is intrinsically related to the deepening economic crisis in the developed countries. Since the 1970s, their economies have been continuously slowing down. With their markets becoming more and more saturated, the giant MNCs that dominate the economies of these countries have been resorting to all kinds of sales gimmicks in a desperate attempt to boost sales.

The most visible part of this sales effort is of course advertising. But in reality, advertising is only one part of a huge marketing exercise which also involves things like: making minor changes in product's appearance, extravagant packaging, making goods fragile (planned obsolescence), frequent model changes, introducing new fashions, targeting, psychological research of consumer behaviour, etc. The aim of this entire sales effort is to manipulate people's desires to push products and rake in profits.

Over the years, advertising and marketing have become indispensable for large corporations—they have, so to say, become a part of the bone marrow of corporate capitalism. Corporations have been pouring in fantastic amounts of resources in an attempt to ensnare people into the 'consumer trap'. Big businesses in the United States now spend well over two trillion dollars a year on marketing![70] Corporations have set up huge research apparatuses, staffed by psychologists and cultural anthropologists, to determine ever newer ways of manipulating peoples' feelings, thoughts and behaviours so as to get them to buy more and more products. There are no moral or ethical limits to be observed. Modern marketing is clearly the greatest concerted attempt at psychological manipulation in all of human history.

Even children are not spared. Not long ago, children were considered vulnerable beings, to be caringly nurtured. However, today's corporation-dominated world increasingly sees kids through an economic lens. Children are now viewed as an economic resource to be exploited, just like bauxite or timber.

Once the race began to target children, it has become unstoppable. Corporations are increasingly targeting younger and younger children, in an attempt to imprint their brand names on their vulnerable minds. Children are easy to take advantage of, because they tend to trust adults. Most children don't grasp the motives behind advertising; they are unable to see it as propaganda. Even the US Federal Trade Commission concluded in 1978 that most children "view commercials simply as a form of 'informational programming'"![71]

Aggressive Marketing Strategies of Coke–Pepsi

Amongst the most aggressive marketeers in the world are the soft drink giants, Coca-Cola Company and PepsiCo. These two corporations make their billions by capitalising on the most basic human physiological need—thirst. Coca-Cola, in its 1993 *Annual Report*, stated:

> All of us in the Coca-Cola family wake up each morning knowing that every single one of the world's 5.6 billion people will get thirsty that day. If we make it impossible for these 5.6 billion people to escape Coca-Cola, then we assure our future success for many years to come.[72]

These two corporations spend over $5 billion (over Rs 25,000 crore) annually on advertising their products, which of course more than pays itself off in increased sales and profits.[73] Coca-Cola Company, ranked as the seventh largest advertiser in the world,[74] spent $2.9 billion on print, radio, television and other advertisements in 2010, thanks to which it sold $35 billion worth of beverages worldwide and its net profits rose a whopping 73 percent to top $11.8 billion that year.[75]

Apart from media advertising, soft drink companies also spend billions of dollars on a myriad of marketing techniques to promote their products, such as corporate social responsibility (CSR) campaigns, sponsorship of concerts, giving away freebies and giving grants to public organisations.

Through their CSR campaigns, the two soft drink corporates are attempting to portray themselves as ethical organisations by associating themselves with good causes. Thus, PepsiCo has launched the Refresh Project in the United States and several other countries around the world. The campaign awards a total of $20 million in grants annually (this figure is for the US alone) to projects that have a positive impact on the community or the country. Anyone can submit an idea for a project online; people are then invited to cast votes on the campaign website, or via Facebook or Twitter, or by SMSes; and the projects receiving the highest votes are funded by the company.

Similarly, to counter the growing campaign by health activists that soft drinks are responsible for the 'obesity epidemic', the two companies are trying to project themselves as 'health friendly corporations' by associating themselves with campaigns and activities promoting healthy lifestyles. One marketing coup for PepsiCo has been becoming a commercial partner since 2009 with the UK National Health Service's *Change4Life* campaign. The campaign is the UK Government's response to obesity and promotes physical activity and healthy eating. As a part of this, Pepsi has been sponsoring ads that use famous soccer players to encourage parents to help their children "have an active lifestyle". Similarly, Coca-Cola has launched a *Live Positively* campaign, wherein it undertakes educational campaigns urging people to live healthy lifestyles, and funds construction or improvement of school playgrounds and public recreation facilities. The aim of such campaigns is to propagate the view that it is not drinking soft drinks, but unhealthy lifestyles that are responsible for the huge rise in obesity.[76]

Similarly, both corporations have been investing heavily to sponsor high profile sports events. Coca-Cola has been sponsoring the football

World Cup since 1978; it has also sponsored the Olympics, the cricket World Cup and other sports competitions. Pepsi is the official partner to Football Association, the governing body of English football; it is also the sponsor of the biggest sports event and the most watched television programme in the USA, the Super Bowl (an annual American football championship).[77]

Marketing Coke–Pepsi to Children

And like other corporations, Coca-Cola and Pepsi too make children a prime target of their indoctrination campaigns. In 1999, Dawn Hudson, Pepsi's chief of marketing, told the *New York Times* that marketing to 8- to 12-year-olds was a priority.[78] Matt Nussbaum, Coca-Cola's youth market representative in Cleveland, Ohio, explains why: "We know... students will continue to drink Coca-Cola products for 50 to 60 years.... We're trying to gain their business for the future."[79]

Beverage and fast food corporations spend billions of dollars on insinuating themselves into every aspect of children's lives. According to one estimate (for the US), these corporations spend over $1 billion per year on advertising directed at children, mostly on television; over $4.5 billion on youth-targeted promotions such as premiums, sampling, coupons, contests and sweepstakes; about $2 billion on youth-targeted public relations, such as broadcast and print publicity, event marketing, and school relations; and an additional roughly $3 billion annually on packaging especially designed for children.[80]

Let us take a look at some of the despicable techniques used by these corporations to hook children on to soft drinks in the capital of the globalised world, the United States.

i) Through the Media

Television literally is an obesity machine, not just because it makes children couch potatoes, but also because of what it shows. The average American child watches around 20 hours of TV programs every week and so around 40,000 TV ads every year.[81] Realising the power of TV marketing in reaching out to children, junk soft drink and food companies have been advertising heavily on TV. Food (including soft drinks) advertising in the developed countries now accounts for around half of all advertising broadcast during children's TV viewing times: three quarters of such ads promote high calorie and low nutrient foods.[82]

Advertisers continuously search for newer and newer ways to paste their products on the minds of children. A popular technique is to pay pop stars, sports-persons and film stars to promote their products. Of late, even recorded music is being used: late in 2002, PepsiCo and Sony Music signed a deal wherein both will promote each other. They have also tied up with popular children's movies. In 2001, Coca-Cola paid Warner Brothers $150 million for exclusive global marketing rights for the film *Harry Potter and the Sorcerer's Stone*;[83] Pepsi, not to be outdone, signed a $100 million contract with Walt Disney to market its film *Monsters Inc.*[84] Another technique used is called product placement, wherein the product is so woven into the story that the viewer would have to view it. Coca-Cola, for example, paid $25 million to AOL Time Warner so that, among other things, characters in the popular TV children's serial *Young American* would gulp down Cokes in each episode.[85] It also paid $26 million so that judges in the popular TV talent show *American Idol* sit behind large red cups emblazoned with the Coca-Cola logo; and contestants wait their turn in the Coca-Cola room, perched on a Coca-Cola sofa.[86] PepsiCo shelled out $60 million to sponsor the equally successful TV music competition *X Factor*.[87]

With children spending an increasing number of hours every day on the internet, marketeers are reaching out to children online too. The most common marketing technique is to set up websites which provide entertainment (games, music, puzzles, etc.) or educative information to children. One of the most popular of these websites is Coca-Cola Company's website, *MyCokeRewards.com*, which averages more than 170,000 unique young visitors per month.[88]

A new company called ZapMe! has extended this strategy to computers. ZapMe! offers free equipment to schools—computers and internet browsers. In return, it advertises to kids, plus it gets a market research gold mine. The company snoops on school children as they browse the internet, and then "breaks down the data by age, sex and zip code. It then sells this information to advertisers and marketeers, who use it to target students in school with laser-like precision" (to quote Associated Press, the news agency).[89]

Marketeers want to engulf children's minds from all angles, like the tentacles of an octopus. Thus, toys have become marketing tools: there are Coke toys such as checker sets and cars that are designed to introduce kids as young as four to the Coca-Cola brand.[90] Coke and Pepsi pop up even when children read! Junk foods now feature so extensively in children's books that Kate Klimo, vice president and publisher of Random House Books for Young Readers, says: "It's not that these books resemble advertising—they are advertising."[91]

The race to 'catch them young' has reached its limits: soft drink companies are now encouraging feeding soft drinks to babies too, by licensing their logos to makers of infant-feeding bottles![92]

ii) Marketeers Go to Schools

Marketeers have even invaded sanctums that were previously off-limits, such as schools.

Cutting government funding to schools is not taking place just in Third World countries like India, it is taking place in the world's richest countries too. And so, to raise funds, schools are allowing soft drink companies (and fast food companies) to sell their toxic products in schools, in return for donations. More than one-third of elementary schools, half of middle/junior high schools and almost three-fourths of senior high schools in the USA have signed such contracts. Incredibly, nearly half of these contracts include financial incentives for schools to sell more Coke or Pepsi. Teachers are even asked to promote soft drink consumption in classrooms to meet sales targets. Schools have become soda pushers!

The contracts can be highly lucrative. For example, a beverage contract with one US school district (a special district in the USA that operates local public primary and secondary schools) has the potential to generate up to $1.5 million per year.

The contracts also allow soft drink companies to advertise in schools. And so, schools and school facilities have become advertising boards. Ads have become omnipresent: on school buildings, school corridors, sports facilities, playing grounds, noticeboards, scoreboards, book covers, student assignment books, school buses, etc.[93]

Marketeers will stoop to any level to sell their products. Thus, the Channel One television news program has tied up with over 12,000 schools in the US to show ten minutes of TV "news" and two minutes of ads every day to a captive audience of over 8 million children. Schools receive free video equipment in exchange for mandatory showing of the program in classrooms. While promoted as "education", the real appeal is to advertisers. Around 70 percent of the commercials shown are for food products, mainly fast food and soft drinks. The junk drink companies are now able to bombard children with their advertisements every day, as knowledge! The atmosphere of the school is an advertiser's dream, says Joel Babbit, former president of Channel One: "The advertiser gets a group of kids who cannot go to the bathroom, who cannot change the station, who cannot listen to their mother yell in the background." Because of such guaranteed effectivity, Channel One charges exorbitant rates for ads. A thirty second TV spot can cost up to two lakh dollars.[94]

4. Why Don't Governments Intervene?

Way back in 1864, referring to the increasing interference of corporations in the political life of the USA, President Abraham Lincoln wrote,

> I see in the near future a crisis approaching that unnerves me and causes me to tremble for the safety of my country. . . . Corporations have been enthroned and an era of high corruption will follow, and the money power of the country will endeavour to prolong its reign by working upon the prejudices of the people until all wealth is aggregated in a few hands and the Republic is destroyed.[95]

Since then, the power of the corporations has multiplied to reach such astronomical heights that they dominate not just the economies of their home countries, but the world economy too.

Because of their enormous financial muscle, it is easy for giant corporations like Coca-Cola Company and PepsiCo to manipulate, distort and suppress scientific research on the toxicity of their products. And if at all some independent scientists and public spirited bodies do defy their power and come up with damning evidence of their crimes, they are powerful enough to influence policy makers and prevent governments from taking action. A few examples:[96]

- **Corrupting Science:** Corporations suppress research, intimidate scientists, set up fake scientific bodies, ghost-write scientific articles, and selectively publish results that suit their interests.
  - Thus, Coca-Cola in March 2004 created a research institute, Beverage Institute for Health and Wellness. This is clearly for public relations, the goal being to convince people that Coca-Cola cares about health issues. On the side, the institute will also aim at downplaying the health risks associated with consuming soft drinks. Many professors of reputed universities are on the advisory council of this research institute.[97]
  - Coca-Cola is also one of the corporate sponsors of the Center for Consumer Freedom, a supposedly non-profit body that campaigns against dietary guidelines recommended by the FDA and other government agencies and medical associations. The Center has also received funding from Monsanto, Philip Morris, Cargill and many other such corporations.[98]
- **Restricting Effectiveness of Regulatory Authorities and Public Bodies:** Companies use their enormous financial muscle to corrupt regulatory bodies, science associations and public spirited organisations, as well as to unashamedly exploit the 'revolving door' between corporate and government employment.
  - Many Coca-Cola executives occupy senior positions (like being a member of the Board of Governors) of numerous US universities.[99] This has helped Coca-Cola sabotage calls for banning soft drinks on campuses.
  - In 2003, the American Academy of Pediatric Dentistry received a $1 million donation from Coca-Cola. The Academy President David Curtis now went on record to state,

"Scientific evidence is certainly not clear on the exact role that soft drinks play in terms of children's oral disease." Before the gift, the Academy had noted the link between soft drinks and tooth decay.[100]

- The WHO, the public health arm of the UN which fights chronic ailments such as diabetes and heart disease, in 2012 accepted a £35,000 donation from Coca-Cola. It has also accepted donations of thousands of dollars from other fast food companies like Nestle and Unilever. These corporations now advise WHO on how to fight obesity![101]
- In 2003, Coca-Cola became a sponsor of the venerable National Parents and Teachers Association (PTA), which for more than a century has promoted the health of children in the USA. Coca-Cola's Senior Vice President for Public Affairs John Downs Jr. even had a seat on the PTA as a Board member for some time![102]

➢ **Influencing Congress:** By spending billions of dollars on lobbying and campaign contributions, corporations influence members of Congress, getting them to delay or scuttle action against their crimes.

- Coca-Cola and Pepsi spend millions of dollars every year on lobbying politicians in state capitals and Washington. Both of them, together with the American Beverage Association, spent around $70 million on lobbying in 2011 to scuttle proposals to impose taxes on soft drinks to counter the obesity epidemic. The bribes had an effect. Attempts to levy such taxes have failed in 30 US states.[103]
- Coke–Pepsi have given millions of dollars in contributions to the campaign coffers of Congressmen of both the Republican and Democratic parties. They have also given generous sums to the candidates of both these parties for the American presidential elections.[104] With such bribes, is it any surprise that when the WHO released a draft report in 2003 suggesting that the consumption of soft drinks are a major cause of obesity in the West, the White House immediately objected, saying that there was not enough evidence to link

the two, and demanded that the offending words be "deleted or significantly revised"![105]

In reality, corporations have become so powerful that Lincoln's worst fears have come true. They now actually control the levers of power in the United States (and other countries too). This is most evident from the way the US presidential elections are now funded. By the time the present round of elections concludes in November 2012, the two main candidates will have together splurged about $2.5 billion. Throw in spending by the two parties, spending on the Congressional races, and 'outside money', and the total would be closer to $6 billion, according to the Center for Responsive Politics, the foremost poll tracker in the United States![106] Obviously, such huge sums cannot come from the general public; they are donated by corporations. The food and beverage industry, which includes corporations like Coca-Cola, PepsiCo and McDonalds, is one of the bigger contributors; it donated $16 million to the 2008 presidential election campaign.[107]

And so, whoever wins the elections will obviously have to return the favour during his presidency. As Joseph Stiglitz has put it, American democracy has become: "Of the 1%, by the 1%, for the 1%."[108]

In such a system, expecting the government to act against corporations to protect the health of people is like expecting the fox to guard the hen house.

5. Coke and Pepsi in India

It's again very similar to the tobacco story. Due to intense campaigning by activist groups, conscientious doctors and public spirited scientists, consumption of carbonated soft drinks has fallen by one-fifth in the United States in the last decade and a half: from 212 litres per person per year in 1998 to 169 litres per person per year in 2011.[109] (This is still the highest in the world.) Sales of CSDs have been weak in Europe too: Coca-Cola reported that sales volume in Europe fell by 5 percent in 2011.[110] Facing stagnant or declining markets in the developed countries, soft drink corporations have been increasingly focussing on the Third World countries, especially China, India and the Latin American countries, to boost their sales.

Coca-Cola Company (once again) and PepsiCo began operations in India in the late 1980s/early 1990s. In just two decades, they have come to dominate the carbonated soft drink market in India, and together account for 95 percent of the total sales. In 2011, total CSD retail sales in India were estimated at 60 billion rupees ($1.05 billion), of which Coca-Cola had a 60 percent share as compared to PepsiCo's 37 percent.[111]

Annual per-capita consumption of CSDs in India is still very low as compared to global figures. According to figures put out by the Coca-Cola Company, while the per capita consumption of Coke beverages in India has gone up from 6 eight-ounce bottles (8 ounces = 237 ml) a year in 2002 to 14 bottles a year in 2012, it is still very low as compared to the global average of 94 bottles.[112] Overall, it is estimated that per capita consumption of soft drinks in India is around 5.2 litres a year, against the world average of nearly 85.2 litres.[113] And so, both companies see a huge potential of increasing sales in India, and have been investing heavily. After investing $2 billion in its India operations over the past two decades, Coca-Cola announced in 2012 that it planned to invest an additional $5 billion in India by 2020.[114] For PepsiCo, India's food and beverage business is already amongst its top five businesses in the world. It invested more than $1 billion over the 12-year period 1998–2010, and in 2010, announced plans to invest another $500 million over the next three years.[115]

Obviously, a significant portion of this investment is going to be in advertising. Both corporations have unleashed a deluge of print, television and outdoor advertising campaigns; hired film stars, pop stars and cricketers for their advertising campaigns; sponsored cricket, football, music, dance and even Navratri events; doled out money to sponsor school and college events, and so on.

There are such fantastic indigenous natural nutritious drinks available in India, such as nimbu pani, butter milk, lassi, panna, sattu, coconut water, kokam sharbat, sugarcane juice and innumerable fruit juices and shakes. Despite their easy availability and cheap cost, despite numerous reports in the media about the presence of pesticides in

Coke–Pepsi soft drinks, the advertising binge unleashed by these two MNCs has led to a sharp rise in consumption of their toxic drinks. And therefore, despite being associated with numerous scams and scandals, India has been one of the fastest growing markets for both corporations in recent years. Sales volumes of soft drinks of both Coca-Cola and Pepsi have been growing at double digit rates.[116]

History of Coke–Pepsi in India

Coca-Cola first came into the country in 1956, when it used to be distributed free at seminars to promote its taste and thus create a demand. By the 1970s, it had established itself in the Indian market. It was kicked out in 1977, due to its refusal to accept Indian laws under which it had to dilute its ownership stake in its Indian subsidiary to 40 percent. Justifying his decision to throw out Coca-Cola, George Fernandes, the then industry minister in the Janata Party Government, stated:

> Coke had 100 percent equity in India. Their investment was not much. They came into the country with 600,000 rupees, which at the present rate of exchange is less than $20,000. On this 600,000 rupee investment, they had taken out of the country, by a modest estimate, 250 million rupees (about $8 million) as profit in the twenty years they had been in the country.[117]

By the late 1980s, the winds of globalisation had started blowing across India, and the Indian Government began welcoming Western MNCs to India. The trickle turned into a deluge after 1991, when the Indian Government, trapped in a foreign exchange crisis and facing external account bankruptcy, entered into an agreement with the World Bank–IMF to restructure the Indian economy and open it up to foreign capital inflows. This surrender of India's economic sovereignty is being glorified under the grandiloquent name of globalisation.

And so, Pepsi and Coca-Cola too entered India. PepsiCo began operations in India in 1988, and Coca-Cola Company re-entered in 1993. The story of their operations since then is very similar to that of other MNCs. They are trampling upon our laws, refusing to implement agreements, thumbing their nose at the judiciary, looting our resources, polluting our environment, destroying people's livelihoods . . . with the connivance of our bureaucracy and politicians, and the silent acquiescence of our courts.

Breaking Agreements, Violating Laws

What a change has taken place in the country! When Coca-Cola Company returned to India, it signed an agreement with the government agreeing to divest 49 percent of its equity holding in its bottling operations to the general public by 2002. However, in 2002, instead of forcing it to honour its commitment or quit India, the government diluted the condition imposed on Coca-Cola! Ironically, when this happened, Fernandes was the defence minister and Atal Bihari Vajpayee the prime minister—Vajpayee was the external affairs minister when the Janata Party Government threw out Coca-Cola in 1977![118]

PepsiCo too made several promises at the time of entering India, such as that it would create 50,000 jobs, that 74 percent of its investment would be in food- and agro-processing (and only 26 percent in soft drink manufacturing), that 50 percent of the value of its production would be exported, and that it would set up a farm research centre in Punjab. Not one of these promises has been fulfilled; the government has meekly swallowed the insult.[119]

In 2003, after the CSE published a report on pesticide residues in soft drinks, Coca-Cola and Pepsi launched a vicious attack to discredit the findings. They questioned CSE's testing methodology, the data analysis, and even raised questions about whether there existed laboratories in the country that could test their products. They threatened to sue CSE for defamation. Their concubine government in Washington too intervened. The US Under-Secretary for International Trade Franklin L. Lavin warned India that a ban on soft drinks could "affect investment". The toadies sitting in Delhi also attempted to bully CSE. Grey-clad men from the Intelligence Bureau visited the CSE office. Taxmen served notices asking CSE to submit details of its accounts and funding sources for the past 20 years.[120]

However, CSE stood its ground, and the public uproar which followed the publication of the test reports eventually forced the government to constitute a Joint Parliamentary Committee (JPC) to review the CSE tests. The JPC report vindicated CSE's findings. The tests, and their vindication by the JPC, led to much noise in the Indian Parliament. But eventually, the only action this hallowed institution took was to ban Coke–Pepsi soft drinks from its canteens.[121]

In 2006, the CSE again undertook a nationwide study of 11 soft drink brands made by the two MNC giants, and found little had changed. The study found pesticide residues in all the samples. Again there was much noise made in the Indian Parliament. But such are the relations of power between MNCs and the Government of India that it again ducked the issue of taking action against these soft drink corporations.[122]

In October 2004, the Rajasthan High Court, in an unprecedented ruling, ruled that Coca-Cola and Pepsi must specify on their labels not just the composition and contents of their beverages but also the presence of pesticides and chemicals, if any. There was actually nothing new in the court order, the court was only asking the companies to implement Indian laws. The requirement to disclose the ingredients of all packaged food items on their labels has been there in the Prevention of Food Adulteration rules in India for a long time. The companies went in appeal to the Supreme Court, which too upheld the High Court order.[123]

These poison companies simply cannot implement the court orders, as if they do so, they will go out of business. And so, they have resorted to the simple stratagem of not implementing the judgement. And the mendicants sitting in Delhi's corridors of power do not have the spine to force these corporations to follow the country's laws.

Destroying People's Livelihoods

Depleting Groundwater

According to Vandana Shiva, the renowned environmentalist, it takes 9 litres of water to make one litre of Coke/Pepsi.[124] These companies of course dispute this figure. Both of them claim that they have reduced their water consumption and that it now takes around 2.5–3.1 litres of water to make one litre of Coke/Pepsi.[125]

But the fact is, these companies are crooks, and simply cannot be trusted with their claims. For, if they have indeed reduced their water consumption, they could have confidently invited independent experts/NGOs into their plants to study and verify their claims. But they are not willing to do this! Obviously, they have much to hide.

Coca-Cola has further gone ahead and now claims that it has become water neutral, that is, it is replenishing every drop of water it uses; while PepsiCo now claims that it has achieved what it calls "a positive water balance". In other words, these corporations are now claiming that they are giving back more water or recharging more water than they use. This is nothing but a public relations exercise—to respond to the growing criticism of their water use practices. Thus, Coca-Cola claims that it is recharging six times more water in Kaladera (in Rajasthan, where one of their bottling plants is located) than it uses; it claims that it is recharging 1.3 billion litres of water annually in Kaladera alone. This is a preposterous claim—the amount that Coca-Cola claims it is recharging in Kaladera is enough to meet the basic drinking water claims of a million people for a year; if that were true, there would be no water shortages in the area, but on the contrary, the water shortages are getting worse. Government data show that groundwater levels have dropped by more than 19 metres in the first eight years of Coca-Cola's operations in the area. When Coca-Cola was asked how does it measure the quantity of water it has recharged, it admitted that it does not have any measuring mechanism![126]

Let us take a look at some more known facts about Coca-Cola and Pepsi's water use in India. These two corporations have set up around 90 bottling plants in India. At each and every location, these plants are drawing out anywhere between 5 to 15 lakh litres of groundwater every day![127] Thus, the bottling plant of Pepsi located in the Pudussery Panchayat in Palakkad district, Kerala is extracting seven lakh litres water per day, according to a report tabled in the Kerala Assembly.[128] A bottling plant of Coca-Cola located in the neighbouring village of Plachimada in the same district was extracting up to 15 lakh litres of water every day, till a powerful agitation of the local people forced the plant to shut down.[129] (For most other plants, we do not have confirmed figures of water extraction by them, as the authorities just do not investigate.)

There are no laws to check groundwater exploitation by private corporations in India. The underground aquifers hold water resources collected over many hundreds of years. As such, they represent the heritage of entire communities. The over-exploitation of this precious resource by these giant corporations for making their toxic products is causing groundwater levels to fall, creating water shortages for people living in the regions where the bottling plants are located. It is not just affecting water supply for agriculture—because of which crop yields are falling, it is affecting drinking water supplies too—wells are going dry, hand pumps no longer work, and women have to go for miles to fetch drinking water. To give a few examples:

- In the village of Plachimada in Palakkad district of Kerala, Coca-Cola Company set up its biggest bottling plant in India to produce 12 lakh bottles of Coca-Cola, Fanta, Sprite, Limca, Thums Up, Kinley Soda and Maaza every day. The company drilled six borewells, each with a depth of between 250–300 metres, and began extracting millions of litres of groundwater. Within months of the plant beginning operations, the water levels in the local wells started falling dramatically, and some of them even ran dry. The water quality of the remaining water deteriorated, and "turned brackish, milky white in colour and tasted bitter." People also started falling sick, with stomach upsets to rashes on the skin. On May 12, 2003, the district medical officer banned people from drinking water from the wells next to the company as the concentration of chlorides, dissolved solids and the hardness of the water was far beyond tolerable limits for human consumption, domestic use or even irrigation.[130] Consequently, women had to walk several kilometres to fetch drinking water.[131] The water shortage started affecting agriculture too. Earlier, a little patch of land would yield up to 500 kilograms of paddy or 1,500 coconuts. Both are water intensive crops, but prior to the arrival of the company, the area had never faced any water shortages. Within three years of the factory being established, the irrigation wells started running dry and agricultural production declined, in some places up to 100 percent.[132]

- Coca-Cola established a bottling plant in the village of Kaladera in Rajasthan in 1999. The village is located in a semi-arid region, and therefore, as it is, the area was water-stressed even before the plant came up in the area. Government records show that while water levels in the area had remained stable from 1995 until 2000, on the whole, they had fallen by 3.94 metres over the ten-year period 1991–2000. But once the plant became operational and began drawing out lakhs of litres of precious groundwater from the aquifers in the region, groundwater levels in the region plummeted by 25.35 metres in the next ten years![133]
- Similarly, in Mehdiganj (near Varanasi), water levels have fallen sharply since Coca-Cola began operations there in 1999. Official data shows that over the 11-year period 1999–2010, groundwater levels dropped 7.9 metres; in the 11 years before that, groundwater levels had actually risen 7.95 metres![134]

If this continues, these regions will soon become *dark zones*, the term used to describe areas that are abandoned due to depleted water resources.

Polluting the Environment

On top of it, these giant corporations have been indiscriminately discharging their toxic waste water into nearby fields and rivers, polluting the groundwater and the soil, rendering the water unfit for human consumption. Coca-Cola has even distributed its solid toxic waste as free fertiliser to farmers!

- BBC presenter John Waite visited Coca-Cola's Plachimada plant and took samples of waste sold as fertiliser to the farmers by Coca-Cola back to the UK, where laboratory tests showed that they contained dangerous levels of cadmium and lead! A short while later, on August 6, 2003, a report by the Kerala State Pollution Control Board confirmed the existence of carcinogenic contaminants in the plant waste.[135]

- The same year, the Central Pollution Control Board of India surveyed eight Coca-Cola bottling plants in the country and tested the sludge at all these facilities. The Board too found that the sludge at all the bottling plants it surveyed contained high levels of toxic heavy metals like lead, cadmium and chromium![136]
- On August 8, 2003, a report by the West Bengal Government stated that it had found toxic metals, including the carcinogen cadmium, in the sludge and liquid effluents from Coca-Cola's plants at Dankuni, Taratala and Jalpaiguri and Pepsi's plant at Narendrapur.[137]
- A few years later, another study by the well-respected Delhi-based NGO, Hazards Centre, found that nothing had changed. In tests conducted in 2006–08, it found high levels of chromium and other pollutants in the soil and water around five Coke and Pepsi plants in northern India: Mehdiganj and Ghaziabad in Uttar Pradesh, Kaladera and Chopanki in Rajasthan, and Panipat in Haryana.[138]

Bottled Loot

This is not the end of the list of crimes of these robber corporations. Apart from extracting groundwater to make soft drinks, they are also (along with other corporations like Nestle and Parle—owner of Bisleri brand) mining millions of litres of groundwater to bottle and sell it to the country's middle classes and elites as 'pure drinking water'.

While this uncontrolled and unregulated exploitation of groundwater is worsening the water woes of India's villages, the corporations are making a killing. Taking advantage of the country's lax laws, they pay virtually nothing for extracting the millions of litres of water from the underground aquifers.[139] Thus, for instance, in Kaladera in Rajasthan, Coca-Cola pays nothing to the local community for all the miseries it has heaped on the people of the village. The only payment it has to make for extracting half a million litres of water from the ground every day is a tiny cess to the government, that too not for extracting water, but for discharging waste water into nearby water bodies—a little over Rs 5,000 a year during 2000–02 and Rs 24,246 in 2003! That works out to just 14 paise per 1,000 litres of water. The purification cost, even with the latest technology, would not be more than 25 paise a litre.[140] And then it bottles and sells it as 100 percent safe drinking water for as much as Rs 15–20 a litre!

With such superprofits to be made, no wonder the bottled water industry is booming. It has become a Rs 1,600 crore business, and is growing at a whopping 40 percent rate annually! The bottled water corporations have set up over 1,200 bottling plants in the country, which are overdrawing water, robbing local communities of their resources and livelihoods. Coca-Cola's Kinley and Pepsi's Aquafina dominate this sector too, together accounting for nearly 50 percent of the market share.[141]

According to a *World Resources Report*, about 70% of India's water supply is seriously polluted with sewage effluents. The United Nations ranks India at 120th among 122 nations in terms of quality of water available to its citizens.[142] Thus, for instance, Delhi's water supply is among the worst in the big cities of the world. Of the 14 lakh villages in India, nearly 2 lakh villages are affected by chemical contamination of water.[143] The result is that lakhs of people fall sick in the country every year due to diseases caused by unsafe drinking water, like cholera, typhoid, jaundice and diarrhoea. The WHO estimates that 7.8 lakh deaths take place in India every year due to unsafe drinking water, inadequate sanitation and insufficient hygiene (estimate for 2002). The majority of these deaths, 4.02 lakh, are due to diarrhoeal diseases (cholera, typhoid and dysentery), which are mainly caused due to ingestion of pathogens in unsafe drinking water.[144] A more recent UNICEF report (2013) estimates that of the 2000 children under the age of five who die every day from diarrhoeal diseases, 24 percent deaths (480 child deaths a day) take place in India; 90 percent of these deaths (432 a day, or 1.6 lakhs a year) are directly linked to contaminated water, lack of sanitation, or inadequate hygiene.[145]

Despite these terrible figures, India's ruling elite is unconcerned. The government is willing to subsidise profiteering of corporations like Coca-Cola by allowing them to extract millions of litres of groundwater for free. But when it comes to spending on providing safe drinking water to people, the government claims it has no money, in the name of a mumbo-jumbo theory that states that 'high fiscal deficit adversely affects growth', and so the Indian Government must rein in its spending.

6. Coke–Pepsi Quit India!

Faced with destruction of their environment and livelihoods, denied access to the very source of life—drinking water, people living around Coke–Pepsi's bottling plants are fighting back. They are demanding that these corporations be held accountable for their crimes. From Kaladera (Rajasthan) to Badauli (Haryana), from Mehdiganj and Ballia and Jaunpur (Uttar Pradesh) to Patna (Bihar), from Mandideep and Peelukhedi (Madhya Pradesh) to Sivagangai and Gangaikondan (Tamil Nadu), from Kudus (Thane district, Maharashtra) to Plachimada and Pudussery (Kerala), tens of thousands of people living in these regions are waging militant struggles, demanding the closure of these bottling plants and compensation for the destruction caused to their health and their lands. They are all raising a common demand: that *Coke and Pepsi should be thrown out of the country.*

However, our rulers, instead of defending the health, environment and livelihoods of the people of our country and taking action against these corporations, are singing eulogies to foreign MNCs. They are telling us that the FDI being brought into the country by these criminal corporations is necessary for our development. In other words, we are being told that we cannot develop ourselves, and that these foreign brigands are coming to help us!

The government is behaving like an agent of foreign MNCs. Wherever people are agitating against Coke–Pepsi, the government has intervened to defend the interests of these corporations and the people have been subjected to severe police repression. Their peaceful demonstrations and rallies have been viciously attacked by lathi-wielding policemen, injuring many. Hundreds have been arrested and false cases foisted upon them. It is back to the colonial days once again. We, the people of India, have become second grade citizens, or non-citizens, in our own land. Helots, as the Roman citizens used to call the others.

Yet the people have refused to cow down. And they have won significant victories too.

Plachimada Struggle

The biggest of these struggles has been the struggle of the people of Plachimada, a small village in Palakkad district of Kerala, against Coca-Cola's bottling plant located in their village. Adivasis constitute the majority of the local population, 80 percent of whom are agricultural labourers. The struggle thus pitted one of the most marginalised sections of the Indian society against one of the most powerful corporations of the world, a David versus Goliath struggle.

Initially, all the political parties, from the left to the right, supported the company. But the people did not give up, they resolutely continued their struggle. Gradually, the agitation spread across the state, and wide sections of the people actively got involved. As public pressure mounted, with even school children getting involved in demonstrations and dharnas, the political parties too were forced to change their position. After a fantastic struggle that lasted for nearly two years, Coca-Cola was forced to shut down its bottling plant in the village in March 2004.

The people however have not remained satisfied with just the closure of the company. They also want compensation for the damage caused to their health, environment and livelihoods. The agitation continued, and eventually, the state government was forced to set up a committee to examine the issue. The committee submitted its report in 2010, recommending that the company should be made to pay Rs 216 crore as compensation to the local people for the losses they have suffered. In February 2011, the Kerala Legislative Assembly unanimously passed a bill to set up a tribunal to go through the claims and award the compensation, which would then be legally binding on Coca-Cola Company. The bill was then sent to the Centre for President's assent in April 2011. But such is the power these MNCs have over the Indian Government that the Centre has sat on the bill since then![146]

While we were editing this essay for this book, the news came that the new BJP Government at the Centre has returned the Plachimada Coca-Cola Victims' Relief and Compensation Claims Special Tribunal Bill back to the Kerala Assembly, saying that the Assembly does not have the power to pass such a bill. The Centre has asked the Kerala Government to approach the National Green Tribunal (NGT) instead. However, the NGT cannot hear the matter because it has become time-barred—the case relates to groundwater and toxic contamination caused by Coca-Cola in Plachimada during the period 2000–04, and the NGT Act prohibits the tribunal from hearing matters more than five years old.[147] The Centre obviously knows this—yet another glaring proof of how India's rulers have become toadies, and are running the country solely for the profit maximisation of giant foreign multinational corporations, betraying the interests of the Indian people.

The Struggle Spreads

As awareness about Coke–Pepsi's crimes has spread, an increasing number of people from all walks of life across the country are coming out in protest, demanding that the government stop bootlicking these corporations and force them to 'Quit India'. At the initiative of the Azadi Bachao Andolan, an Allahabad-based Gandhian activist group fighting the assault on our country's sovereignty by foreign corporations:

- On February 1, 2001, 3.5 lakh students of 500 educational institutions participated in forming a 300-kilometre long human chain connecting the cities of Allahabad, Varanasi and Jaunpur.[148]
- On January 29, 2003, over 10 lakh students and village folk participated in forming an even more unbelievable 1200-km long human chain that passed through 22 districts of Rajasthan, UP, Haryana and Punjab as well as the union territory of Chandigarh to gherao Delhi's rulers. Students

from 2000 schools and colleges participated in the human chain, braving the cold wave sweeping the region.

- On January 20, 2005, nearly 50 bottling plants of Coke and Pepsi spread over 14 states were gheraoed by people by forming human chains. People also organised 'peoples' courts' at the factory gates wherein evidence was presented charging the factories with destroying people's livelihoods and the environment.

In another exhilarating development, students, teachers, college principals and vice-chancellors of several universities and colleges have openly come out and announced a boycott of these two criminal corporations. Tens of thousands of students, together with their teachers, at the Anna University in Chennai, the Avinashlingam Deemed University for Women in Coimbatore, the Gujarat Vidyapeeth of Ahmedabad and Kashi Vidyapeeth of Varanasi have imposed a people's ban on the entry of these junk drink companies into their campuses. Several dozens of colleges across the country have also declared their campuses as 'Coke–Pepsi Free Zones'.

[*Why have we not heard of these movements? We did not hear because the national newspapers didn't find the news worth printing.*]

The Struggle Goes Global

The struggle against Coca-Cola's crimes in Plachimada, Mehdiganj, Kaladera and elsewhere in India, as well as its crimes against people in other countries around the world such as Colombia and Turkey, has drawn support from students and ordinary people around the world:[149]

- ✓ Students at several universities in the UK, including universities at Leeds, Sussex and Manchester (one of Europe's biggest universities with 36,000 students) have banned Coca-Cola Company's drinks from their student union's shops and bars in protest against the American company's abuses of human rights and the environment in India, Turkey and Colombia.[150]
- ✓ By early 2006, 12 universities in the USA, including the New

York University, the largest private university in the US with over 50,000 students, and the University of Michigan, had thrown out Coca-Cola products from their campuses. University of Michigan and New York University were Coca-Cola's largest campus markets in the US; Coca-Cola's annual contracts with the University of Michigan alone were worth around $1.4 million in sales.[151]

- ✓ Worldwide, anti-Coke campaigns are active in more than 130 campuses. Dozens of schools and colleges, in countries from Ireland to Italy and Germany to Canada, have banned Coke from their campuses for its crimes.[152]
- ✓ Federations and unions across the United States and Canada have passed resolutions protesting Coke's labour and human rights violations, banning Coke machines and products from union halls, and demanding that schools remove Coke machines. These include various locals of the Postal Workers, Communication Workers, Service Employees, Automobile Workers and Steel Workers. In April 2005, the Representative Assembly of the New York State United Teachers, a 525,000-member teachers union, adopted a resolution to ban serving or selling Coke products at its offices, events and meetings.[153]

Plachimada Declaration

In January 2004, representatives of peoples' movements from all over the world participated in the World Water Conference held in Plachimada. Over 2,000 people attended the three-day conference. The *Plachimada Declaration* issued at the end of the conference affirms:

- ☞ Water is the basis of life; it is the gift of nature; it belongs to all living beings on earth.
- ☞ Water is not private property. It is a common resource for the sustenance of all.
- ☞ Water is the fundamental right of all human beings. It has to be conserved, protected and managed. It is our fundamental obligation to prevent water scarcity and pollution and to preserve it for generations.

- ☞ Water is not a commodity. We should resist all criminal attempts to marketise, privatise and corporatise water. Only through these means can we ensure the fundamental and inalienable right to water for people all over the world.
- ☞ The right to conserve, use and manage water is fully vested with the local community. This is the very basis of water democracy. Any attempt to reduce or deny this right is a crime.
- ☞ The production and marketing of the poisonous products of Coca-Cola and PepsiCo corporations lead to massive destruction and pollution, and it also endangers the very existence of local communities.
- ☞ The resistance that has come up in Plachimada, Pudussery and in various parts of the world is the symbol of our valiant struggle against the devilish corporate gangs who engage in piracy of our water.
- ☞ We, who stand in full solidarity with the struggle of the people of Plachimada, exhort people all over the world to boycott the products of Coca-Cola and PepsiCo.

Let Us Join the Struggle Too: Coke–Pepsi 'Quit India'!

Friends, Coca-Cola and Pepsi are symbolic of all MNCs. Multinational corporations are seeking to acquire control over what we eat, what we drink, what we read, what we see and what we think, so that they can maximise their profits. They are bombarding us with their propaganda, and we are becoming victims of it. We must throw off this yoke of mental slavery.

Our government is grovelling before these foreign corporations. Therefore we need to act. The least we can do is BOYCOTT COCA-COLA and PEPSI soft drinks.

We must join the boycott of Coke and Pepsi:

- not just because they are harmful to our health;
- not just because through their manipulative advertising techniques they entice people into drinking their toxic brew;
- not just because they are destroying the livelihoods of

thousands of people in Plachimada, Mehdiganj and other places;

We must support the movement to throw Coke and Pepsi out of India also because:

- We need to assert that foreign corporations who do not implement the agreements they have signed with our government, who do not respect the laws of the country, who do not respect and honour the judgements of our judiciary, cannot be allowed to operate in the country;
- We need to assert that our country's natural resources are common property; giant cash-rich corporations cannot be allowed to acquire control over it;
- *Most Importantly*: We need to affirm that Water is a Fundamental Right, and corporations cannot be allowed to plunder it.

Let us therefore join this struggle and:

- Boycott all Coke and Pepsi soft drinks.
- Organise campaigns against Coke and Pepsi in our schools, colleges, offices, workplaces and residential colonies.
- Impose a ban on Coke and Pepsi in our college canteens, office canteens, union offices, etc.
- Organise cycle rallies, form human chains and adopt other such forms to reach out to people in the area we live in and make them aware of the crimes of these robber corporations.

Let us unite to KICK OUT COKE–PEPSI from India!

Appendix

The Story of How Aspartame Got US FDA Approval[154]

- 1965: Searle Pharmaceuticals accidentally discovers aspartame.
- 1967–71: Searle conducts tests to assess effects of aspartame on primates. Of seven monkeys fed aspartame, one dies and five others have epileptic seizures. Another study shows that it caused holes in the brains of infant mice.
- 1973: Searle suppresses these reports and applies for FDA approval, citing over 100 safety studies.
- 1974: Scientists and consumer groups file objections to Searle's test reports, citing evidence that aspartame could cause brain damage, particularly in children.
- 1975: FDA appoints a task force to examine accuracy of Searle's test reports. Its report points out that Searle had done faulty and fraudulent product testing, and had knowingly misrepresented and manipulated test data.
- 1976–77: FDA appoints a new task force headed by Jerome Bressler to further investigate Searle's aspartame studies. The Bressler Report, submitted in August 1977, affirms the findings of the first task force. The report investigated three key aspartame studies conducted by Searle. It found that in one study 98 of the 196 animals died but weren't autopsied until later dates, making it impossible to ascertain the actual cause of death. Tumours were removed from live animals and the animals placed back in the study. It noted many other errors and inconsistencies.
- January 1977: FDA requests the US Attorney's office to investigate whether indictments should be filed against Searle for knowingly misrepresenting findings and 'concealing material facts and making false statements' in aspartame safety tests. This is the first time in FDA's history that it requests criminal investigation of a manufacturer.
- March 1977: Searle hires Donald Rumsfeld, ex-Congressman and former defence secretary (in the Ford administration), as new CEO. Rumsfeld brings several influential Washington

politicians into top management.

- July 1977: Samuel Skinner, the US Attorney in charge of the Searle investigation, resigns and joins Searle's law firm.
- July–December 1977: William Conlon replaces Skinner. Conlon stalls prosecution of Searle till December, the maximum time by which legal proceedings needed to be initiated as per the statute of limitations, and the investigation is dropped. A year later, Conlon too joins Searle's law firm.
- August 1977: Following the submission of the Bressler Report, FDA sets up yet another task force, headed by senior scientist Jacqueline Verrett, to review the Bressler Report.
- September 1977: The third task force exonerates Searle of any wrongdoing in its testing procedures. [A decade later, Jacqueline Verrett testifies to the US Senate that her team had been pressured into validating data from experiments that were clearly a 'disaster'. (The Senate maintained a stony silence on her charges.)]
- 1979–80: FDA establishes a public board of inquiry (PBOI) comprising three scientists to review scientific objections to the approval of aspartame and rule on safety issues surrounding the sweetener; the PBOI too votes unanimously against aspartame's approval.
- January 1981: Reagan sworn in as US President. Rumsfeld is on his transition team (he later becomes defence secretary); the team nominates Dr. Arthur Hull Hayes Jr. as the new FDA commissioner. Searle re-applies to the FDA for approval for aspartame.
- May 1981: Hayes appoints a five-member commission to review issues raised by PBOI. Three of the five FDA scientists on it advise against approval of aspartame, stating on record that Searle's tests are unreliable and not adequate to determine the safety of aspartame.
- July 1981–July 1983: Hayes overrules his own internal FDA team and PBOI findings, and gives approval for use of aspartame in dry goods in July 1981; in October 1981, FDA approves aspartame as a tabletop sweetener and for use in tablets, breakfast cereals, instant tea and coffee, etc.; and in July 1983, aspartame

is approved for use in carbonated beverages.

- September 1983: Hayes resigns as FDA commissioner to eventually become senior scientific consultant with Burston-Marsteller, the chief public relations firm for Searle. Newsreports later reveal that more than 10 federal officials involved in granting approval to aspartame have taken up private sector jobs linked to the aspartame industry.
- 1984: Numerous complaints begin to come in regarding adverse effects of aspartame. FDA requests the US Government health agency Centers for Disease Control and Prevention (CDC) to investigate. CDC's review of public complaints notes that aspartame adversely affects the nervous system in sensitive individuals; nevertheless, CDC concludes that aspartame is safe to ingest!
- 1985: Monsanto purchases Searle.
- 1986: US Supreme Court rejects petition filed by consumer groups against FDA approval to aspartame. Court is headed by Justice Clarence Thomas, a former Monsanto attorney.
- 1991: The US National Institutes of Health publishes a bibliography of 167 studies documenting adverse effects associated with aspartame.
- April 1995: Activists use the US's Freedom of Information Act to force the FDA to release an official list of adverse effects associated with aspartame ingestion. Culled from 10,000 consumer complaints, the list includes four deaths and more than 90 unique symptoms, a majority of which are connected to impaired neurological function.
- June 1995: FDA announces it has no further plans to continue collecting adverse reaction reports or monitoring research on aspartame.
- 1996: FDA approves use of aspartame as a 'general-purpose sweetener', meaning that it can now be freely used in any food or beverage.

REFERENCES

1. "MSSD Releases Tip List for Top 10 Healthy Foods", September 30, 2012, http://www.kten.com; "Corporate Clout: The Influence of the World's Largest 100 Economic Entities", http://www.globaltrends.com.
2. "Corporate Clout: The Influence of the World's Largest 100 Economic Entities", ibid.
3. John Bellamy Foster et al., "The Internationalization of Monopoly Capital", *Monthly Review*, June 2011, http://monthlyreview.org; *Oligopoly, Inc. 2005*, Communique, ETC Group, November–December 2005, http://www.etcgroup.org.
4. Andy Coghlan and Debora MacKenzie, "Revealed – The Capitalist Network That Runs the World", October 24, 2011, http://www.newscientist.com.
5. "Richest 1% Will Own More than All the Rest by 2016", January 19, 2015, http://www.oxfam.org.
6. "Forbes Releases 28th Annual World's Billionaires Issue", March 3, 2014, http://www.forbes.com. Global GDP for 2014 estimated at 72.6 trillion dollars – taken from: "Global Gross Domestic Product (GDP) at Current Prices from 2004 to 2014", http://www.statista.com.
7. http://www.unwater.org/statistics_san.html; "Solving the Energy Poverty Problem", February 28, 2011, http://leadenergy.org; "Resources: We Need a Plan to Make Poverty History", 2010, http://www.makepovertyhistory.ca.
8. "New and Improved: The Story of Mass Marketing in America", http://www.businessweek.com.
9. Ibid.; David B. Yoffie, "Cola Wars Continue: Coke and Pepsi in the Twenty-First Century", Harvard Business School, January 27, 2004, http://www.platform.bilkent.edu.tr.
10. Richard Girard, *Corporate Profile: Coca-Cola Company – Inside the Real Thing*, Polaris Institute, August 2005, http://www.polarisinstitute.org.
11. Harry Magdoff, *The Age of Imperialism*, Monthly Review Press, New York, reprinted by Aakar Books, Delhi, 2010, p. 126.
12. Neeraj Jain, *Globalisation or Recolonisation?* Lokayat publication, Pune, 2006, pp. 11–20, available on the internet at www.lokayat.org.in.
13. Beverly Bell, "Cola Wars in Mexico", October 6, 2006, http://www.inthesetimes.com.
14. *Coca-Cola – The Alternative Report*, War on Want, London, March 2006, http://www.waronwant.org.

15. Valentin Angelkov et al., *Pepsi's Strategy in the Carbonated Soft Drinks Market*, University of Texas, April 30, 2003, p. 3, http://www.mcafee.cc.
16. "Future Success Strategies for Carbonated Soft Drinks (CSDs)", September 2010, http://www.reportlinker.com.
17. *Coca-Cola Company – CorporateInformation.com*, http://www.corporateinformation.com.
18. "Carbonated Soft Drinks: Global Industry Guide", *MarketLine*, March 2012, http://www.researchandmarkets.com; "Global Carbonated Soft Drinks", *MarketLine*, March 30, 2012, http://www.marketresearch.com.
19. Michael F. Jacobson, *Liquid Candy: How Soft Drinks Are Harming Americans' Health*, Center for Science in the Public Interest, Washington, D.C., p. 1, http://www.cspinet.org.
20. Ibid., p. 9.
21. Ibid., p. 8.
22. "The Health Dangers of Soda", *Heal With Hope*, http://www.healwithhope.com; *Soft Drinks – "The Liquid Candy"*, April 6, 2008, http://cleaneatingdiet.blogspot.in; Sumei FitzGerald, "Physiological Effects of Carbonated Drinks", *eHow.com*, http://www.ehow.com.
23. *Soft Drinks – "The Liquid Candy"*, ibid.; Dr. Eileen Silva, "Soft Drinks: America's Other Drinking Problem", 2006, http://www.streetdirectory.com; Joel Fuhrman, "Diet Soda Depletes Calcium and May Increase Heart Attack Risk", April 24, 2012, http://www.diseaseproof.com.
24. "All Not Well with Cola Consumption", *The Tribune*, August 26, 1999, http://www.tribuneindia.com/1999.
25. *Caffeine Content for Coffee, Tea, Soda and More*, Mayo Clinic staff, http://www.mayoclinic.com. Several other sources on the internet also give similar figures.
26. Michael F. Jacobson, *Liquid Candy: How Soft Drinks Are Harming Americans' Health*, op. cit., p. 17; "Colas like Coke, Pepsi Are Injurious to Health, Assert Mexican Consumer Watchdogs", August 25, 1999, http://www.rediff.com.
27. Michael F. Jacobson, ibid., pp. 17–18.
28. Ibid.
29. Ibid., pp. 17–18; "Colas like Coke, Pepsi Are Injurious to Health, Assert Mexican Consumer Watchdogs", op. cit.
30. "Caffeine is Not Good for Your Health", http://www.healingnaturallybybee.com; "July 31, 1997, Letter to the FDA on Caffeine", http://

www.cspinet.org/new/cafdalet.htm.

31. Michael F. Jacobson, *Liquid Candy: How Soft Drinks Are Harming Americans' Health*, op. cit., pp. 4–5. According to this article, a 12-ounce can contains 10 level teaspoons of sugar.
32. *The Surgeon General's Call to Action to Prevent and Decrease Overweight and Obesity*, 2001, http://www.surgeongeneral.gov.
33. Gary Ruskin, *The Fast Food Trap: How Commercialism Creates Overweight Children*, Public Citizen's Commercial Alert, October 31, 2003, http://www.commercialalert.org.
34. Jeremy Laurance, "Obesity Now a Bigger Threat than Smoking", *The Independent*, January 5, 2010, http://www.independent.co.uk.
35. Kim Severson, "Researchers Link Soft Drinks to Diabetes/Drinking a Soda a Day Led to Weight Gain in Medical School Study of 90,000 Women", August 26, 2004, http://www.sfgate.com; "Diet and Regular Soda's is a NO NO", September 2, 2010, http://puremotivation.yourtalk.com.
36. *The Nutrition Source: Sugary Drinks and Obesity Fact Sheet*, http://www.hsph.harvard.edu.
37. Kim Severson, "Researchers Link Soft Drinks to Diabetes/Drinking a Soda a Day Led to Weight Gain in Medical School Study of 90,000 Women", op. cit.
38. *Research Links Soft Drinks with Obesity and Diabetes*, Canadian Obesity Network, http://www.obesitynetwork.ca.
39. *National Diabetes Fact Sheet, 2011*, www.cdc.gov.
40. Gary Ruskin, *The Fast Food Trap: How Commercialism Creates Overweight Children*, op. cit.
41. *Global Status Report on Noncommunicable Diseases 2010*, WHO, 2011, pp. 23–24, http://www.who.int.
42. Kate Kelland and Deena Beasley, "Global Diabetes Epidemic Balloons to 350 Million", June 25, 2011, http://www.reuters.com.
43. *Framingham Observational Study Notes Greater Incidence of Metabolic Syndrome Among Adults Consuming Soft Drinks*, July 23, 2007, http://www.nih.gov; Tara Parker-Pope, "Exploring a Surprising Link Between Obesity and Diet Soda", *Wall Street Journal*, July 24, 2007, http://online.wsj.com.
44. John Phillip, "Soda Consumption Dramatically Increases Risk of Stroke and Vascular Disease", May 12, 2012, http://www.naturalnews.com; *Study Finds Soda Consumption Increases Overall Stroke Risk*, April 20, 2012, http://my.clevelandclinic.org.
45. *Fact Sheet: Sugary Drink Supersizing and the Obesity Epidemic*, June

2012, http://www.hsph.harvard.edu.; Frank B. Hu, *Healthy Beverage Choices and Prevention of Obesity, Diabetes, and Cardiometabolic Diseases*, Harvard Medical School, http://www.projectwet.org.

46. "High Fructose Corn Syrup Linked to Liver Scarring, Research Suggests", *ScienceDaily*, March 23, 2010, http://www.sciencedaily.com; "The Truth About High Fructose Corn Syrup (HFCS)", http://www.natural-health-restored.com; Dan Hammer, "The Dark Cola Drink Versus Water!" http://www.aging-no-more.com.
47. Michael F. Jacobson, *Liquid Candy: How Soft Drinks Are Harming Americans' Health*, op. cit., pp. i, 2.
48. Jennifer L. Harris et al., *Sugary Drink FACTS: Evaluating Sugary Drink Nutrition and Marketing to Youth*, Rudd Center for Food Policy and Obesity, October 2011, http://www.sugarydrinkfacts.org.
49. Michael F. Jacobson, *Liquid Candy: How Soft Drinks Are Harming Americans' Health*, op. cit., p. i.
50. *Overweight and Obesity in the U.S.*, Food Research and Action Center, http://frac.org/initiatives.
51. Kristin Leigh, *Physical and Psychological Consequences of Obesity in Children*, May 26, 2011, http://www.livestrong.com; "Childhood Obesity Facts", Centers for Disease Control and Prevention, USA, http://www.cdc.gov; Freedman D.S. et al., "Cardiovascular Risk Factors and Excess Adiposity Among Overweight Children and Adolescents: The Bogalusa Heart Study", *J Pediatr. 2007*; 150(1):12–17: cited in: "Childhood Obesity: It's Everyone's Business", National Business Group on Health, Washington, D.C., http://www.businessgrouphealth.org.
52. Malathy Iyer, "Soda a Day May See 20% Rise in Heart Attack Risk", *TNN*, April 8, 2012, http://articles.timesofindia.indiatimes.com.
53. Gary Ruskin, *The Fast Food Trap: How Commercialism Creates Overweight Children*, op. cit.; Kristin Leigh, *Physical and Psychological Consequences of Obesity in Children*, op. cit.; *Type 2 Diabetes and Kids: The Growing Epidemic*, http://www.centrahealth.com.
54. Kristin Leigh, *Physical and Psychological Consequences of Obesity in Children*, ibid.
55. Michael F. Jacobson, *Liquid Candy: How Soft Drinks Are Harming Americans' Health*, op. cit., pp. 13–14; *Diet Soft Drinks for Healthy Kids*, http://healthy-kids.com.au; *Caffeinated Soft Drinks Are Weakening Children's Bones*, http://www.medicdirect.co.uk.
56. Figures for 2003. Cited in: *The Obesity Crisis in America*, Statement of Richard H. Carmona, Surgeon General, US Public Health Service, July 16, 2003, http://www.surgeongeneral.gov.

57. *The Obesity Prevention Source, Economic Costs*, http://www.hsph.harvard.edu.
58. "Diet and Dental Health", *BBC – Health*, http://www.bbc.co.uk; "Dental Health", *Nutrition Australia*, http://www.nutritionaustralia.org.
59. Pat Thomas, "Behind the Label: Diet Coke", June 1, 2006, http://www.theecologist.org.
60. Daniel J. DeNoon, "Cancer in Colas' Caramel Coloring?" *WebMD Health News*, March 5, 2012, http://www.webmd.com; Bonnie Vanaman, *Health Effects of Caramel Colorings*, June 29, 2011, http://www.livestrong.com; "Caramel Color", *Wikipedia*, accessed on October 16, 2012, http://en.wikipedia.org.
61. *Pesticides in Soft Drinks*, http://www.cseindia.org.
62. "The Top 10 Bestselling Soft Drinks", May 29, 2013, http://www.therichest.com; Amanda Chan, "Diet Soda Linked to Weight Gain", *Huffington Post*, June 29, 2011, http://www.huffingtonpost.com; Ethan A. Huff, "Study: Drinking Diet Soda Actually Causes Weight Gain, Blood Sugar Spikes", July 24, 2011, http://www.naturalnews.com; Joel Fuhrman, "Diet Soda Depletes Calcium and May Increase Heart Attack Risk", op. cit.; Mark Hyman, MD, *Artificial Sweeteners Could Be Sabotaging Your Diet*, October 19, 2014, http://drhyman.com.
63. *Framingham Observational Study Notes Greater Incidence of Metabolic Syndrome Among Adults Consuming Soft Drinks*, op. cit.; Tara Parker-Pope, "Exploring a Surprising Link Between Obesity and Diet Soda", op. cit.
64. "More Weight Gain for Diet Soft Drinks than Regular Ones: A Wake-Up Call for Soda Drinkers", April 2008, http://www.live-in-green.com; John Phillip, "Soda Consumption Dramatically Increases Risk of Stroke and Vascular Disease", op. cit.; Nathan Gray, "Daily Dose of Diet Soda May Increase Heart Attack Risk: Study", February 2, 2012, http://www.foodnavigator.com.
65. Soft drink companies also use acesulfame potassium as a calorie-free sweetener, but it is no less harmful. Several animal studies show that it can cause hypoglycemia, lung tumours, breast tumours, rare types of tumours of other organs (such as the thymus gland), several forms of leukaemia and chronic respiratory disease, even at low doses. References: Jennifer Hill, "Acesulfame-K – Such Sweet Poison", July 30, 2010, http://www.stopkillingmykids.com; Dr. Janet Hull, "Aspartame – Most Dangerous of All Artificial Sweeteners", http://www.sweetpoison.com.
66. Dan Hammer, "The Dark Cola Drink Versus Water!" op. cit.; Pat Thomas, "Aspartame – The Shocking Story of the World's Bestselling

Sweetener", *The Ecologist*, http://www.wnho.net; Pat Thomas, "Behind the Label: Diet Coke", op. cit.; "Aspartame is, by Far, the Most Dangerous Substance on the Market That is Added to Foods", November 6, 2011, http://articles.mercola.com.

67. Richard York, "Manufacturing the Love of Possession", *Monthly Review*, February 2004, http://monthlyreview.org.
68. Harry Magdoff and Fred Magdoff, "Approaching Socialism", *Monthly Review*, July–August 2005, http://monthlyreview.org.
69. Chris Harman, *A People's History of the World*, Orient Longman, 2005, pp. 3–9.
70. Michael Dawson, "Why Marketing Always Grows, and Why That Matters", November 29, 2005, http://mrzine.monthlyreview.org.
71. Gary Ruskin, *The Fast Food Trap: How Commercialism Creates Overweight Children*, op. cit.
72. Cited in: Richard Girard, *Corporate Profile: Coca-Cola Company – Inside the Real Thing*, op. cit.
73. Jeremiah McWilliams, "Coca-Cola Spent More than $2.9 Billion on Advertising in 2010", March 1, 2011, http://www.ajc.com; Natalie Zmuda, "Pepsi Plays Catch-Up with Coke, Adds $500M in Spending", *Advertising Age*, January 30, 2012, http://adage.com.
74. "Global Advertising Growth Continues as Latin America and Asia Pacific Compensate for Weakening Europe", March 12, 2012, http://www.zenithoptimedia.com.
75. "Coca-Cola Profit Skyrockets 73 Percent in 2010", *Atlanta Business Chronicle*, February 9, 2011, http://www.bizjournals.com.
76. Lori Dorfman et al., "Soda and Tobacco Industry Corporate Social Responsibility Campaigns: How Do They Compare?" *PLOS Medicine*, June 2012, http://www.plosmedicine.org.
77. These facts and much more are available on Wikipedia. See for instance: "Coca-Cola", *Wikipedia*, http://en.wikipedia.org.
78. Michael F. Jacobson, *Liquid Candy: How Soft Drinks Are Harming Americans' Health*, op. cit., p. 20.
79. Richard Girard, *Corporate Profile: Coca-Cola Company – Inside the Real Thing*, Polaris Institute, op. cit., p. 17.
80. Mary Story, Simone French, "Food Advertising and Marketing Directed at Children and Adolescents in the US", *International Journal of Behavioral Nutrition and Physical Activity*, 2004, http://www.ijbnpa.org.
81. Mary Story, Simone French, ibid.; Gary Ruskin, *The Fast Food Trap: How Commercialism Creates Overweight Children*, op. cit.; Martin Donohoe, "Weighty Matters: Public Health Aspects of the Obesity

Epidemic: Part II—Treatment and Approaches to Combating the Problem", *Medscape Ob/Gyn and Women's Health*, 2008. Document available on internet at www.medscape.com.

82. *Health Groups Warn: World's Children at Risk from Junk Food Marketing*, Food Commission, UK, July 29, 2003, http://www.foodcomm.org.uk.
83. Gary Ruskin, *The Fast Food Trap: How Commercialism Creates Overweight Children*, op. cit.
84. "PepsiCo Has Teamed Up with Walt Disney as Marketing Partner (for Film Monsters Inc)", March 15, 2001, http://www.accessmy library.com.
85. John Bellamy Foster and Robert W. McChesney, "The Commercial Tidal Wave", *Monthly Review*, March 2003, http://monthlyreview.org.
86. Katherine Neer, *How Product Placement Works*, http:// money.howstuffworks.com.
87. Mike Esterl, "Pepsi Thirsty for a Comeback", *Wall Street Journal*, March 18, 2011, http://online.wsj.com.
88. Jennifer L. Harris et al., "Sugary Drink FACTS: Evaluating Sugary Drink Nutrition and Marketing to Youth", op. cit.; Mary Story, Simone French, "Food Advertising and Marketing Directed at Children and Adolescents in the US", op. cit.
89. Gary Ruskin, *Why They Whine: How Corporations Prey on Our Children*, http://www.mothering.com.
90. *Statement at the Coca-Cola Annual Meeting of Shareowners*, April 19, 2005, http://commercialfreechildhood.org.
91. Gary Ruskin, *The Fast Food Trap: How Commercialism Creates Overweight Children*, op. cit.
92. *Liquid Candy: Highlights*, http://www.cspinet.org; Mike Adams, "Soft Drink Company Marketing Tactics: The Experts Sound Off", January 8, 2005, http://www.naturalnews.com.
93. Mary Story, Simone French, "Food Advertising and Marketing Directed at Children and Adolescents in the US", op. cit.; Gary Ruskin, *The Fast Food Trap: How Commercialism Creates Overweight Children*, op. cit.; Judith Valentine, *Soft Drinks – America*, http://www.globalhealing center.com.
94. Gary Ruskin, *Why They Whine: How Corporations Prey on Our Children*, op. cit.; Mary Story, Simone French, "Food Advertising and Marketing Directed at Children and Adolescents in the US", ibid.
95. "Tokyo War Crimes Indictment Against George W. Bush", March 1, 2004, http://globalresearch.ca.
96. For many more such cases, see: *Heads They Win, Tails We Lose*, Union

of Concerned Scientists, February 2012, http://www.ucsusa.org.
97. Richard Girard, *Corporate Profile: Coca-Cola Company – Inside the Real Thing*, op. cit., pp. 10, 13.
98. *Heads They Win, Tails We Lose*, Union of Concerned Scientists, op. cit.
99. Richard Girard, *Corporate Profile: Coca-Cola Company – Inside the Real Thing*, op. cit., pp. 11–13.
100. Michael F. Jacobson, *Liquid Candy: How Soft Drinks Are Harming Americans' Health*, op. cit., p. 22.
101. "World Health Organisation 'Taking Cash Handouts from Coca-Cola to Plug Black Holes in Budget'", *Mail Online*, October 19, 2012, http://www.dailymail.co.uk.
102. Gary Ruskin, *The Fast Food Trap: How Commercialism Creates Overweight Children*, op. cit.
103. "How Cola Companies Are Winning the War Against Obesity", March 16, 2012, http://www.trefis.com.
104. "Food and Beverage", *OpenSecrets.org*, http://www.opensecrets.org; Spencer MacColl, "Business Favors GOP, Poll Shows Tie Amongst Parties, and More in Capital Eye Opener", September 21, 2010, http://www.opensecrets.org.
105. Sarah Boseley, "What Are Fizzy Drinks Doing to Our Children?" *The Guardian*, January 9, 2003, http://www.guardian.co.uk; Gary Ruskin and Juliet Schor, *Junk Food Nation: Who's to Blame for Childhood Obesity?* August 11, 2005, http://www.commercialalert.org.
106. "2012 Election Will Be Costliest Yet, with Outside Spending a Wild Card", August 1, 2012, http://www.opensecrets.org.
107. "Food and Beverage", *OpenSecrets.org*, op. cit.
108. Stewart Lansley, "The Price of Inequality", July 5, 2012, http://www.timeshighereducation.co.uk.
109. Michael F. Jacobson, *Liquid Candy: How Soft Drinks Are Harming Americans' Health*, op. cit., p. 1; "U.S. Soda Consumption Fizzles", April 2, 2012, http://www.foodproductdesign.com.
110. Alan Rappeport, "Coke Sales Hampered by Weak Europe", July 17, 2012, http://www.ft.com.
111. Nikhil Gulati and Rumman Ahmed, "India Has 1.2 Billion People but Not Enough Drink Coke", July 13, 2012, http://online.wsj.com. Similar percentages in: "Soft Drinks in India – India Food Brief", *Datamonitor*, http://www.indiafoodbrief.com.
112. "Coca-Cola: Per Capita Consumption of Company Beverage Products", http://www.coca-colacompany.com.
113. "Soft Drinks in India – India Food Brief", op. cit.

114. Nikhil Gulati and Rumman Ahmed, "India Has 1.2 Billion People but Not Enough Drink Coke", op. cit.
115. Uttara Choudhury, "Pepsi Will Ramp Up Investment to Leverage the India Opportunity", April 2, 2010, http://www.dnaindia.com.
116. Piyali Mandal and Viveat Susan Pinto, "Consumers' Thumbs-Up to Coke, Pepsi", March 28, 2012, http://business-standard.com; Nikhil Gulati and Rumman Ahmed, "India Has 1.2 Billion People but Not Enough Drink Coke", op. cit.; Uttara Choudhury, "Pepsi Will Ramp Up Investment to Leverage the India Opportunity", ibid.
117. "Thanda-Hearted Matlab: Coca Cola in India", 2003–04, http://www.ashanet.org.
118. Paranjoy Guha Thakurta, "How Coke Arm-Twisted the Indian Government", *Rediff.com*, June 21, 2003, http://www.indiaresource.org; V. Sridhar, "Playing with Regulations", *Frontline*, September 13–26, 2003, http://www.frontlineonnet.com.
119. V. Sridhar, "Playing with Regulations", ibid.
120. *Pesticides in Soft Drinks*, http://www.cseindia.org; "Cola Majors Resort to Misinformation to Counter the CSE Report", http://www.cseindia.org; Praful Bidwai, "Coke, Pepsi Face Public Ire", September 6, 2006, http://www.indiaresource.org; "Coca-Cola–Pepsi: Three Years Have Passed Since the Day We Released Our First Study on Pesticides", *Down to Earth*, August 2, 2006, http://www.biobased.us.
121. *Pesticides in Soft Drinks*, ibid.; "Parliamentarians Say No to Colas", *Economictimes.com*, August 6, 2003, http://articles.economictimes.indiatimes.com.
122. *Pesticides in Soft Drinks*, ibid.; "Govt Rules out Action Against Cos for Now", *TNN*, August 11, 2006, http://articles.economictimes.indiatimes.com; "Colas Continue to Be Toxic", *TNN*, August 3, 2006, http://articles.economictimes.indiatimes.com.
123. Sonu Jain, "Court Orders Coke and Pepsi to State Pesticide Levels on Label", *Indian Express*, October 21, 2004, http://www.indiaresource.org; "The Verdict is out", December 31, 2004, http://www.downtoearth.org.in; Vandana Shiva, *The Law for Food Fascism*, February 22, 2005, http://www.countercurrents.org.
124. Vandana Shiva, "India: Soft Drinks, Hard Cases", *Le Monde Diplomatique*, March 2005, http://www.mindfully.org.
125. "PepsiCo Receives Recognition for Its Water Replenishment Initiatives Wins the CII and UNESCO Award", December 30, 2008, http://www.pepsicoindia.co.in; Surajeet Das Gupta, "Coke, Pepsi Effect Big Cuts in Water Use", August 30, 2010, http://www.business-

standard.com; "Pepsi Takes Fight with Coca-Cola into Potato Fields", October 19, 2010, http://www.theguardian.com.

126. Amit Srivastava, "Coca-Cola's Lies About Sustainability Have Gone Too Far", India Resource Center, September 24, 2009, http://www.alternet.org; Melanie Warner, "How Do We Know PepsiCo Saved Huge Amounts of Water in India?" May 28, 2010, http://www.cbsnews.com; "Deception with Purpose: Pepsico's Water Claims in India", India Resource Center and Community Resource Centre, November 30, 2011, http://www.indiaresource.org; Amit Srivastava, "Coca-Cola's Latest Scam – Water Neutrality", India Resource Center, November 25, 2008, http://www.indiaresource.org.
127. Alexandra Alter, "Yet Another 'Footprint' to Worry About: Water", February 17, 2009, http://online.wsj.com.
128. Dipin Damodharan, "Ground Water Exploitation with Govt Support: Pepsi Extracts 7 Lakh Litres Water Per Day in Palakkad", May 1, 2010, http://www.groundreport.com.
129. Arjun Sen, "Heat on Cold Drinks", *Statesman*, August 19, 2003, http://www.countercurrents.org.
130. Mahesh Menon, "Lessons from Plachimada for Water Law: Who Should Own the Groundwater", Royal Institute of Stockholm, May 2013, http://www2.lwr.kth.se; Vandana Shiva, "India: Soft Drinks, Hard Cases", op. cit.
131. Vandana Shiva, "India: Soft Drinks, Hard Cases", ibid.
132. Mahesh Menon, "Lessons from Plachimada for Water Law: Who Should Own the Groundwater", op. cit.
133. "Coca-Cola: Drinking the World Dry", November 19, 2007, http://www.waronwant.org; "Water Levels Continue Dropping Sharply Around Coca-Cola Plant in Kala Dera", India Resource Center, September 21, 2011, http://www.indiaresource.org.
134. "Sharp Drop in Groundwater Levels Around Coca-Cola Bottling Plant", India Resource Center, April 25, 2011, http://www.indiaresource.org.
135. Arjun Sen, "Heat on Cold Drinks", op. cit.
136. "India: Coke Faces Charges in India, Including 'Greenwashing'", http://www.asiawaterbusiness.com.
137. Arjun Sen, "Heat on Cold Drinks", op. cit.
138. "Water and Coca-Cola in India", http://www.gits4u.com; "Soft Drink Plants Cause Chromium Pollution", June 5, 2010, http://www.thehindu.com.
139. "Coca-Cola and Water Use in India: 'Good till the Last Drop'", March 11, 2010, http://scienceblogs.com; Laxmi Murthy, "Boond-Boond

Mein Paisa: Bottled Water is Big Business", October 2005, http://infochangeindia.org.

140. Chandra Bhushan, "Bottled Loot", *Frontline*, April 8–21, 2006, http://www.frontlineonnet.com.
141. Laxmi Murthy, "Boond-Boond Mein Paisa: Bottled Water is Big Business", op. cit.; *Project Profile on Packaged Drinking Water*, Micro Small and Medium Enterprises-Development Institute, Government of India, 2011, http://www.dcmsme.gov.in.
142. Y.P. Gupta, "Poor Water Quality, a Serious Threat", April 13, 2010, http://www.deccanherald.com.
143. Ibid.
144. *Safe Water, Better Health*, WHO, 2008, http://whqlibdoc.who.int.
145. "Children Dying Daily Because of Unsafe Water", UNICEF, March 22, 2013, http://www.unicef.org.
146. "Call for Presidential Assent to Plachimada Bill", June 5, 2012, http://www.thehindu.com; "Case Against Coca-Cola Kerala State: India", The Rights to Water and Sanitation, http://www.righttowater.info; P.M. Ravindran, "Plachimada: The Struggle for Water and … Life!" January 7, 2012, http://www.vijayvaani.com.
147. M. Suchitra, "Plachimada Bill: Centre Asks Kerala to Approach National Green Tribunal", December 29, 2014, http://www.downtoearth.org.in.
148. "300 Kilometers-Long Human Chain by 3 Lac School Youth", Press Release, Azadi Bachao Andolan, March 20, 2001, http://www.mindfully.org; http://azadibachaoandolan.freedomindia.com/update9.htm.
149. Note that all this information is for the years 2005–07. It is not clear from information available on the internet whether all the bans mentioned here are still in force. But what we know for sure is that in at least 50 campuses worldwide, Coke continues to be banned: Jason Farbman and Blair Ellis, "NYU Campaign to Kick out Coke ... Again", May 3, 2010, http://socialistworker.org.
150. "Manchester Students Ban Coke in Human Rights Protest", March 12, 2007, http://www.polarisinstitute.org; Maxine Frith, "Coca-Cola is Banned from Students' Union Over 'Unethical Practices'", August 19, 2006, http://www.independent.co.uk.
151. Scott Jaschik, "At More Campuses, Coke Isn't It", January 3, 2006, http://www.insidehighered.com; "Coca-Cola Faces Another University Ban", http://www.icmrindia.org; "New York University Joins Anti-Coke Campaign", http://uk.oneworld.net.
152. "Campaign to Stop Killer Coke Update: Landslide Votes Ban Coke

Products", March 3, 2007, http://ymlp.com/zptSdB; Michael Blanding, "The Case Against Coke", *The Nation*, April 13, 2006, http://www.thenation.com.

153. Bryan G. Pfeifer, "Killer Coke's Deadly Policies Exposed", June 30, 2005, http://www.workers.org.
154. Pat Thomas, "Aspartame – The Shocking Story of the World's Bestselling Sweetener", op. cit.

About Us: LOKAYAT

The Directive Principles of the Constitution direct the Indian State to orient its policy towards:

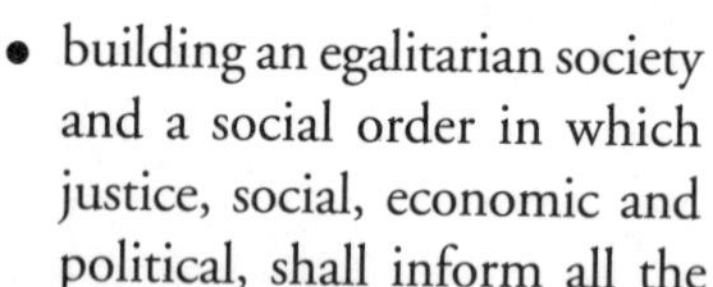

- building an egalitarian society and a social order in which justice, social, economic and political, shall inform all the institutions of the national life [Article 38 (1)];
- ensuring that all citizens have the right to an adequate means of livelihood [Article 39 (a)];
- minimising inequalities in income and ensuring that there is no concentration of wealth [Articles 38 (2) and 39 (c)];
- ensuring that children are given opportunities and facilities to develop in a healthy manner and in conditions of freedom and dignity [Article 39 (f)];
- regard raising the standard of living of the people, improvement of public health and making effective provision of education for all children as among the primary duties of the state [Articles 41 and 47].

Unfortunately, the major political parties that dominate the Indian Parliament have decided to abandon this vision of the founding fathers of the nation, and secede from the people of the country. Ever since India's ruling classes decided in 1991 to globalise the Indian economy and open it up to foreign multinational corporations, they have been running the economy solely for the profit maximisation of giant foreign and Indian business houses:

- Giant corporations have launched a ferocious assault to dispossess the poor of their lands, forests, water and resources—to set up mining projects, huge infrastructural projects, golf courses, residential complexes for the rich, etc.
- Public sector corporations, including banks and insurance companies, are being privatised and handed over at throwaway prices to these scoundrels.
- Indian agriculture, on which 60 percent of the Indian people still depend for their livelihoods, is being deliberately strangulated—so that it can be taken over by giant agribusiness corporations. The consequence: more than three lakh farmers have committed suicide since the 'reforms' began.
- Lakhs of small businesses have downed their shutters.
- Welfare services are being privatised and transformed into instruments of naked profiteering:
    - government hospitals and municipal schools are being privatised; medicine prices have zoomed; college fees have gone through the roof; electricity prices are rising; bus fares are rising; the ration system designed to make available foodgrains and other essential items to the poor at affordable rates is being eliminated.
- There are simply no decent jobs for the youth; probably nearly half the population is unemployed or underemployed.
- The country is heading towards an ecological catastrophe: corporations are being allowed to cut down entire forests, destroy coastal lands in the name of aquaculture, over-exploit groundwater, pollute our seas–rivers–soil–groundwater–air, damage the health of not just the living but also of those yet to be born . . .

These policies have produced the most obscene inequalities, that are becoming worse by the day:

- While on the one hand, the rich are becoming extremely rich—the wealth of India's 56 billionaires equals 10 percent of the country's GDP, and the wealth of India's richest 7,800 people equals 50 percent of the country's GDP;

- On the other hand, the poor are becoming even more poor. According to the government's own statistics:
    - 75.5 percent of the rural and 73 percent of the urban population are not able to eat two full meals a day;
    - 50 percent children below the age of five are malnourished;
    - 42 percent children drop out of school without completing basic schooling;
    - Lakhs of children die every year due to entirely preventable diseases; . . .

As the economic system becomes more and more sick, the social and political system is also becoming more and more degenerate. All-pervasive corruption; an educational system that makes us think we are incompetent fools; continuation of the age-old caste-based social system because of which atrocities on Dalits take place almost daily, and which is exploited by politicians to make the upper caste youth believe that the reservation system is responsible for lack of jobs; a communal political system that divides people in the name of religion and fills them with hatred against each other; a value system that promotes crass selfishness and unconcern and apathy for others; a society where cynicism and moral bankruptcy permeate every nook and cranny—this is the reality of today.

The common people have not been silent spectators to this betrayal of the Indian Constitution. Like flowers spring up in every nook and corner with the onset of spring, people are coming together all over the country, getting organised, forming groups and raising their voices in protest. Though these struggles are presently small, scattered and without resources, the future lies in these magnificent struggles. As more and more people join them, they will strengthen, join hands and become a powerful force which will transform society.

We must stop being sceptics, dream of a better future, believe that it is possible to change the world. *Yes, Another World is Possible!* But to make it a reality, we must start our own small struggles. These will ultimately unite, like the small rivulets hurtling down the

Himalayas which ultimately form the mighty Ganges, to build a new society in accordance with the dreams of our freedom struggle that are embedded in the Directive Principles of the Indian Constitution. And so, we have started this forum, *Lokayat.*

The deepening economic crisis due to globalisation has been accompanied by a gradual growth of fascist forces in the country. With the coming to power of the BJP in 2014, not only is it implementing the globalisation policies of the previous government at an accelerated pace, it is also implementing a very regressive fascist social agenda, wherein it is attempting to promote backward, feudal, unscientific, irrational and even Brahminical values amongst the people and divide the country on communal lines. It is even attacking very conception of India as a sovereign, socialist, secular and democratic republic as visualised by our country's founders and enshrined in the Constitution of India. To fight this vicious fascist offensive and provide a political alternative to the people, it is necessary for all progressive forces to unite. At the national level, Lokayat is affiliated with the Socialist Party (India). Unlike the mainstream political parties, Socialist Party (India) has consistently opposed globalisation and communalisation, and has not made any unprincipled compromises to somehow win political power.

We organise a wide range of activities/programs in Pune colleges, schools, city and slums, including:

- Seminars, talks, film screenings, street campaigns, street plays, poster exhibitions, solidarity hunger fasts, rallies and dharnas on various issues of deep concern to common people, such as: rising inflation; privatisation of essential services; destruction of the environment and livelihoods of common people in the name of development; the deepening crisis of global warming; Pune's transportation problems; the attack on labour laws to enable corporations to hire-and-fire workers at will; the growing fascist offensive against secularism and democracy; the rising number of atrocities on Dalits; and so on.
- Lokayat's women's wing, named Abhivyakti, actively

campaigns and organises programs on various aspects of gender inequality and the social roots of violence against women.

- Lokayat has a very active cultural wing which makes use of a wide variety of cultural forms—including songs, rock concerts, street plays, dramas, dance and traditional folk art—to reach out to people, raise their cultural consciousness, stimulate them to question the present decadent social–cultural order and its decadent values, and motivate them to come together and act for social change.

Dear friends, if you would like to know more about us, or participate in our activities, you may contact us at any of the addresses given below.

Contact Phones:

Neeraj Jain 94222 20311
Abhijit A.M. 94223 08125

Website and E-mail:
www.lokayat.org.in
lokayat.india@gmail.com

Contact Address:

Lokayat, Opp. Syndicate Bank, Law College Road,
Near Nal Stop, Pune 411 004.

INDEX